The Business Planning Guide

The Business Planning Guide

Creating a Plan for Success in Your Own Business

8th Edition

DAVID H. BANGS, JR.

Upstart
Publishing Company®
Specializing in Small Business Publishing
a division of Dearborn Publishing Group, Inc.

"A small business is one where you can bring your dog to work."
—David H. "Andy" Bangs, Jr.

Acquisitions Editor: Danielle Egan-Miller
Managing Editor: Jack Kiburz
Interior Design: Lucy Jenkins
Cover Design: Scott Rattray, Rattray Design

Published by Upstart Publishing Company, a division of Dearborn Publishing Group, Inc.

Printed in the United States of America
98 99 00 10 9 8 7 6 5 4 3 2 1

Library of Congress Cataloging-in-Publication Data

Bangs, David H.
    The business planning guide: creating a plan for success in your own business / David H. Bangs, Jr. — 8th ed.
        p.   cm.
    Includes index.
    ISBN 1-57410-099-8 (pbk.)
    1. Business planning—Handbooks, manuals, etc. 2. Business—Handbooks, manuals, etc. 3. Business enterprises—Finance—Handbooks, manuals, etc. I. Title.
    HD30.28.B362 1998
    658.4'012—dc21
                                                                98-13586
                                                                CIP

Upstart books are available at special quantity discounts to use as premiums and sales promotions, or for use in corporate training programs. For more information, please call the Special Sales Manager at 800-621-9621, ext. 4384,or write to Dearborn Financial Publishing, Inc., 155 N. Wacker Drive, Chicago, IL 60606-1719.

Praise for Earlier Editions of *The Business Planning Guide*

Named the favorite best-selling small business book of 1996 by *Forbes* magazine. "It works. Excellent charts, tables."—*Forbes*

"This is a new edition (is) . . . evidence that it's done the job for many entrepreneurs. It's about how to create a business plan that secures you the financing you need to get started or grow. Many lists, charts, graphs, tables."—*Business Week*

"Written by a small business owner for small business owners, the guide provides plenty of examples and worksheets to help readers begin the planning process."—*Nation's Business*

"An easy-to-use complete overview of how to put a business plan together. Users don't have to plow through a lot of hard-core business jargon or complicated formulas, yet still evolve with a sophisticated plan that would impress any banker or venture capitalist."—*In Business*

"Easy-to-use guide for growing businesses seeking financing for expansion—or for start-ups. Contains updated, simply-worded approach to organizing financial data for a business proposal . . . sample financial charts for the plan . . . and much more."—*Boardroom Reports*

"A detailed step-by-step approach to generating a successful business plan. I highly recommend this book to any start-up entrepreneur."—*Business Age*

"An excellent step-by-step guide to writing a business plan and financing proposal, complete with worksheets and case examples . . . an underground bestseller."—*Working Woman*

"A clear, simple explanation of how to write a business plan and financing proposal. I highly recommend this book."—*Small Press magazine*

"Comes complete with examples, forms, and worksheets."—*The St. Louis Countian*

"Portsmouth author David H. "Andy" Bangs, Jr. continues to preach the way to entrepreneurial success with the release of the sixth edition of his *Business Planning Guide: Creating a Plan for Success in Your Own Business*. The guide takes entrepreneurs step-by-step through the process of writing a business plan, and has sold more than 300,000 copies worldwide through its five previous editions."—*Business New Hampshire*

To my wife, Lacey Smallwood Bangs, for her wonderfully supportive and loving help over the decades—and to black Lab wonder dogs Hinckley (1976–1987) and Thud (1987 and still going strong), my constant companions in the peculiar and solitary business of writing. I'm not sure how they put up with me, but they do—and I'm very grateful! Thanks, Lacey! Thanks, Thud!

C O N T E N T S

The Business Planning Guide has been developed to help you construct a logically arranged and reasonably complete business plan and financing proposal that will:

- serve your need for business analysis;
- help you design a business plan for your business;
- provide you with a set of financial forecasts based on your rational assumptions about the future and on your hard-won business experience;
- set budgeting guidelines—including a working capital budget and a breakeven analysis for your business;
- help you determine the amount and kinds of financing most appropriate for your business; and
- give your financing sources the most useful and persuasive information about your business—information they need to make swift, accurate, and helpful decisions.

The suggested outline is flexible and you should tailor it to your own needs. It is based on the critical analysis and evaluation of thousands of business plans and financing proposals, and on a wide range of resources such as Small Business Administration pamphlets, bank guidelines, textbooks, periodicals, and conversations with experienced business owners, proposal writers, and many readers' comments.

This planning process is deliberately not computerized. All of the available planning software programs, without exception, are too restrictive. They force a shape and a size on all businesses, ignoring the fact that each business is unique. This fill-in-the-blanks approach abrogates the planning process, sacrificing thought and thoroughness in favor of an apparent gain in ease. Unfortunately, planning isn't easy. It takes work, time, and effort—though perhaps not as much as you may think at the beginning of the process.

The business planning process is much more important than the end result of a written business plan. General Eisenhower put it best: plans aren't important. Planning is.

If your plan requires additional information—a time/cost study, for example—include it. If you have trouble understanding how to complete your plan, seek assistance.

A business plan and a financing proposal are closely related. In fact, a good business plan that is updated periodically makes the most powerful financing proposal a small business can have. If you follow the guidelines (remembering to adapt them to suit your particular business situation), then you will not only know exactly how much money you need to make your business work, you will also know and understand what kind of financing to seek and who is most likely to provide it.

This knowledge alone helps you establish credibility with the potential sources of your financing. The complete financing proposal, which is a modification of your finished business plan, will establish maximum credibility. By presenting a clearly thought out, well-documented financing proposal, you show that you know what you want to do, how to do it, and how the loan will be repaid or how the investment will appreciate.

HOW TO USE THIS GUIDE

The Business Planning Guide is divided into major sections, some or all of which will be useful to you depending upon your specific needs. The first section is a general discussion of business problems and highlights the main points of the other sections. It is intended to help identify problem areas and will help you decide which of the other sections will be most useful in problem solving. A glossary defining some of the terminology is included at the end of *The Business Planning Guide*.

The Business Planning Guide can be used both by people contemplating going into business and those already in business.

The Business Planning Guide is not a substitute for other kinds of assistance but rather points out the need for and strongly encourages the use of competent legal, banking, and accounting services as well as other specialized forms of assistance.

The Small Business Administration (SBA) provides many superb resources for small business owners. The SBA is listed in the white pages of your phone book under the heading "United States Government." Call them for local phone numbers and addresses. Check out their home page on the Web at http://www.sbaonline.sba.gov. The SBA itself has many free or low-cost publications, as well as limited financing programs (including loan guarantees) and direct technical management assistance programs. Three of their resources follow:

1. **Small Business Development Centers** (SBDC). To find the SBDC nearest to you, go to http:/www.smallbiz.suny.edu/roster (their Web address). SBDCs offer one-on-one counseling in all aspects of small business management, ranging from prestartup business financing and market planning to advice on how to sell a business. SBDCs come as close to a one-stop, full-range assistance center as one could hope for and are usually staffed with people who have run businesses of their own. If you have an SBDC available to you, use it.

2. **Service Corps of Retired Executives** (SCORE). SCOREs home page on the Web is at http:/www.score.org. These are staffed by retired volunteers who have had extensive practical experience that they are eager to share with you. SCORE chapters' special expertise varies from one chapter to the next so you may want to shop around. They provide one-on-one counseling and put on seminars, workshops, and other educational programs.

3. **Small Business Institutes** (SBI). A former SBA program that has gone "private," SBI programs are located on a few college campuses. Go to http:/www.sbaer.uca.edu/Others/sbida to find a listing of colleges currently offering this program. They provide more specialized kinds of help than SBDCs (for example, one SBI I'm familiar with offers engineering advice) and are more academic. Most SBI assistance is provided by students under the close direction of a qualified faculty member. These projects have to fit into an academic calendar, so sign up in advance. A few years ago the University of New Hampshire SBI wrote, conducted, and interpreted a comprehensive telephone survey of 600 potential bank clients for Upstart. Their findings saved us from making a major marketing blunder. Our costs were limited to off-hour use of our WATS lines and some out-of-pocket copying and travel expense.

If at any point in using *The Business Planning Guide* you need further help, seek it out. There are various groups in most areas that exist to provide free or low-cost assistance to small businesses. Ask your banker about organizations in your area that might be helpful to you.

Each section of *The Business Planning Guide* is divided into three parts:

1. Major points of concern, and why each is important to the business
2. How to do whatever is required to complete that section
3. Examples from an actual business plan

When you have finished the process, you will have a complete, coherent document that serves your needs and the needs of others who may require information from you about your business.

SOME REQUIREMENTS FOR USING *THE BUSINESS PLANNING GUIDE*

You must do the planning.

This means that you must make the time available. If you are already in business, this may seem impossible. However, while you can hire people to do the work in your business, you cannot hire someone to do the planning. The plan is for your business and must be based on your ideas, experience, and assumptions. Others can assist you in the process, but you must do the actual planning.

If you are not in business but are trying to determine whether your business idea makes sense—or are getting ready to get started—following the planning process is the most important thing you can do. It will help you avoid mistakes and save you grief, time, and money.

Plan what's going to happen.

Then do it.

AN EXPLANATION OF THE EXAMPLE USED IN THIS BOOK

The sample plan that is used throughout *The Business Planning Guide* is based on an actual business plan for a business that was being started when we originally developed the book. Dealing with their real problems helped to ensure that we were staying on the right track. The planning represented here was accurate and effective.

Actual performance turned out to be quite in line with the original projections.

Finestkind Seafoods, Inc. sells fish to both retail and wholesale customers and is located in southern Maine. Since their original modest beginning, Finestkind has successfully established their original location, developed and sold a second, and is considering further expansion.

While Finestkind conducts a retail, perishable business in the Northeast, the principles expressed in their planning are universally applicable.

All businesses, in every part of the country, face the same challenges that Finestkind faced. Whether you manage a hardware store, a job shop, a division of a large company, a professional practice, or offer a service, you still must know where you want to go, how you will get there, and what benchmarks are important. You still must work with and through people. You still must use financial controls to manage your business and keep it growing and healthy. Above all, you still must have customers—customers keep you in business.

Finestkind's complete business plan is provided in Appendix 3: Sample Business Plans.

You will find two other sample business plans in Appendix 3. The first is the World Beat Tours business plan, a specialty tour packager. The second is Mediverse Products, Inc. (MPI), a distributor of health care related products.

Your business plan will be shorter or longer, more complex or simpler than the samples, because your plan will reflect the operating and financial details of your business, not somebody else's.

ABOUT UPSTART

Upstart Publishing Company is committed to serving the needs of small businesses everywhere. We can provide a wealth of information to those who are planning to start a business, those who are currently in business, and those who have an interest in and serve small businesses.

For more information and a free catalog, all us toll-free at 800-235-8866.

ACKNOWLEDGMENTS

This is the *eighth* edition of *The Business Planning Guide.* I am amazed and gratified at the growing list of patient and resourceful friends, critics and users who have sent along their comments and suggestions for improvement since the first edition was published in 1976.

Andrea Axman, who has edited most of my books with a sure touch and occasional pain, deserves a lot of credit for the style and directness of this book. Karen Billipp has given me a great deal of supportive criticism, stylistic and aesthetic. Thanks are also due Brad Ketchum (father and son), Steve White, Jean Kerr, Spencer Smith, Peter Rainsford, Dewey Johnson, Jim Howard and Country Business Inc., Peter Worrell, Bill Eldridge, Neil Herring, Bill Wetzell, Patricia Peacock, Bill Duncan, Joan Gillman, Stuart Devlin, Don Kuratko, Bill Naumes, Bill Pincowicz, Dick Schafer, Mary Shuter, Jere Calmes, and Jack Savage, all of whom have made helpful and substantive suggestions to improve the book over the years. Fellow writers—especially Laurie Zuckerman and Roger Parker—have traded war stories and ideas with me. The directors and consultants at hundreds of Small Business Development Centers, Service Corps of Retired Executive chapters, and Small Business Institutes have offered many useful suggestions that have been integrated into successive editions. Bankers, including Steve Beck and the late Halsey Smith, have helped me polish the financing sections and restrained me from certain rhetorical excesses.

My new editor at Dearborn Financial Publishing, Danielle Egan-Miller, has been a joy to work with. She and Robin Nominelli, my long-time friend and occasional sailing partner, came up with some excellent reviews as well as helpful hints for improving this edition of *The Business Planning Guide.* Rich Wright of Omega Publishing Services did a great job cleaning up seven editions' worth of accumulated errors. They make my job much easier!

Most of all, I want to thank Michael Goslin, the founder and part-owner of Finestkind Seafoods in York, Maine, for allowing me to use his business as a running example for more than 20 years. He's shown the finest kind of grit and stamina, qualities no small business owner can survive long without. Finestkind is on Route 1, just off the first exit on the Maine Turnpike. Call Mike at 207-363-5000 if you want to order fresh live lobsters, wholesale or retail. He's now shipping internationally, a far cry from the original small retail operation alongside Route 1.

Overview of the Business Plan

Why should you go to the trouble of creating a written business plan? There are three major reasons:

1. The process of putting a business plan together, including the thought you put in before beginning to write it, forces you to take an objective, critical, unemotional look at your business project in its entirety.
2. The finished product—your business plan—is an operating tool that, if properly used, will help you manage your business and work effectively toward its success.
3. The completed business plan communicates your ideas to others and provides the basis for your financing proposal.

The importance of planning cannot be overemphasized. By taking an objective look at your business you can identify areas of weakness and strength, pinpoint needs you might otherwise overlook, spot opportunities early, and begin planning how you can best achieve your business goals. Your business plan also helps you see problems before they grow large and helps you identify their sources—thus suggesting ways to solve them. Your business plan will even help you avoid some problems altogether.

This handbook has been designed with these considerations in mind. But you must do the work. A professionally prepared business plan won't do you any good if you don't thoroughly understand it. That level of understanding only comes from being involved from the very start.

The depth of understanding that you gain by writing your own business plan precludes the advantages you might hope for in using a computerized business plan. Your business needs its own unique business plan—and the weight attached to each piece of your plan should dictate the content, not the artificial restraint of a preformatted computer plan. The flexibility that comes from doing your own financials—especially the cash flow budget—on Excel™ or Lotus 1-2-3™ is not available in any prepackaged financial template. The best way to write your plan and financials is to use paper and pencil while doing the thinking, then turn to a computer to produce the final draft.

Use your plan. Don't put it in the bottom drawer of your desk and forget it. Going into business is rough—over half of all new businesses fail within the first ten years. A major reason for failure is lack of planning. The best way to enhance your chances of success is to plan and follow through on your planning.

Your business plan can help you avoid going into a business venture that is doomed to failure. If your proposed venture is marginal at best, the business plan will show you why and may help you avoid paying the high tuition of learning about business failure. It is far cheaper not to begin an ill-fated business than to learn by experience what a business plan would have taught you at the cost of several hours of concentrated work.

Finally, your business plan provides the information needed by others to evaluate your venture, especially if you will need to seek outside financing. A thorough business plan can quickly become a complete financing proposal that will meet the requirements of most lenders.

The best way to enhance your chances of success is to plan and follow through on your planning.

OUTLINE OF A BUSINESS PLAN

- **Cover Sheet: Name of business, names of principals, address and phone number**

- **Statement of Purpose or Executive Summary**

- **Table of Contents**

- **Section One: The Business**

    A. Description of Business

    B. Product/Service

    C. Market

    D. Location of Business

    E. Competition

    F. Management

    G. Personnel

    H. Application and Expected Effect of Loan (if needed)

    I. Summary

- **Section Two: Financial Data**

  A. Sources and Applications of Funding

  B. Capital Equipment List

  C. Balance Sheet

  D. Breakeven Analysis

  E. Income Projections (Profit and Loss Statements)

    1. Three-year summary

    2. Detail by month for first year

    3. Detail by quarter for second and third years

    4. Notes of explanation

  F. Cash Flow Projection

    1. Detail by month for first year

    2. Detail by quarter for second and third years

    3. Notes of explanation

  G. Deviation Analysis

  H. Historical Financial Reports for Existing Business

    1. Balance sheets for past three years

    2. Income statements for past three years

    3. Tax returns

- **Section Three: Supporting Documents**

  Personal résumés, personal balance sheets, cost-of-living budget, credit reports, letters of reference, job descriptions, letters of intent, copies of leases, contracts, legal documents, and anything else relevant to the plan.

The following pages elaborate and explain each of the above categories.

Three Parts to the Business Plan

Concept

- What business are you in?
- Why is it the right business for you to be in?
- What would you like your business to be famous for?
- What do you sell?
- Why will people buy from you?
- Who are your competitors?
- How can you stand out from the crowd?

Customers

- Who are (and will be) your customers?
- What benefits do you (can you) provide them?
- How many of them are there?
- How many customers do you need?
- What are their buying patterns?
- Where do they currently buy?
- How will they know about you?

Capital (or Cash)

- How much capital do you need?
- How can you maintain cash flow and liquidity?
- How much working capital do you need?
- What kind of budgets should you follow?
- How can you control your finances?
- How much growth can you afford?

THE COVER SHEET

The cover sheet should

- identify the business and the document;
- identify the location and telephone numbers of the business or where the principals can be reached; and
- identify the person who wrote the business plan.

A Sample Cover Sheet

FINESTKIND SEAFOODS, INC.
123 Main Street
Anytown, ME 04112
207-432-1111

Business Proposal for Mike Gosling and Mike Swan

The cover sheet should not be elaborate. It should be neat, attractive, and short. If the plan is to be used as a financing proposal, use a separate cover sheet for each bank or capital source you submit it to. See below for a suggested cover sheet for a financing proposal.

A Sample Cover Sheet for a Financing Proposal

FINANCING PROPOSAL FOR
FINESTKIND SEAFOODS, INC.

To be Submitted to
The Great Bay Bank and Trust Co.

Mike Gosling
Mike Swan
Finestkind Seafoods, Inc.
123 Main Street
Anytown, ME 04112
207-432-1111
October 31, 19—

STATEMENT OF PURPOSE

The first page of your plan should state your objectives as simply as possible. If the plan is for your sole use, the statement should be a brief description of how you intend to use the plan once it has been developed. For example: "This plan will be an operating and policy guide for Finestkind Seafoods, Inc."

If the plan is also to be used as a financing proposal, the statement of purpose becomes more complex. It should include responses to the following seven questions:

1. *Who is asking for money?*
2. *What is the business structure [for example: sole proprietorship, partnership, corporation, LLC (Limited Liability Corporation), Subchapter S corporation]?*
3. *How much money is needed?*
4. *What is the money needed for?*
5. *How will the funds benefit the business?*
6. *Why does this loan or investment make business sense?*
7. *How will the funds be repaid?*

The deal you propose—the loan or investment, its use and expected effects on the business, and how you will repay it—will be supported by the rest of your plan. If you are not seeking a loan, the plan should still support and justify the use of your own money (or the money of partners, friends, or family).

Keep the statement short and businesslike. It will usually be no longer than half a page, but can be longer if necessary. Use your own judgment.

A Sample Statement of Purpose

Finestkind Seafoods, Inc. seeks loans totaling $120,000 to purchase equipment and inventory; purchase property and buildings at 123 Main Street, Anytown, Maine; perform necessary renovations and improvements; and maintain sufficient cash reserves to provide adequate working capital to successfully expand an existing wholesale/retail seafood market. This sum, together with an additional $30,000 equity investment by the principals, will finance transition through the expansion phase so that our business can operate at a higher level of profitability.

Notice that this sample statement of purpose contains responses to the checklist items. The last statement is intended to assure the bank that the deal is viable.

The statement of purpose cannot be completed until you have calculated your capital needs. It can be written, but the exact amount needed won't be known until the projections in Section Two: Financial Data have been worked through.

TABLE OF CONTENTS

The Table of Contents should follow your Statement of Purpose, which is expanded and supported in the remainder of the business plan.

There are three main sections of your plan:

1. The Business
2. Financial Data
3. Supporting Documents

The Table of Contents serves as a guide to writing and organizing your business plan.

These sections may be broken down further if necessary. Because a business plan, even for a modest deal, can run to 20 or more pages, you want to help readers find their way to sections or subsections of particular interest. The Statement of Purpose states what your deal is. The Table of Contents makes it easy to find supporting material.

A format of this kind makes it easy to find the section of most interest to you at any given time. You will have to fill in the actual page numbers as you go along, but the Table of Contents serves as a guide to writing and organizing your business plan.

A BRIEF NOTE ON FINANCING

Most of the cash required to start a business is provided by the business principals themselves. However, you may need additional funds to launch your business or provide for its growth once it gets started.

Outside funds come in two forms: equity or debt.

Equity funds come from selling a portion of the business to yourself or another person. The amount you have to sell to acquire the needed funds reflects the amount of risk that the investor perceives. If your venture seems very risky, you may have to sell a substantial share. If it is not seen as very risky, you won't have to give up as much ownership. Hence it is greatly to your advantage to make the perceived risk as low as possible—and a business plan can do this.

It is greatly to your advantage to make the perceived risk as low as possible—and a business plan can do this.

Debt is a loan, usually from a bank, that the lender expects you to repay at some determinate time. The lender will ordinarily receive a return for the use of the funds in the form of interest. The interest rate reflects the lender's perceived risk. The higher the perceived risk, the higher the rate. Your plan must take into account the need to repay both principal and interest as agreed. This has far-reaching effects on your profits and cash flow, so borrow with care.

A Sample Table of Contents

If you use an outside equity investor, you don't have to repay the funds, but you give up a share of ownership and will have to share decision making and profits. If the business grows to the point where you wish to sell out, the real cost of an equity investor can be far greater than interest on a loan.

If you use bank debt, you may find yourself subject to loan agreements that effectively compel you to share decision making with your creditors. For example, an agreement may limit the amount of debt you can incur relative to the net worth of the business, which can force you to find new equity money in order to grow.

Just about every small business goes to the bank for money sooner or later. The sample business plans presented in this handbook are tailored to the need to make as strong a case to a banker as possible. More exotic sources of investment, such as venture capital firms, are highly unlikely to be interested in the kind of business banks invest in.

You will find that more advice on these kinds of concerns will be very helpful. Your banker or accountant can provide this advice (and in any case you should be in close communication with both your banker and your accountant as you plan your business).

A brief discussion of different types and sources of financing is included in Section 3: The Financing Proposal.

The Business

*T*his is the most important and most difficult part of your business plan. The objective of this section is to make a clear statement of the following:

- What the business is (or will be)
- What products and/or services you plan to offer
- What markets you intend to service, the size of those markets, and your expected share
- How you can service those markets better than your competition
- Why you have chosen your particular location
- What management and other personnel are available and required for the operation
- Why (if appropriate) debt money or someone's equity investment will make your business more profitable

A rule of thumb: If you can't describe your idea clearly and simply, you haven't thought it through.

These seven statements are crucial. Together they will form the written policy of your business, rules you shouldn't deviate from without compelling reasons. Policy establishes direction and lends stability to your business. Direction and stability are as important to a business as to a tightrope walker—so give them a great deal of thought and planning.

In describing your business idea, aim for clarity and simplicity. A rule of thumb: If you can't describe your idea clearly and simply, you haven't thought it through.

Remember that the technical support for your business idea will be found primarily in the Financial Data and the Supporting Documents sections. In the section on The Business, refer to the supporting information as needed. Too much detail gets in the way of explaining your idea.

A. DESCRIPTION OF BUSINESS

The objective of this section is to explain the following:

- What your business is
- How you are going to run it
- Why you think your business will succeed

Deciding what your business is—and what it will be in five years—is the most important single decision you have to make.

Any business will be involved in more than one activity: If so, your judgment of what the central activity is (or what the central activities are) is crucial. Your entire planning effort is based on your perception of what business you are in. If you make a serious error at this point, your chances of success will be sharply diminished. So be sure to think this decision through.

The Description of Business section answers these seven basic questions:

1. *What business are you in?* Is your business primarily merchandising, manufacturing, or service? What are your products and/or services? Who are your customers? Where is your industry on the industry life cycle? (See Figure 1.1 on page 13.)
2. *What is the status of the business:* A startup? An expansion of a going concern? A takeover of an existing business? A division of a larger business?
3. *What's the business's form:* sole proprietorship, partnership, corporation? (Your attorney's advice is essential if you are starting up a business. Use the sample partnership agreement and corporate checklist in Appendix 1 as a guideline. Because the legal and tax implications are so complex, you need your attorney's and accountant's advice.)
4. *Why is your business going to be profitable (or continue to grow)?*
5. *When will (did) your business open?*
6. *What hours of the day and days of the week will you be (are you) in operation?*
7. *Is your business seasonal?* If it is or if the hours will be adjusted seasonally, make sure the seasonality is shown in your replies to Questions 5 and 6.

The first question is the toughest to answer concisely because it is the linchpin of your plan and it involves the questions mentioned above. It certainly calls for more detail than a simple "Finestkind Seafoods, Inc. merchandises seafoods to local wholesale and retail markets" kind of statement. (See page 17 for a more detailed example.)

Knowing exactly what your business does and how it operates enables you to plan effectively for profits. This means you must be able to clearly identify the goals of your business at the beginning of your planning. Once the goals are clear, then you can start figuring out ways to

Your entire planning effort is based on your perception of what business you are in.

FIGURE 1.1 Industry Life Cycle

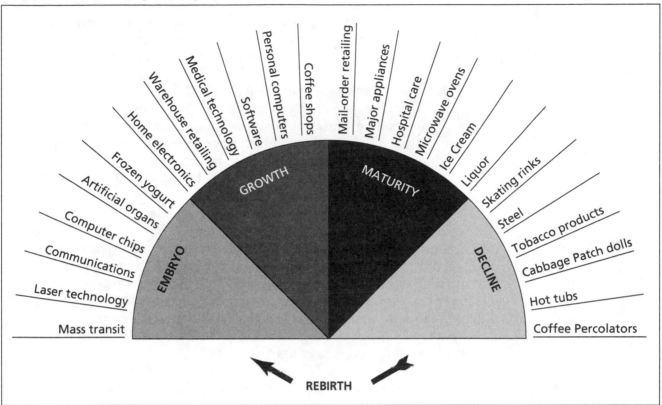

make a profit. As the business progresses, the question of how to make profits must be continuously asked and answered. (Making profits is what business is about. Even nonprofit organizations must have revenues that exceed expenses to survive.)

Focus is the aim. The tighter your focus, the less time and money you'll waste. If you know what business you are really in, you'll concentrate your efforts and use your resources efficiently.

Attention to profit planning will help you identify what is special about your business and why it won't be one of the 50 percent or more that disappear before their second anniversary.

You will not yet have a complete answer to Question 4 because it will be partially answered in the financial projections in Section Two: Financial Data. Keep in mind that the answers will come out as your business plan progresses.

Questions 5, 6, and 7 are particularly important for merchandising and service businesses. These are marketing questions that will be addressed later in the plan.

Because startups and takeovers face different kinds of problems, they are treated separately on the following pages. The following checklists supplement Questions 1 through 7.

For a New Business

Your Description of Business section should be based on responses to the following questions (as well as the basic seven). These questions will come up again and again—and as your business grows, your answers will change.

1. *Why will you succeed in this business?*
2. *What is your experience in this business?* Lack of experience is one of the leading causes of business failure. Fortunately, it's a risk you can avoid. Before you launch your own business, gain experience and learn the ins and outs of your proposed business by working for someone else. Ideally, you would work in management for at least a year. All businesses are more complex when seen from within than when viewed from the outside.

Both of Finestkind's owners had the necessary experience before they opened their store. In the fish business, for example, buying is critical and a function of how well you get along with fishermen. Who are the wholesalers? Do restaurant and retail customers want their seafood whole or filleted? How do you transport such a fragile, perishable commodity and keep it fresh and appealing? The list is endless, but the point is that you don't learn these skills overnight.

3. *Have you spoken with other people in this kind of business? What did you learn from them?*
4. *What will be special about your business?* Business is competitive—and standing out from the competition is increasingly important. Many business owners fail to take advantage of possible competitors' insights and experience. Competitors are your best single source of information and will often give you valuable advice for nothing more than a chance to show their expertise. Talking with them (and observing their business practices) will also help you define what the special advantages of your own business will be.
5. *Have you spoken with prospective trade suppliers to find out what managerial and/or technical help they will provide?*
6. *Have you asked about trade credit?* Trade credit is a source of funds. Terms such as "2/10, net 30" allow you to use the supplier's money for the 30 days—it's like a non-interest-bearing loan for that period. However, this also means that you forego the cash discount allowed for payment within 10 days. Taking discounts can represent a substantial savings on the cost of the product: By paying within 10 days, you save 2 percent of net. This cash discount represents an annualized rate of 36 percent. (Saving 2 percent by paying 20 days sooner is the same as earning 2 percent for a 20-day period—and there are 18 such periods each year.) If you can borrow funds somewhere else for less interest, you should take advantage of the savings.

Take advantage of possible competitors' insights and experience.

Trade credit is often not available until a business has been in operation long enough to establish a reputation for paying on time.

Many suppliers offer free services as an inducement to buy their product. For instance, store fixture suppliers provide free layout advice; utility companies give hints on how effective use of lighting can create more sales.

7. *If you will be doing any contract work, what are the terms?* Reference any firm contract or letter of intent, and include it as a supporting document.

This is especially important for anyone contemplating contract work: Find out how and when you will be paid. Get a feel from other contractors about their experiences. A slow-paying customer can put you out of business if you aren't prepared. If slow payment is a fact of life for your business, plan for it.

8. *How will you offset the slow payment of your customers?* Build your cost of funds into all contracts. At a minimum, adequate capital and careful credit and collection policies will be needed.

For a Takeover

Your Description of Business should contain a brief history of the business you plan to take over and reflect answers to the following questions.

Make sure you can answer these thoroughly: Your banker and other investors will want detailed knowledge. If you don't have these answers, chances are you won't get the financing. Protect yourself.

1. *When and by whom was the business founded?*
2. *Why is the owner selling it?*
3. *How did you arrive at a purchase price for the business?* Businesses that are strong and growing are rarely offered for sale and most sellers will give (not necessarily deliberately) misleading reasons for selling their business.

Determine exactly what you are buying.

Protect yourself. Ask your banker to check out the business. This is a normal bankerly activity, and bankers can get information you may not have access to. If your lawyer or accountant has had a lot of experience buying and selling businesses, get their advice. (They will be involved anyway: Buying a business is a major financial commitment, and you will want all the help you can get.)

A strong case can be made that buying a going business with a positive cash flow is a lot less risky than starting a business from scratch. You might want to involve a professional business broker to help you find the right business or provide you with their updated listings of businesses you might be interested in buying.

Pricing a business—especially a small or closely held company that is not publicly traded—is a delicate and demanding process. It calls for both expertise and ethics. Paying for a professional appraisal may turn out to be an excellent investment as it not only establishes a fair price for the business but also provides justification for the price should outside financing be needed.

The simplest way to establish a justifiable and understandable price for a business is to reconstruct its financial statements, cleansing them of any extraneous or misstated entries to get a clear picture of the earning capacity of the business. Every business accumulates unnecessary expenses over time. Some of them are compensation to the owner (company car, insurance and retirement plans, travel and entertainment expenses). Some are just poor habits, such as doling out contracts to favored suppliers without soliciting comparison bids. Inventories and property have to be evaluated; real estate may be understated, while inventories may be stale and lose value. Risk and desirability factors will also affect the value.

Include a copy of the appraisal as a document supporting the price. The price should reflect the value of the assets of the business, the rate of expected return on your investment (including new investment in the business during the first few years), and some "going concern" or good-will figure.

Because you will be repaying the purchase price out of profits, make sure that you get what you pay for. Be careful—and seek professional help.

4. *What is the trend of sales?*
5. *If the business is going downhill, why? How can you turn it around?*

Questions 4 and 5 should be supported by income statements and tax returns. Remember, if a business is sliding downhill, there may be reasons that aren't immediately apparent. Check out the owner's reasons for selling. Ask his bankers. It is difficult to restore a tarnished reputation, and it can't be done overnight.

6. *How will your management make the business more profitable?* If you can turn around a faltering business, the rewards can be great. Just make sure that you have the skills, capital, and patience turn-arounds require before you commit yourself.

Some additional suggestions to keep in mind as you check out the business are as follows:

- Evaluate and determine the age of the inventory.
- Check with trade creditors.
- Determine the age of the receivables.
- Determine the age and condition of the operating machinery and physical plant.
- See if the business owes money. (If it does, will you inherit the liabilities?)
- See if there any legal problems pending.

You are planning to put your money on the line. Don't be afraid to ask for advice before you commit yourself to any deal. A good attorney and accountant are essential at this point to make sure the transaction benefits both sides—especially if seller financing will be involved, as is usually the case.

Note that this description answers most of the questions posed on the various checklists on pages 12 through 15. (But remember that the checklists are meant to provide a guideline, not a straitjacket.)

It should be apparent that Finestkind has a well-defined marketing strategy. They will be selling premium-quality seafood to two target markets: wholesale (restaurants, markets, institutions) and retail (mainly tourists at the 123 Main Street store). Long term, they will concentrate more heavily on the wholesale market because they feel their chances of penetrating that market are better than their chances of increasing retail trade.

A Sample Description of Business

Finestkind Seafoods, Inc. is a fish market specializing in selling extremely fresh (no more than one day from the boat) seafood to local retail and wholesale customers. At present, about 60 percent of sales are retail. Finestkind plans to concentrate more heavily on the wholesale trade (restaurants and grocery chains) in the future. Although margins are lower in the wholesale trade, profits are higher due to lower personnel costs and faster inventory turnover.

Finestkind began business in September 19—. The store is open seven days a week from 10:00 AM to 8:30 PM (6:00 PM in the winter) for retail business and from 6:30 AM to 8:30 PM year-round for wholesale.

The retail demand is seasonal and fluctuates according to weather (the store is located on a tourist route). The wholesale demand is constant and increasing. We feel that the latter can be improved by more direct selling efforts. Our customers agree (see letter from Nightlife Clambakes in the Supporting Documents). The quality of our seafood is exceptional, and because Mr. Swan is a former fisherman with many personal friends in the fishing industry, we do not anticipate trouble maintaining good relations with our suppliers. We have made a policy of paying premium prices in cash at dockside for the best, freshest seafood.

This is a careful strategic move. They think they see a way to develop a competitive advantage in a market niche, based on their experience and analysis of the competition. Shifting marketing emphasis has problems, but doing so deliberately and thoughtfully makes sense. The shift toward wholesale would be most hazardous if done without a clear idea of where the opportunities are, where the profits are greatest, and what resources are needed to take advantage of the opportunities in their marketplace.

Finestkind should be prepared to explain to a loan officer what "exceptional quality" means and how they plan to be competitive if they continue to pay premium prices for their seafood. These are the areas in which Finestkind stands out from their competitors, but they may prove to be economically self-defeating.

B. PRODUCT/SERVICE

Most businesses are built around products and/or services that already are available. A fish market such as Finestkind has a very simply described product line (seafood); the service element involves how they process the product and satisfy their customers.

If your products or services are unique, state-of-the-art or otherwise noteworthy, take advantage of it. Such differentiation is valuable, tends to be fleeting, and attracts imitators.

The products and/or services offered by most businesses are generic. While you may believe your products and services are special, that perception is not necessarily shared by your market, and no amount of advertising is apt to change their perception. A hardware store sells hardware; a lawyer sells legal services; seafood markets sell fish.

Differentiating your products and services from those of the competition starts with thorough product or service knowledge. One of the most important aspects of business management is giving your markets reasons to buy your products—and one of the best reasons is that the benefits you offer meet the market's desires. People tend to buy what they want, not what you think they need.

Product Research on the Internet

As an example of the power of the Internet for various aspects of market research, a quick search for "Maine + seafood + product + new + retail" yielded over 60,000 responses. Don't faint—of the 60,000 responses only the first 20 had much to offer, including descriptions of seafood products, services, and trade association studies. Some of the other listings observed were very specific: other seafood retailers (all over the place, even though "Maine" was a qualifier) with a description of their prices and products. Some were general: aquaculture in New England showed up.

The important point is that the Internet has a huge wealth of information that can help you to better understand your product or service and its place in the market.

Even if you mention your products and services only in passing in your business plan, you should go through the exercises below. They will help you understand better how to position your business—and can make a difference when your banker asks what's so special about your venture.

The key question is not: "What are your products or services?" The questions are:

1. *What are you selling?* You may think you're selling hardware in your hardware store, that is, hammers and saws and nails and buckets of paint. Your customers, on the other hand, think they're buying (along with the hammers, saws, nails, paint) savings, improved homes, fulfillment of a do-it-yourself ethic—and they choose your hardware store because it's convenient, clean, staffed with polite clerks, has convenient parking, and so on.

The same applies to a lawyer: People seldom buy legal advice. They want to buy solutions to legal problems, a sympathetic ear, a champion of their cause, redress of a problem, and so on.

Finestkind sells good taste, convenience (delivery and filleting fish to order, for example, are conveniences), accessibility, adventure (they were the first to sell Mako, monkfish and mussels in their market area) along with the fresh seafood they thought they were selling.

2. *What are the benefits (as opposed to the features) of what you are selling?*
3. *How do your products and/or services differ from competitive products and/or services?* Customers buy benefits. Features make those benefits possible—the freshness of Finestkind's seafoods is a feature. The taste and the perception that these foods are fresh, natural, healthy foods are benefits that customers (including wholesale) infer in the product line. Other stores offer other benefits—more convenient locations, proven reputation (habit is powerful), long-term vendor relationships with wholesale markets. Finestkind can't compete on every front; they hope to dominate one niche of the seafood business in a local market by a strategy of product differentiation.
4. *If your product is new or state-of-the-art or otherwise unique, what makes it different? Desirable?* Educating a market to a new product is fraught with danger and unexpectedly high costs. Ask yourself where your product or service is on its life cycle. Is it new and growing, or old and obsolescing? Check its industry life cycle. (See Figure 1.1 on page 13.)
5. *If your product or service line is not special, why would people buy from you?* Convenience? A wide product line? Special knowledge of how to use the products you sell?

Business success comes from satisfying market needs. In only a very few businesses does that edge come from product superiority or high technology. Most business—whether retail, wholesale or service—is pretty mundane.

Don't rely on your "superior" product or service. Do rely on satisfying your markets' needs. The first step toward this goal is to understand all about your products or services: What are their features? What benefits can they provide the customer? How can you use your product or service knowledge to differentiate your business from competing businesses?

The second, more important step comes in the next section of the business plan: What do your customers want?

C. THE MARKET

Two important maxims to keep in mind throughout this section are:

* minimize opportunities for customer dissatisfaction; and
* marketing wars are never won—they are always lost.

In this section you will develop a marketing strategy, a plan within a plan. You want to make sure you don't lose the marketing war by making avoidable mistakes. Your business succeeds or fails according to how well you satisfy your market's perceptions, wants, and expectations. This means that you have no option but to learn who your customers and prospects are, why they buy from you or from someone else, and what you can do about getting more customers.

You must be thoroughly knowledgeable about your market, the people who buy or will buy your service, product or merchandise. You need a stream of customers who will buy your goods and services, at a price that yields you a profit, over a sufficient period to keep your business healthy and growing.

Your first challenge is to: Define your target markets.

Who uses your goods and services? Start with your current customers. They find what you offer them to be of value. If you are in a startup business, who do you think your customers will be? Your aim is to know in detail what your customers want that your business can profitably provide them.

Marketing has the customer as its sole focus.

Marketing has the customer as its sole focus. Everything in your business, whether it's a startup or a going concern, old or new, big or small, revolves around your customers and prospects (people you plan to have as customers). Your product or service has to be tailored to *their* perceptions of what is worth buying. Your location and working hours have to fit *their* needs. Management and personnel have to be selected and trained with one goal in mind: satisfying the customers and keeping them coming back. Even the capital structure of the business revolves around the customer. If you can persuade your bankers, investors, and suppliers that you have a strong and stable customer base, you won't lack capital.

It sounds so simple: Put the customer first and the profits will follow. In practice, of course, it's far more difficult.

Four Basic Marketing Moves

1. Sell old products to old customers. This is the least risky strategy.

2. Sell new products to old customers.

3. Sell old products to new customers.

4. Sell new products to new customers. This is the most risky strategy.

Your marketing plan gives you a way to define, understand, and satisfy your target markets. Write it down. It involves too many variables and is too important to be left to chance.

Marketing is the process of creating and retaining customers. Your strategic marketing plan is built on realistic answers to three basic questions:

1. *What business are you in?* Look at your mission statement again. Your mission statement helps you position your business in the marketplace. What makes your business unique? The concept of positioning is critical to your promotional and advertising efforts and will be considered below. What do you want your business to become?

2. *Who are your target markets?* You can't serve everyone. There used to be a store near Keene, New Hampshire, that proudly boasted "We have Everything for Everybody!" Not even the largest international corporation can claim everyone as their prospect. The focus implied by target marketing ripples over into finding ways to limit your markets because you have only so many hours and so many dollars to find and satisfy your customers and prospects. Who is your ideal customer?

3. *What do your customers buy? Or: What benefits do your customers think they receive from your products and/or service?*

Providing informed answers to these questions is difficult. Marketing is a mixture of art (in the guise of your hunches and experience, insights and vision) and science (in the form of careful research and attention to facts). If marketing were simple, no business would ever fail. Your marketing plan helps you make sure that you keep all the pieces of the marketing puzzle in balance.

What goes into a marketing plan? There are at least eight pieces. While they will be presented here as if they come one after another, in the real world they are so interrelated that you can't separate them. As a simple example, your pricing decision will be driven by how your markets perceive the benefits they gain from what you offer them. Their perceptions are influenced by (and will influence) your positioning and promotion efforts, which you adopt at least in part in response to what your competition is up to. And this is just the beginning.

Don't be daunted. You can start anywhere. The following descriptions and question lists are intended to stimulate your thinking. For a much fuller treatment, see *The Market Planning Guide* (5th edition, Chicago: Upstart Publishing Company, 1998).

1. Customers

This is where your market planning begins. Customer focus is the crux of your marketing efforts. There is no substitute for thoroughly understanding your markets. Start with your current customers.

Questions you must be able to answer include:

1. *What are your markets?*
2. *Which ones are buying from you now?*
3. *What products/services are they buying?*
4. *Who are the people who are buying from you?*

These are baseline questions. It's easy to broadly characterize markets you now serve. Finestkind has at least three: the wholesale market (restaurants, groceries, other institutional accounts) and two retail markets (local and tourist). These constitute their current markets, and their purchasing habits can be fairly readily ascertained by observation and some sampling. Determining a market's characteristics are favorite tasks for business school classes—and can cost you as little as the out-of-pocket costs for the students and their professor.

The simplest demographic segmentation of your target markets will vault you ahead of most of your competitors, who rely on habit and inertia rather than analysis of their markets. *Demographic segmentation* is a marketing analysis that targets groups of prospects by factors such as sex, age, marital status, income, occupation, lifestyle, family size, and education.

If you have customers already, start with them. See who patronizes your competition. Pore through trade journals, the more specific to your business the better. Call up the editor of your trade magazine—market analyses, with customer profiles and other useful information, are a stock-in-trade for these experts, and they will be glad to steer you to more information. These indirect sources of customer information are especially useful for startups.

You want to be able to identify your best (most profitable to you) prospects and understand them well enough to be able to satisfy their perceived needs. If you are marketing primarily to businesses, this process has a few added dimensions: First identify the kind of company you are successfully selling to, then find the persons within those businesses who influence or make the buying decision, and then find out more about these individuals. People make decisions to buy products—even if their title is "Purchasing Agent" or "Restaurant Owner."

Sample Demographic Segmentation Criteria

For Individuals

- Age
- Gender
- Race and ethnic group
- Hobbies
- Lifestyle
- Reading, listening, and viewing patterns (newspapers, magazines, TV, radio)
- Education
- Social class
- Occupation
- Income level
- Family life cycle

For Businesses

- Kind of business: manufacturer, retailer, service, wholesaler
- SIC (Standard Industrial Code)
- Position on business life cycle
- Buying motivation
- Location(s)
- Structure (corporation, partnership, d/b/a, sole proprietor)
- Sales level
- Distribution patterns
- Number of employees

5. *How would you characterize your markets?* Some market segmentation criteria that might help are listed on page 23. These are suggested as starting points only. Your markets will have criteria specific to them.

*S*egmentation of your markets provides the basis for all subsequent marketing and promotional efforts.

Why is this so important? *Segmentation of your markets provides the basis for all subsequent marketing and promotional efforts.* If you know who your best prospects are, then you can find out what they want and use their point of view to guide all of your business activities. There is no other way to put the customer first or focus on the customer.

If you do not know who your customers are (or will be), there is no way to find out what they want. You can't advertise effectively; you can't develop products or services that meet their needs; you can't get ahead of your competitors. What you can do—if you think that you know it all already and so don't have to go to the effort of analyzing and understanding your markets—is trust to dumb luck and correct your inevitable blunders by following behind the market leader, thus relegating your business to (at best) an also-ran position.

Segmenting and categorizing your customers and prospects makes sense for even the smallest business. It is a necessity for a new business or one in transition or a business in a rapidly changing market where the experience-based "feel" for the customer base is lacking or no longer applies. That feel is a poor substitute for segmentation but is better than nothing. Augmented by segmentation analysis, your sense of who the market consists of becomes a powerful competitive weapon.

2. Product Benefits

As noted above in B: Product/Service, customers don't buy products or services. They buy benefits. The benefits they perceive are very often not those that you might have spotted, which is why surveys and other methods to find out what your customer wants are so important.

"What's in it for me?" is the question every prospect implicitly asks. They may not express it in this way, but all of us want to know "what's in it for me? If I buy this product or service, what do I gain?" Your prospects have needs, they see a variety of ways of meeting those needs, and if you manage to present your goods and services to them in such a way that they think you can satisfy those needs best, or fastest, or most economically or pleasurably, you'll get their business. (This, by the way, is one way to define positioning. See below for more.)

This knowledge does not come from sitting back in an armchair and theorizing about what the customer might want—or worse, should want. Buying behavior is just not that rational. It's one of those areas where guesses don't pay off but research does.

The simplest research: Just ask them. Go to your customers and ask what they do and do not like about your products, services, facility or store, sales methods, and so on. People like to have their opinion solicited.

You want answers to the following questions:

- *Why do these people buy from my company?*
- *Why do they buy from us and not from the competition?*

Unless you know who your customers, prospects, and competition are you can't even begin to ask these questions. You can get help with marketing surveys from Small Business Development Centers, marketing courses at local business schools, and from your trade association. Check out http://www.princeton.edu/~abelson/index.html (the Survey Research Center home page) to see how surveys are constructed and analyzed. Surveys can be tricky. Customers don't always give straight answers to direct questions, and interpreting the data can be a challenge, so use whatever help you can get.

You will be surprised at what surveys turn up. Customers buy from you because your location is convenient, or your sales force is polite and well informed, or because they think your competitors are arrogant, rude, brusque, and disdainful. Your services may or may not be perceived to be superior; your goods may or may not be price competitive. But there will be reasons why you get their trade and your competitors do not. On the other hand, when you lose customers to the competition you want to know what you are doing wrong—or what they are doing better than you.

- *What are they buying from us? On what cycle?*

There are two levels to this question. On the surface, they buy the things you sell them—hours of a service, a bed for the night, two pounds of haddock.

Service businesses have nontangible inventories, which presents a problem. An airplane seat is either sold for this flight or it is not; a hotel room is either booked for the night or not; a hairdresser either is booked this half-hour or not. They still have to manage their inventories carefully—and this comes from knowing when people are most apt to schedule a flight, visit a hotel, patronize the beauty shop. The buying cycle of their customers affects their scheduling. The most obvious application of this is in retailing. Jewelry stores do as much as 80 percent of their annual sales during the Christmas season. They stock their shelves and staff their counters with that customer buying cycle very much in mind.

All businesses have such cycles. The cycles may be subtle, but your customers buy your goods and services in patterns you can understand if you take the effort to observe them.

The second level is concerned with perceived benefits. You have to look at what you sell through the eyes of your customers and prospects. People buy benefits, the gains or rewards they expect to receive from your products. This is always complex. Max Factor, the cosmetics king, said "Our factories make cosmetics. We sell hope." The things *sold* (lipstick, perfume, eye shadow, mascara, and so forth) have physical characteristics or features such as color, weight, fragrance, and texture. The customer could care less about these physical characteristics. She is *buying* hope—hope for approval, hope for beauty, hope for a new mate or retaining the old one, and so forth. Features are only important insofar as they convey benefits to the prospective buyer.

By focusing on the perceived benefits (the "what's in it for me?") you make positioning your business much simpler. You may be selling door locks with features such as "weighs one pound, made of brass, has clever tumblers, and is highly polished," but your customer is buying security, a sense of achievement (do-it-yourself), and savings. And so on.

The key exercise: What features of your goods or services convey benefits to the customer? How does your customer perceive your offerings? What are the benefits you ultimately provide that customer?

Don't beat this into the ground. Use your common sense. Place yourself in your customer's shoes. Ask questions. Listen to the responses. Once you know what benefits your business should provide, provide them. Your business will flourish.

- *How can we find more people (businesses, buyers) like these?*

This question drives your future strategies. It is always easier to sell to current customers than to new ones, but you have to constantly look for more customers to replace those you lose through normal attrition and to competitors, to say nothing of the new customers you need to grow more profitable.

People cluster by interests and expectations. Once you know what people are buying, why they buy from you, and who those people are (by description as well as direct personal acquaintance), you can find more people like them.

3. Sales and Distribution

*M*ake it easy for your customer to buy from you.

Distribution is a highly important and very visible part of your marketing efforts. The type of distribution channel you choose may be direct (to the end user) or indirect (through middlemen, wholesalers, distributors, or jobbers to the retailer). The right channel for *your* business may consist of more than one channel of distribution, a decision not to be made lightly. What do other people in your industry do? Should you alter this, or (more likely) follow the trade?

The challenge is to deliver your goods and services to the customer economically. Part of this is a function of your location. A good location (see D: Location of Business below) makes it easy for customers to find you and makes it possible for you to present your goods and services to those customers in a favorable way. The other part is concerned with sales practices, how you persuade the prospect that you do indeed have the solution to his or her needs. While that subject is well beyond the scope of this book, the idea behind strategic sales and distribution efforts is simple: Make it easy for your customer to buy from you.

Ways to make it easy for your customers to buy from you range from using 800 numbers to providing charge accounts or using credit cards. A major office supplier, Quill, used a $15 electronic link to make ordering easier for their customers. Not coincidentally this tied the customer and Quill together.

A Brief Note on Credit

Will you offer credit to your customers? If you give credit to your customers, you are making them a loan. Can you afford to do this? Do you have to extend credit? Can you evaluate credit risks? Can you collect slow-paying credits? Can you afford to write off bad debts?

Customer credit can result in an unexpected cash drain on your business. If you must offer credit because it's customary in your line of business, because you think that sales and profits increases will outweigh the costs of offering credit, or because a competitive market situation demands that you offer credit, make sure that your financial plans include the effects of offering credit.

Offering credit costs you money. It can have a negative effect on your cash flow, especially in the early stages. You may have to borrow money for working capital to carry customer credit. You may strangle your business by tying up funds you could have used more profitably elsewhere.

Check with your banker. Judicious use of bank credit cards is much less expensive and far safer than setting up your own credit department. You may find that there are other methods that don't deny you the benefits of offering credit but let you pass on the costs to a bank or other financial institution that knows how to deal with credit risks.

---

4. Competition

Who are your competitors? Look for companies that are selling similar products and chasing similar customers and prospects.

You can learn a lot from your competitors: What do they do better than you? Less well than you? How do they please their customers? What is their pricing policy? Where and how do they advertise—and does it work?

Your suppliers will have insights into what your competition is doing and what people in your line of business in noncompetitive areas (another city or state, for example) are doing. If you feel bold enough (or are in a startup or transitional business) take a trip and visit businesses like yours. Small business owners love to talk about their businesses if (a) they aren't talking to direct competitors and (b) you make an appointment at their convenience and (c) let them know beforehand what you are going to ask.

Information is power. Most small business owners do not take the time to painstakingly assemble competitive information. There is nothing wrong or immoral about scouting the competition—athletes and armies do it all the time. So should you. This will give you a strong competitive edge.

5. Positioning, Publicity, and Promotion

In *Ogilvy on Advertising* (New York, Crown Publishers, 1983), David Ogilvy, founder of a hugely successful advertising firm, wrote that of the 32 things his advertising company had learned, the most important was positioning. Positioning is a marketing method in which you determine what market niche your business should fill and how it should promote its products or services in light of competitive and other forces.

Positioning is important for all businesses but especially for small businesses that lack the depth of resources to weather a major marketing blunder. The importance of establishing a market niche is hard to overstate. Pick a market big enough to support you and allow you to grow your business, yet small enough to defend against competitors. You simply cannot afford to aim for huge markets. The economics are overwhelming.

So your recourse is positioning. Pick a niche in which you can become a presence. This can be as simple as locating your convenience store where there is little competition except major supermarkets, keeping hours to suit the convenience of your customers, and stocking the things they want at odd hours. Or if your local laws allow, become the only hairdresser who makes house calls. The idea is to differentiate your business from competing businesses, which means you must know what they are up to (hence the study of the competition) and who your customers are and what they want that other businesses aren't providing.

A market niche is much like a target market except (for most cases) a little more tightly defined in terms of how you can reach that market. Finestkind advertises in local newspapers, on local radio, and uses location and signage to reach its local markets. Several specialty woodworkers in Boston advertise in the Boston Symphony Orchestra program and in alumni magazines; they find that this is far more economical than buying space in a major daily newspaper or using network television. They zero in on their markets, using the proverbial rifle rather than a shotgun approach.

Targeted promotions to targeted markets is the safest way to stretch your promotional dollars and gain market share. By this point you should be able to decide what image and message you want to project: What will make your customers and prospects think of your business when they want to buy whatever it is you sell?

Promotion and Advertising Note

Because you know who your prospects are (the target market, in your market niche) you can determine where your prospects are on the Promotion Pyramid. The notion behind the pyramid is that you can move people along one step at a time. If they don't know that you're in business, let them know. If they know you are in business, what does it take to persuade them that you are going to be able to meet their needs? What will it take to get them to act? Do they understand what you want to sell them, or will you have to educate them first?

For some businesses, this is quite easy. Finestkind has been around for some years now, so people know who they are and what they sell, and they are convinced that they can get excellent seafood (and service) at the Route 1 store. Therefore Finestkind can advertise specials: New species of shark! or Fresh lobster! or whatever they think would move their market to act.

For other businesses, it can be complicated. Here's where niche marketing and positioning become vitally important. If you are selling a new technical consulting service to nuclear engineers, you will find it easier to educate a few engineers than all the engineers in the Western world. Then you can move them up the Promotion Pyramid one step at a time.

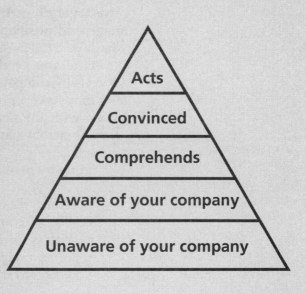

As you figure out how to promote your company using all the tools available to you, including public relations and advertising, there are three myths to avoid. If you are already in business, you probably know these; if you are new to business, they are hazardous to your economic well-being.

The first myth is "You can rely on 'word-of-mouth' advertising." This is usually an excuse not to invest in advertising rather than a good way to gain customers. Passive word-of-mouth advertising is always ineffective. Happy customers tell an average of 0.7 other people if they have had a positive experience with you. Unhappy customers tell 7 to 11 other people! That is why minimizing opportunities for customer dissatisfaction is so important. Word-of-mouth advertising can be made to work, but it requires discipline and a programmatic effort: Ask customers for referrals. Make it easy for them—give them brochures, flyers, samples, or whatever it takes to make your case. Then follow up.

The second myth is that only highly creative and clever advertising works. Not true. Clearly positioned and consistent advertising does work, though it is mainly supportive rather than the clinching argument for customers. Consider McDonald's. They make a deliberate attempt to meet 105 percent of their customers' expectations, not more, not less. People do not like surprises. You know that McDonald's will have clean rest rooms and fast service at a low price. You know just what to expect, and they deliver. They advertise what they actually provide, not more, not less.

Third, "You can save money by doing your own advertising." This is a costly mistake made by many beginners. Ineffective advertising is expensive. Advertising that does work, that informs your markets honestly, accurately, and effectively, is worth its apparently high initial costs. Advertising includes space ads in newspapers, home pages on the Internet, radio or television spots, signage, logos, stationery and business cards, everything that the public gets as an image of your business. Your image and positioning is far too important to do yourself. And besides, you have a business to run.

Hire a professional advertising agency or consultant to set up your advertising campaigns. It pays off. Check with your local SCORE chapter; they may have a professional who will help you in these matters for free. Check with the nearest college (including junior college) business program; they may have free or low-cost help for you. But do not try to do it yourself.

Some more questions to answer include:

- *What is the size of your markets?*
- *What percent of the market do you (will you) have?*
- *What is the market's growth potential?*
- *As the market grows, will your share (percentage) increase or decrease?*
- *Is the market competitive? If not, why not?*

You can obtain information on the size of your markets from chambers of commerce, trade publications, marketing consultants, other business persons, schools, and colleges. The Federal Census Report, which will be in your local library, provides detailed information down to a block-by-block analysis of buying patterns for most areas.

Get help in assessing your prospective markets from such sources rather than trying to guess by watching passing traffic and hoping for the best. Good marketing strategies are planned. Good plans are based on good information.

Marketing Research on the Internet

More and more, astute market researchers are turning to the Internet as a primary research tool. The only limits are your own ingenuity. If there is secondary data out there, it will be on the web. If you want to find books about marketing research (or any other topic) try Amazon (http://www.amazon.com/). It's an astonishingly excellent bookstore that has a powerful search engine built in so you can browse their millions of books.

Here are seven key sites to help you get started:

1. *American Demographics,* the monthly magazine, has an excellent home page at http://www.marketingtools.com/. *American Demographics* is the magazine of record for demographic research. They make using census data simple and effective.

2. *Home Office Computing* (http://www.smalloffice.com/) is to my mind the best small business magazine. HOC has practical, down-to-earth advice on topics ranging from market research to what computer programs to use for research. Plus a lot more. Other magazines with useful home pages are *Inc., Forbes,* and *Fortune,* though they tend to be somewhat less directly helpful than HOC.

3. Prentice Hall's *Directory of On-Line Information* (http://www.bizinfosearch.com/) is a good place to conduct specific market research.

4. Princeton University's *Survey Research Center* home page (http://www.princeton.edu/~abelson/index.html) is a must-visit. It contains a number of links to other sites, as well as being of value in itself.

5. The *National SBDC Research Network* home page (http://www.smallbiz.suny.edu/) is your entry into the SBDCs' extraordinary wealth of information.

6. *SCORE On Line* (http://www.scn.org/civic/score-online/) has one-on-one marketing research advice as well as plenty of helpful links.

7. *Hoover's Online* ("The ultimate source of information on businesses") is terrific for getting financial information on publicly traded companies. (http://www.hoovers.com/)

Don't forget search engines such as Lycos, Gopher, WebCrawler, NetSearch, and so on. You can find just about any kind of information on the Internet—but you do have to be careful to delimit your search. A few hours spent learning how to use these search engines is time well spent.

6. Pricing

Pricing is a widely misunderstood strategic tool. Lack of courage in pricing may be the biggest single marketing error small business owners make. There is a widely held perception that price drives all purchasing decisions, so in order to gain market share you have to slash prices below the competition. Wrong! This is the worst strategy possible. You cannot afford to be the low-cost producer or cut-rate king.

Price and perceived value work together. Price *is* important. But it is not the main reason people buy things. Ryobi, a manufacturer of construction tools, did a pricing study to learn how to penetrate the construction trade market. They found that workmen compared products on reliability, durability, and guarantee before price came into play.

Look at it this way. Do you buy everything on price? Medical care? Cars? Food? Education for your children? You will find the following kind of matrix helpful in thinking through your pricing strategies. Any product or service can be compared to competitive offerings this way. Think of cars. A basic model, no radio, secondhand will be low price, low quality. A Cadillac or Mercedes will be high price, high quality. If status is the selling point, high price becomes a selling point. Think of perfume or jewelry. You want to provide the level of pricing your customers expect. K-Mart pricing won't work at Tiffany's.

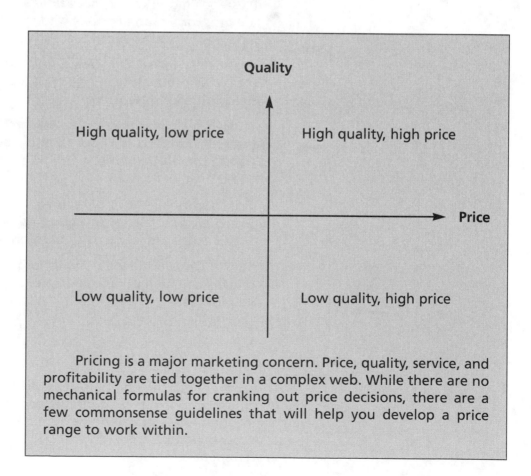

Pricing is a major marketing concern. Price, quality, service, and profitability are tied together in a complex web. While there are no mechanical formulas for cranking out price decisions, there are a few commonsense guidelines that will help you develop a price range to work within.

Pricing is inherently strategic, so be clear on your objectives.

1. *Price = Product + Service + Image + Expenses + Profit.* The prices you set on your goods and services should reflect not only the product or service itself but also an intangible image factor. In an ideal situation, you would know how your customers and prospects perceive the value of whatever you sell and price accordingly. You also have to cover costs and profits.

2. *Determine your pricing objectives.* Identify your objectives. Are you trying to buy market share with low prices? (It won't work but you can always try!) Maximize profits? Remain competitive? Build up a new product line? Your general marketing objectives apply here. Pricing is inherently strategic, so be clear on your objectives.

3. *Establish price ranges.* This is defensive. Make sure that you charge enough to cover your costs. A breakeven analysis (see Section Two: Financial Data) will help you establish the low end of your price range. You have to cover your fixed costs with enough margin to survive—and this can be calculated in terms of both unit sales and dollars, thus helping you establish minimum prices.

At the high end, build your desired profit levels into the breakeven equation and compare the prices you arrive at (on an item-by-item or product-line basis) to your sense of what the market will bear. Your customers won't pay more for your goods and services than they have to—and their perception of the value of your goods and services makes a very effective upper price limit.

4. *Choose a flexible pricing approach.* The four basic pricing approaches are full-cost pricing (which reflects your costs), flexible markups, gross margin pricing (which takes operating costs and marketing factors into account), and suggested or going rate. The last of these is the least desirable; it involves you in an endless game of follow-the-leader and ignores your cost structures. All of these approaches have their merits, however, and it makes sense for you to understand all of them.

For a fuller description of these pricing approaches, check with your accountant. A review of your pricing strategy is a valuable addition to your planning and should be part of your periodic financial and accounting reviews.

7. Goals and Budgets

In Section Two: Financial Data you will establish budgets that include money for marketing. The amount you budget for advertising (the most visible but by no means most important part of marketing) depends on what you are trying to accomplish in the business as a whole. A startup needs to spend more for marketing than a well-established business because the markets need to be informed that you are in business, where and when, and what products or services you will provide. A very rough guide to marketing expenditures can be gained by looking at trade figures, but keep in mind that the average percent of gross sales (a common measure) is based on a wide range of businesses with different markets, different positioning within those markets, and at different stages on the corporate life cycle. A company milking a cash cow will spend less than a company aggressively seeking a share of a new market.

Your safest course is to look at your sales and profit goals, then work backward to see what marketing goals and budgets will help you reach those sales and profit levels. Your goals might include training salespeople, opening a new branch in another city, or changing your distribution patterns. The key point: Tie your marketing goals and budgets to your business's goals, not to an artificially chosen or arbitrary percent of gross sales plucked from a trade or financial publication.

Tie your marketing goals and budgets to your business's goals

Make sure that goals you set are "believable, achievable, and measurable" so they can be communicated clearly. If they are not believable, they will be ignored. If they are not achievable, they will backfire. If they are not measurable, how will you know whether progress is being made toward them?

An old saw tells us: It takes money to make money. Your advertising and promotion budget is an investment in future sales, not an expense that can be cut at the slightest sign of a drop in profitability. Note that if you know who your target market is, and how to reach them, you can control some of these promotional costs—but in a brand new market you would still have to get your message out more vigorously than to a market that knows your business and your products and services well. Think of all the steps in the Promotion Pyramid you have to move brand new customers along.

8. Strategies

Pick the simplest strategy you can.

"Coddle your customer" is the best strategy for any small or new business. If put into effect it will automatically differentiate your operation from your competition because most businesses are run for the sake of the owner and employees, not the customer.

"Minimize opportunities for customer dissatisfaction" is another excellent strategy. It puts your customers where they belong, at the center of all your business efforts, and reminds you and your employees that the customer is the reason you are in business in the first place.

Why pick a simple strategy? Because simple strategies work.

Why pick a simple strategy? Because simple strategies work. Complex strategies get shelved or miscommunicated. Napoleon always closeted himself with the dumbest general under his command and explained to a jealous Maréchal Ney (his most brilliant general) that "If he understands it, the dumbest private will. . . ."

That's all you want from a strategy. Clear and complete communication with employees and markets, based on a comprehensive customer focus.

Finally, your strategy has to address these two questions:

1. *How will you attract and keep your target markets?*
2. *How can you profitably expand your market niche(s)?*

A Sample Description of the Market

Finestkind will continue to provide premium-quality seafoods to both wholesale and retail customers. We plan to switch the balance from 60 percent retail/40 percent wholesale to 40 percent retail/60 percent wholesale as we grow. Retail business should grow over the next few years, but the greatest growth will be in wholesale accounts.

Our goal is to provide the freshest seafood at competitive prices to customers within 25 miles of York. This market has a total population of over 100,000 people and a potential of over 300 commercial wholesale accounts.

Customers will be attracted by:

- Direct approach to local restaurants, groceries, and other potential wholesale accounts

- A local radio and newspaper advertising campaign

- Word-of-mouth advertising from our present customer base

- Our location and signs on Route 1, a heavily traveled tourist route

As a footnote: In the past month distributors from four countries (Turkey, Germany, Poland, and Belgium) have purchased significant amounts of fresh and frozen lobsters from us. This may represent a low-risk growth opportunity because these accounts pay in advance of shipment. While we came across these accounts by a fluke, we think they could be an entry into a wider market. We are currently exploring this opportunity with our advisers and exporters recommended by the SBA.

These bring in further questions, such as how and where to advertise, the suitability of your location, the attractiveness and accessibility of your store or office or plant, and the fit between your business and its chosen markets. You can't answer them without knowing your markets in great detail, which presupposes that you have gone to the trouble of first defining, then segmenting, your markets.

Use your mission statement to test your strategy. This is easy to do: State your strategy, then see if it forwards the achievement of your mission. If the answer is no, discard it.

Think of McDonald's. Their motto (a statement of their mission) is QSC: Quality, Service, and Cleanliness. Constant and consistent reference to QSC guarantees that all of McDonald's activities have a customer-centered marketing focus.

Note that Finestkind has included strategies consistent with the policy stated in the above example (see page 35). Finestkind's marketing strategy is limited to a specific geographical area, the area they feel they can service without incurring prohibitive travel and spoilage costs. Their advertising will be on local radio stations (four 50,000W FM stations cover the area) and in local papers. Advertising can be costly, and they plan to invest their advertising budget wisely.

They are wise to approach export markets carefully. The financial and marketing structures of export businesses are very different from Finestkind's structures and could lead to a loss of focus: Are they in retail, wholesale, or export?

Finestkind's pricing strategy is pegged to competitive prices. This strategy is questionable because they pay top dollar for their product and provide a superior level of service. They could justify a higher price, on the basis of higher quality and better service.

D. LOCATION OF BUSINESS

Proper site location can help your business make money. If you are going into business, first try to locate the ideal site, then figure out how close you can come to it. Remember:

Rent = The Costs of Space + Advertising

Information about specific areas is available from chambers of commerce, industrial development commissions (they may also have information about tax breaks and financing incentives for businesses that will employ substantial numbers of people in towns under their commission), trade sources such as magazines and associations, planning commissions, bankers, and lawyers. Try these first.

Then ask commercial real estate brokers, once you have a feel for how much space you need and about location cost requirements.

Do not go into business in a given spot simply because the price is low. Rent and purchase prices are fixed by market forces, and a low price usually reflects low desirability. Although for some operations this doesn't matter, for others—merchandising and restaurant businesses in particular—the three most important success factors are said to be location, location, and location.

Different businesses have different needs. Manufacturers and wholesalers value low space costs and good access to transit routes over exposure to and accessibility by the public. For retail operations, access and exposure are very important. Traffic studies may be available for the area you are interested in and can give you information to make the right location decision for your business.

Your banker may be your most helpful reference. Some locations seem to be jinxed, and bankers are apt to know why and will tell you.

In this section of your business plan, you should answer the following nine questions:

1. *What is your business address?*
2. *What are the physical features of your building?*
3. *Do you lease or own your space?*
4. *What renovations are needed, and how much will they cost?* Get written quotes from more than one contractor. Include these as supporting documents.
5. *Does zoning permit your kind of business in the neighborhood?*
6. *What other businesses (kinds of businesses) are in the area?* For example, car dealers tend to cluster. So do art businesses, restaurants (especially fast-food restaurants), jewelry stores, and financial businesses.
7. *Why did you pick this site over others?*
8. *Why is this the right location for your business?*
9. *How will the choice of location affect your operating costs?* A bad site can put you out of business, while a good site will increase your profits. Choose wisely.

A Sample Description of the Location

Finestkind is currently leasing a one-story, wooden frame building with cement floor (2,000 square feet) at 123 Main Street, Anytown, Maine, for $550/month with an option (in writing) to buy for $105,000. The area is zoned for commercial use. Main Street is part of U.S. Route 1, a heavily traveled tourist route with most nearby businesses catering to the tourist trade. Finestkind has performed major leasehold improvements, such as installing rough-sawed pine board walls and a walk-in freezer. The building is divided into (1) a sales/counter area (1,200 square feet); (2) a cutting area (100 square feet); (3) a multipurpose area, including toilet with separate entry, storage space, and room for some expansion of the freezer and processing areas (700 square feet in all). See the diagram in Appendix 3: Sample Business Plans.

Once you get started, or if you are already in a good location, keep a constant eye on changes in your location—new roads get built, populations change, people move, zoning ordinances change, and your business needs may change too. Prepare to anticipate these changes. Compare census reports over a period of time to find long-term shifts. Keep in touch with real estate people who have to know what's happening.

This section needn't be too involved. Except for serving as a reminder of things to look out for, once the location has been chosen a brief statement is all that's necessary when you update your business plan. Suggested alterations may not be made for reasons you forget between periods of updating your plan, so it may be wise to make a note of them as they come up.

E. THE COMPETITION

If you have decided on your target markets and found that they are large enough to be profitable and contain reasonable expansion possibilities, the next step is to check out your competition, both direct (those operations similar to yours) and indirect.

There are three times you should be concerned about the competition.

1. *When you are planning to start up or buy a business, or planning to enter a market that's new (to you).* You'd best check up before sitting down with your investors and banker—because the first question they'll probably ask is, "What competition do you face?" Business is inherently competitive, and because there is very little that's new in business, most worthwhile markets are already being worked by someone. In fact, if you think you've found a brand new untapped market, think carefully before entering it. If there are no competitors, it's probably because the market can't support a business.

2. *When a new competitor arrives on the scene.* When you study the competition under these circumstances, you probably won't have the flexibility you had earlier. New competition can come from direct competitors (old rivals as well as new ones). But it can also come from outside your line of business. (A classic example would be the assault television made on the movie business for people's free time.)

3. *All the time.* This ongoing monitoring of the competition is an inexpensive form of preventive maintenance, and is your best strategy for protecting your customer base. While forestalling competition and ensuring your survival is very important, being in a position to recognize and take advantage of new opportunities is even more important. Constant monitoring of the market will allow you to keep ahead of your competition, whether new or old.

To analyze your competition, consider the following questions:

- *Who are your five nearest competitors?*
- *How is their business—steady, increasing, or decreasing?*
- *How are their operations similar and dissimilar to yours?*
- *What have you learned from watching their operation? What works for them? What doesn't?*
- *How will your operation be better than theirs?*

To make gathering this information easy, set up competitor files, simple manila folders into which you put any scrap of information about your competitors. You will be surprised how quickly you gain a clear picture of what your competition is up to. Collect and date their ads, brochures, trade show handouts, and any other printed material. Jot down their radio jingles. Check local community home pages to see if they are listed. Look for their home page (if they have one) on the Internet and visit it frequently. For example, if you were planning to open a restaurant in Portsmouth, New Hampshire, you could go to http://www.portsmouthnh.com/ to see what other restaurants are offering by way of price, product, specialties, and service levels. Put in notes of rumors about their financial condition, want ads, activities in the community. Anything that helps you form a clear picture of their plans is germane.

Then review each competitor file weekly or monthly. This has to be done systematically or the full benefits will be lost. Who are they advertising to? How? What are they trying to sell? The benefits they stress will be a good indicator. Where do they advertise? And so on.

The objective of this section is to enable you to pick up the good competitive practices and avoid the errors of your competitors. A common error is opening a business in a market that is already more than adequately serviced. Carefully viewing the competition can lead you to alter your basic strategy or to change existing operations to compete more effectively. This has to be an ongoing practice because markets are continually changing and success attracts competitors.

How should you compete? Knowledgeably. There are many alternatives to price competition, for example, that small business owners could profitably use. These are based on knowing how your business compares to competing businesses.

You won't be able to fight on every front. Choose the areas where you can gain a competitive advantage, one based on your business's strengths (people, product, and service are the three most important). Try to match your strengths against your competitors' weaknesses—which of course means you have to know what these matchups are.

For a quick comparison, fill in the form on page 40.

The number of competitors (five) mentioned in the first question is arbitrary. Use your own judgment. Perhaps there are no direct competitors (Finestkind has three) and the main competition is indirect.

But make sure to regularly keep abreast of the competition. Business—any business—is too competitive to allow your attention to lapse.

Customer Seeks	Competition Offers	You Offer
Quality		
Exclusivity		
Lower prices		
Product line		
Product service		
Reliability		
Delivery		
Location		
Information		
Availability		
Credit cards		
Credit line		
Warranty		
Customer advice		
Accessories		
Knowledgeability		
Polite help		

By looking carefully at their competition, Finestkind has the basis for a competitive marketing strategy. They seek information about competitors' strengths (to learn from) and weaknesses (to avoid). They aim to find a market segment that is being underserved or undersatisfied, to form a strategy taking advantage of that competitive oversight, to gain a niche, and then to defend it. An advantage for a small business is being able to operate profitably in a market too small for big businesses to consider.

A Sample Description of the Competition

There are three seafood operations competing directly with Finestkind:

1. **Ferd's Fish**—a scattered operation with one truck making the rounds and a small counter leased from a supermarket in Anytown. We have cut into their sales by making promised deliveries on time and at the agreed price. As a result, their operation has become marginal.

2. **Kingfisher**—a clean, three-man operation in Rye specializing in cheaper fish. Kingfisher has trouble with their suppliers because they aren't willing to pay top dockside prices in cash—the owner likes to haggle over price. The operation is well financed and managed, has modern equipment, and sells directly to homes from a fleet of three trucks (very convenient). They have some wholesale business that they want to expand. Their sales are apparently growing because they have been serving the same routes for five years and have an excellent reputation. Rumor has it that Kingfisher is interested in buying Ferd's Fish or adding another delivery truck or two.

3. **Job's Seafoods**—currently rebuilding because of a disastrous fire but will be our most serious competitor when their new store opens. Job's has been in business for 25 years in Anytown and has a good location on a scenic bridge two miles south of Finestkind. Job's has good relations with suppliers and serves most of the supermarkets. Currently, they have no retail business but plan to open a retail store in their new building. However, the owner needs a major eye operation and may be willing to part with some of his wholesale business because he is getting on in years.

Indirect competition is from major processors in Portland (45 miles east) and Boston (60 miles south). Because we fall between their primary market areas we can purchase from both on consignment basis.

F. MANAGEMENT

According to various studies of factors involved in small business failures, 98 percent of the failures stem from managerial weakness. Two percent of the failures are due to factors beyond control of the persons involved.

Your business plan must take this into account. If you are preparing a financing proposal you should make sure that your prospective financing source is aware of what steps you have taken or are taking to correct any weakness in your managerial staff (yourself and any other managers involved); if you are to use your business plan to its fullest, you should use this segment to highlight both strengths and weaknesses of management for your own sake.

The failure factor breakdown provides a guide:

Managerial incompetence	45%
Inexperience in the line	9%
Inexperience in management	18%
Unbalanced expertise	20%
Neglect of business	3%
Fraud	2%
Disaster	1%
Total	**98%**

There is no known cure for incompetence—but there are two very direct cures for inexperience and/or unbalanced experience: Get the necessary experience yourself; get a partner or employee who has the requisite experience. (An important Small Business Administration study showed a high correlation between small business success and having a partner as opposed to being a solo act.)

The final three items represent managerial failures because neglect of business, fraud, or being put out of business by disaster could almost always have been prevented by foresight. Insurance, for example, can protect a business against both fraud and disaster, while neglect of business is a form of business suicide.

In preparing the management section, there are five areas to cover:

1. Personal history of the principals
2. Related work experience
3. Duties and responsibilities
4. Salaries
5. Resources available to the business

Personal History of Principals

This segment should include responses to the following seven questions:

1. *What is your business background?*
2. *What management experience have you had?*
3. *What education (including both formal and informal learning experiences) has a bearing on your managerial abilities?*
4. *What is (are) your age(s), special abilities and interests, reasons for going into business, where do you live and have you lived, and so on.* The personal data needn't be a confession, but it should reflect where your motivation comes from. Without a lot of motivation, your chances of success are slight. It pays to be ruthlessly honest with yourself—even if you don't put the results on paper.
5. *Are you physically up to the job?* Stamina counts.
6. *Why are you going to be successful in this venture?* Keep in mind that your family will be affected by your decision to go into business. Try to assess the potential fallout—while your family may be supportive now, will they continue to be when you're putting in 80-hour weeks for very little money?
7. *What is your personal financial status?* A personal balance sheet must be included as a supporting document in your business plan if the plan is to double as a financing proposal.

Bankers and other providers of capital want to see as much collateral as possible to secure their investment. There are no small business loans; there are only loans to small business owners, and under most circumstances the personal creditworthiness of the principals will be the major factor in your banker's decision.

You will undoubtedly be expected to guarantee the loan personally. This means that your personal assets may be taken if the business fails—even if the business is a corporation. Your banker doesn't want to be in the secondhand house business—but centuries of experience indicate that if you are personally tied to the business, you'll be less apt to walk away from it if things get tight.

Related Work Experience

This segment is a detailed response to the experience factors mentioned earlier. It includes (but is not limited to) responses to the following:

1. *What is your direct operational experience in this kind of business?*
2. *What is your managerial experience in this kind of business?*
3. *What other managerial experience have you had—in different businesses, in a club or on a team, in civic or religious organizations, or in some other area?* Many managerial skills are transferable. Others are not—but the more evidence and analysis of your managerial experience you can show, the better. You'll be able to use this to plug managerial gaps.

Unbalanced managerial experience can cause serious problems. For example, the talents required of a financial specialist are quite different from those of a used car salesman. A combination of both sets of talent in one individual is rare.

Duties and Responsibilities

Once you have written down the experience and skills (and have a feel for the weaknesses) of the proposed management, this segment becomes much simpler. Follow the rule: Always build on strengths and seek to alleviate weaknesses.

This is a variant on "you can't make a silk purse out of a sow's ear"—attempting to make a salesman out of a retiring clerk is folly. Attempting to make a sales manager out of your star salesman may also be folly. Use skills to advantage.

The scarcest asset you will have is time. To make the most of it, make sure that you budget your time carefully by spelling out, in advance:

- Who does what
- Who reports to whom
- Who makes the final decisions

Make sure you allot adequate time for the following:

- Planning and reviewing plans
- Major operating duties (purchasing, sales, personnel, production, distribution, promotion and advertising, marketing, and so forth as needed in your business)
- More planning

The purpose of your business plan is to make your business run more smoothly, more profitably, and more easily. If you find that you spend a lot of time solving yesterday's problems, stop. Get out of the shop, sit down somewhere quiet and begin to plan. That time investment—anywhere from a few hours to a few days—can make all the difference.

Allocating duties and responsibilities is critical. If the chain of command is unclear to your employees, you will have the worst kinds of personnel problems. This is a major management responsibility and must not be evaded under the hopeful guise of "we can work it out later when we see where the problems are." By then it will be too late.

Salaries

A simple statement of what the management will be paid is sufficient. Just remember to cut the fat from your personal budget, add 15 percent for contingencies, and then stick to it. Many deals never get going because bankers feel the principals are getting paid more than they should; other deals self-destruct when the rock-bottom salary figures, unrealistic to begin with, are altered without planning, thus throwing the budgets into disarray. Be realistic. Don't be greedy. Your payoff comes in the future, after your business becomes successful.

To help you figure out what you need to live on, we have provided some Cost of Living Budget forms in Appendix 4.

Knowing what you need, as distinguished from thinking you know what you need, takes effort—but one sure way to damage a small business is to bleed it for family necessities. If your business can't afford to pay you a living wage, and you have no other income or savings, you had better think your deal over again.

If you are preparing a financing plan, your banker will need the cost of living budget to help justify your salary requirements. Remember: Be realistic.

Resources Available to the Business

All businesses, no matter how tiny, need the following:

- An accountant
- A lawyer
- A banker
- An insurance agent or broker

If you have to be told why you need these, you shouldn't be contemplating going into business.

Other sources of assistance include the following:

- Chambers of commerce, regional planning commissions and councils
- Business, trade, and civic organizations
- Small Business Administration technical assistance, SCORE, and SBDC programs
- Consultants
- Colleges, universities, and schools
- Federal, state, and local agencies
- Your board of directors

Some small business owners have found that judicious use of online bulletin boards and chat rooms can lead to linkage with other owners in similar businesses. For example, a Berwick, Maine, woman with a computer-driven service for small contractors was able to link up with a woman in Mississippi who had a similar business several years further along. They "met" via a chat, and ended up phoning one another to discuss their ventures.

Don't forget: Your banker can be among the most helpful of all due to the nature of the job. Bankers trade in information as much as in credit, and banks have a wealth of information about businesses that you can tap simply by asking.

You won't have to use all of these resources (except the first four), but it is a good idea to know what help will be available if you need it, and to know where it is (and who it is) well ahead of time.

List these resources, and make yourself known to them. You can plug many gaps in your experience and increase your chances of success by relying on the experience of others. Tapping into many of these resources will cost you no more than time and a phone call.

Summary

This section is intended to make you aware of the availability of management skills in and outside your business. If you keep in mind the necessity of managing your business rather than letting your business manage you (and constantly review and reevaluate the results of this analysis in the future), you will drastically reduce the odds against you. Keep this section short, direct, and honest.

A Sample Description of Management

Mr. Gosling was born in Anytown, Maine, and has lived there all his life. After graduating from local schools and serving in the U.S. Navy for three years, he became a self-employed carpenter, taking night courses in small business management and sales at the University of Maine, with the aim of owning and managing a retail store. He currently serves on the local zoning board. He and his wife (a medical secretary) live in Anytown with their two children.

Mr. Swan was born in Wisconsin, attended schools in Utah, Alaska, and Florida, and served four years in the Marines (rank upon separation: E-3). He test-drove motorcycles for a year, then served as parts manager for Wheely Cycles, Inc. before joining the Fatback Fish Division of Tasty Foods as a packer in March 1989 in their East Machias, Maine, plant. In June 1991 he resigned as line foreman of the Frozen Food Filleting Department to join Mr. Gosling in Finestkind. He is unmarried and lives in Anytown.

Both men are healthy and energetic. They believe their energies complement each other and will help them make Finestkind a success. In particular, Mr. Swan knows all of the fishermen while Mr. Gosling is a well-known member of the community. Because Mr. Swan has had experience in cost control and line management, he will be responsible for the store and inventory control. Mr. Gosling will be primarily responsible for developing the wholesale business. They will set policies together. Personnel decisions will be made jointly.

Salaries will be $950/month for the first year to enable the business to pay off startup costs. Mr. Gosling's wife earns enough to support their family; Mr. Swan's personal expenditures are low because he shares a house with five other men. In the second year they will earn $1,200/month; in the third year $1,500/month with any profits returned to the business.

In order to augment their skills, they have enlisted the help of Smith & Farley (CPAs), Dewey Cheatham & Howe (attorneys), and Halsey Johnson, a retired banker who will be on their advisory board. Other advisory board members are Andrew O'Bangfo, business consultant; the University of Maine's Venture Incubator Division's Etienne LeBlanc; and Gene Brudleigh of FROG (Fish Retailers Organized for Growth). This board will provide ongoing management review.

G. PERSONNEL

Personnel management is a major stumbling block for small business owners. Personnel management is a demanding profession that few people learn; the assumption that "I can manage people because I've been around" is dangerous. You may find it valuable to hire a consultant to set up your personnel systems, help in hiring and training, and educate you in personnel management. While the cost may seem high initially, the cost of a poor hiring process can be catastrophic.

A Sample Description of Personnel

Finestkind will hire one part-time salesperson within six months to sell seafoods over the counter to the retail customers. He or she will be paid $4.00/hour for weekend work; no fringe benefits or overtime are anticipated. We will also employ, on an as-needed basis, one cutter at $6.75/hour to help process seafood for the wholesale trade. We think the counter help will be needed for 10 weeks during the summer and the cutter will be needed for about 20 hours/week for 16 weeks. (This should take care of the second summer as well. For the third year, we plan on two counter helpers plus a full-time summer cutter.) In the second year we'll add one full-time employee at $850/month, with a raise to $900/month in the third year.

No further employees are planned for unless business grows more rapidly than we have forecast.

Businesses stand or fall on the strength of their personnel. Good employees can make a marginal deal go; poor employees can destroy the best business.

As with other management tasks, personnel management requires careful planning. Here are eight questions to think about as you outline your personnel needs for the future:

1. *What are your personnel needs now? In the near future? In five years?*
2. *What skills will your business need?*
3. *Are the people with those skills available? Where?*
4. *Will you have full- or part-time employees?*
5. *Will your employees be salaried or hourly?*
6. *What fringe benefits will you offer?*
7. *Will you pay overtime?*
8. *Will you have to train people?* If so, at what cost to your business (time, interrupted work flow, money)?

Be careful. Training can be a hidden cost that you didn't expect.

Hire people only when it will result in added profitability for your business, and think before hiring whether the job is really necessary. If it is, then careful selection of the right person for that job will pay off. Salaries are a fixed expense, and you want to be sure that the expense is really necessary.

Personnel Management on the Internet

The Internet is a boon for the small business owner looking for personnel management information. You can find wage and salary ranges, sample forms and contracts, job descriptions, and even receive expert human resource assistance from a variety of providers.

Check your state and local department of labor or department of employment security (or whatever they call it in your state) for wage and salary advice, as well as availability of trained personnel for a specific job listing.

Sylvia Ho is a human resources attorney with a wonderful home page (http://www.ultranet.com/~windog/hr/index.html) called HR in a BOX. To understand how valuable a resource her site will be for you, pay it a visit. You can e-mail Sylvia at Sylvia.ho@snet.net.

SCORE provides a wealth of personnel management expertise. SCORE On Line (http://www.scn.org/civic/score-online/).

The Small Business Administration has many free or low-cost publications, including some of the best material for small business personnel management. Visit it at http://www.sbaonline.sba.gov.

H. APPLICATION AND EXPECTED EFFECT OF LOAN

This section is important whether you are seeking a loan, outside equity, or planning to finance your deal yourself. In determining how much money you'll need and for what purposes it will be used, do not rely on guesses when exact prices or firm estimates are available. If you must make an estimate, specify how you arrived at your figures.

It is often helpful to make a three-column list.

Bare Bones	Reasonable	Optimal
(What you can just scrape by with—secondhand, makeshift—the bare minimum.)	(What you will most likely get—some new, some used, some fancy, some plain.)	(What you'd like if money were no problem.)
1. Bicycle with large basket (Schwinn '52 at $12.50)	Pickup truck with insulated camper adapted for icing fish ('91 Ranchero $3,885)	Custom-made truck with new freezer unit (new El Dorado $68,500)
2. Used desk ($7.00)	Inexpensive desk ($55)	New teak desk ($750)

Fill out the Bare Bones and Optimal columns first, then make your reasonable choice. It may be important for you to have a luxury item or two, but weigh the cost. This tabular worksheet is particularly handy for a startup business and can be used whenever a purchase of additional equipment is contemplated.

Make sure that this section contains responses to the following seven questions:

1. *How is the loan or investment to be spent?* This can be fairly general (working capital and new equipment, inventory, supplies, and so on).
2. *What items will be purchased?*
3. *Who is the supplier?*
4. *What is the price?*
5. *What is the specific model name and/or number of your purchase?*
6. *How much did you (will you) pay in sales tax, installation charges, freight or delivery fees?*

Your banker may be interested in using whatever it is you are buying as collateral for the loan. By having a list, your loan can be processed faster.

You should consider the possible advantages of leasing some of the capital equipment you need and definitely look into the advantages of renting rather than owning your place of business. If you have the money to buy, owning may (or may not—ask your accountant) be less expensive than leasing. If you are short of cash, a lease arrangement may enable you to ease your cash problems by lowering your investment in fixed assets (perhaps a sale/leaseback deal would help if you already own the building).

Leases also have great flexibility: As your business grows, you may want to change some of the fixed assets. Leases also have certain tax advantages. Once more, check with your accountant.

Most importantly, ask yourself:

7. *How will the loan make your business more profitable?*

Interest is an expense that directly reduces profits. If you propose borrowing money or investing your own, you must know how well that money will work for you.

Make sure the loan earns more than it costs.

The exact figures in the Application and Expected Effect of the Loan or Investment section won't be available until you have worked through the financial data—but the fixed assets you plan to acquire and some working capital needs can and should be addressed here. You can always pare back from reasonable to bare bones (for example) if your finances demand it.

The sample is modest. For a more complicated deal, much more detail would be needed. Be guided by your judgment in this section. The hard figures in the Financial Data section will provide support for a loan proposal, but the objective here is to give the reader, either you or your banker, a qualitative insight into the expected effect of the loan on the business.

Notice that Finestkind has asked that $14,350 be reserved as a line of credit to allow them to take advantage of opportunities that may arise in the future. Frequently a small business grows too fast, and when it turns to its bank for additional financing, the funds are denied. By reserving funds ahead of time, those funds will be available, but because they aren't disbursed, they won't incur additional interest expense. Finestkind is looking ahead to forestall cash-flow problems, a good example of careful planning.

I. SUMMARY

The purpose of this section is to summarize the ideas you have developed in the preceding sections. This summary will help you make sure that the different parts of the analysis make sense, that they support each other logically and coherently, and that they will leave the reader with a concise, convincing statement that the project and plan are feasible.

A Sample of Application and Expected Effect of Loan or Investment

The $120,000 will be used as follows:

Purchase of Main Street property $75,000
Equipment:
      Used Ford pickup with insulated body 3,885
      Dayton compressor (used, serial #45-cah-990) 365
      Sharp slicer (used, Speedy model) 400
Renovations (see contractor's letter in Supporting Documents) 12,500
Working capital 12,000
Inventory 1,500
Cash reserve 14,350
Total: **$120,000**

    Finestkind can purchase the 123 Main Street property at a substantial savings under the terms of a lease/purchase agreement. An independent appraiser has calculated the value of the property, including leasehold improvements already done by Finestkind, at $135,000. The monthly payment for a 15-year mortgage ($75,000 at 11.5 percent interest) will be $875/month, a net increase of $325/month over the current rent. See the Financial Data section for the effect on the business.

    The truck will be used to deliver merchandise to our wholesale customers, retard spoilage, and maintain the quality of the seafood.

    The compressor will replace the one now used for the freezer and will lower electrical costs and provide a measure of insurance against loss of refrigeration. (We'll keep the old compressor as a spare.)

    The slicer will save four man-hours of work daily. The time released will be used for soliciting more business and processing a greater volume of whole fish. With the slicer, relatively untrained help can fillet flounder with minimal waste.

    The renovations are: a deep-water well required by the state, a toilet and wash sink separate from the work area, and replacement of the current obsolete heating system to reduce fuel expenses.

    The working capital will enable Finestkind to meet current expenses, offset negative seasonal cash flow as shown in the Cash Flow Projection in the Financial Data section, and ensure the continued growth of the business.

    The inventory is to take advantage of bulk rates on certain fresh-frozen packaged goods such as red snapper or South American spiny lobster.

    The bank will hold the reserve as a line of credit. It will be used to take advantage of special opportunities or to meet emergencies.

A Sample Summary

Finestkind Seafoods, Inc. is a fish market serving retail and wholesale markets in and around Anytown, Maine. Mike Gosling and Mike Swan, the owners, are seeking $120,000 to purchase the 123 Main Street property, perform necessary renovations and improvements to the property, maintain a cash reserve, and provide adequate working capital for anticipated expansion of the business. This amount will be sufficient to finance transition through a planned expansion phase so the business can operate as an ongoing, profitable venture.

Careful analysis of the potential market shows an unfilled demand for exceptionally fresh seafood. Mr. Gosling's local reputation will help secure a sizable portion of the wholesale market, while Mr. Swan's managerial experience assures that the entire operation will be carefully controlled. Mr. Gosling's current studies at the University of Maine will provide even more control over the projected growth of Finestkind and complement the advice of a thoughtfully selected advisory board.

The funds sought will result in a greater increase in fixed assets than may be shown, as Mr. Gosling will be performing much additional renovation and improvements himself. The additional reserve and working capital will enable Finestkind to substantially increase their sales while maintaining profitability.

Guidelines for the Summary Section

The following checklist will help you make sure that important points are covered in your summary. These guidelines are a suggestion; your business plan may need to emphasize different points. If so, make sure that they are included.

Description of Business

1. Business form: proprietorship, partnership, or corporation?
2. Type of business: merchandising, manufacturing, or service?
3. What is the product and/or service?
4. Is it a new business? A takeover? An expansion?
5. Why will your business be profitable?
6. When is your business open?
7. Is it a seasonal business?
8. What have you learned about your kind of business from outside sources (trade suppliers, bankers, other business owners, publications)?

Product/Service

1. What are you selling?
2. What benefits are your customers buying?
3. Which products are rising stars? Which are steady cash cows? Which are in decline or investments in ego?
4. What is different about your goods and services?

The Market

1. Who buys from you? Define your target markets.
2. Are your markets growing, steady, or declining?
3. Is your market share growing, steady, or declining?
4. Have you segmented your markets? How?
5. Are your markets large enough for expansion?
6. How will you attract, hold, and increase your market share?
7. Are you planning to enter or leave any markets?
8. How do you price your products?

Location of Business

1. Where are you (or should you be) located?
2. Why is it a desirable area? A desirable building?
3. What kind of space do you need?
4. Are any demographic or other market shifts going on?

The Competition

1. Who are your nearest direct competitors?
2. Who are your indirect competitors?
3. How are their businesses similar to and different from yours?
4. What have you learned from their operations? From their advertising?

Management

1. How does your background/business experience help you in this business? For your own use, what weaknesses do you have and how will you compensate for them? What related work experience do you have?
2. Who is on the management team?
3. What are their strengths and weaknesses?
4. What are their duties?
5. Are these duties clearly defined? How?
6. What additional resources are available to your business?

Personnel

1. What are your current personnel needs?
2. What skills will your employees need in the near future? In five years?
3. What are your plans for hiring and training personnel?

Application and Expected Effect of Loan (Investment)

1. How will the loan (investment) make your business more profitable?
2. Should you buy or lease (equipment, your place of business, and so on)?
3. Do you need this money? Establish a procedure for making borrowing decisions, and plan your borrowing.

Financial Data

*P*olicy and control are key ingredients of any successful business. Policy establishes what your business will do. Control measures the accomplishment of policy goals.

The heart of the operation is in the accounting system. Before you start your business, it is essential that you have a competent accountant set up a system to give you adequate accounting records. If you can't afford this, you are simply too undercapitalized to be in business. If you don't understand the need for accounting records, you don't have enough management experience to be starting a business. This is a common problem area for many small businesses.

Control is essential. If you don't control your business, it will control you.

The overriding policy of your business is:

- to find out what your markets want,
- to satisfy those wants, and
- to make a profit while doing so.

The implementation of your policy depends on planning and using your plan as a means of controlling your business. The first step toward managing your business for profits is to establish a bookkeeping system that provides you with the raw data for the five control documents (balance sheet, breakeven analysis, income statement, cash flow analysis, and deviation analysis) that will be developed in this section.

Your bookkeeping system should be simple enough for you or an employee to keep up to date on a daily basis with provisions made for weekly, monthly, quarterly, and yearly summaries. The system must contain cash controls (a checkbook and a cash register tape are part of your

If you don't control your business, it will control you.

bookkeeping system). Beyond this, your method of bookkeeping should be suited to your specific needs.

Because your bookkeeping system is the basis of your business information (control) system, and because only you know what kind of information you will require beyond the demands of this section, no attempt is made in this handbook to set up a system for you.

There are three resources for setting up your bookkeeping system:

1. You or an in-house bookkeeper
2. Business service firms
3. Accountants

Each has advantages and drawbacks. You should decide which suits your needs best. The do-it-yourself systems are lowest in cost but require more time and often provide less information than professional business service firms and accountants provide. However, business service firms and accountants cost considerably more. Your best bet is to check out all three before making your decision. Keep in mind that business service firms and accountants act as outside staff (management consultants) for your business as part of their services. This extra service alone often justifies their higher costs.

The kind of insights a good accountant (whether with a business service firm or a CPA firm) can bring include analysis and interpretation of your financial statements, wide experience with many other small businesses, knowledge about people and markets, advice on choosing and using up-to-date computer power, and other general managerial tools. They also provide tax advice—which should be the least of your worries. (Sometimes a good tax accountant can actually make you more money in tax savings than he or she costs in fees.)

The five control documents mentioned earlier provide the structure for your planning efforts. Properly used, they act as a budgeting tool, an early warning system, a problem identifier, and a solution generator. Used inconsistently or not at all, they are worthless. Used incorrectly they are dangerous. Misleading financial information can lead to making bad or disastrous decisions.

Develop your financial statements with an eye on your information needs.

These documents needn't be very complicated. Develop your financial statements with an eye on your information needs, using your common sense and your accountant's experience as guides to the level of detail needed. (It's also possible to suffer from too much information.)

These statements should be used systematically. Make it policy to spend at least several hours (preferably free from distractions) each month checking them over, once your business is underway. By doing so your information will be fresh and of greatest value to you and help you plan profitable strategies, make good business decisions, and set reasonable objectives for the future.

Ultimately, your accounting system should be a working model of your business. A business manager has two concurrent objectives (which may conflict): to make a profit and to pay bills as they come due. These objectives are reflected in the two most important financial statements, the income statement and the cash flow projection. The income statement (also called the profit and loss statement) is designed to show how well the company's operations are being performed over time by subtracting expenses from sales (profit or loss). The cash flow projection is designed to show how well the company is managing its cash (liquidity) by subtracting disbursements (actual cash outlays) from cash received.

The balance between profitability and liquidity can be hard to maintain. Fast growth (with high profits) can deplete cash, causing illiquidity. Companies have been known to fail even while they are profitable. The role of projected income and cash flow statements is to help you spot these kinds of severe problems in time to do something to forestall them such as raise new capital or arrange for the right kind of financing. Your banker will be helpful here; ask.

The breakeven statement is based on the income and cash flow statements. Breakeven analysis is a technique that no business can afford to ignore. Basically, the breakeven shows the volume of revenue from sales you need to exactly balance the sum of your fixed and variable expenses. This document can be used to make decisions in such critically important areas as setting prices, whether to purchase or lease equipment, projecting profits or losses at different sales volumes, and even whether or not to hire a new employee.

The balance sheet records the past effect of such decisions. More to the point, it records what the cash position (liquidity) of the business is and what the owner's equity is at a given point in time. These are directly affected by the cash flow and income statement, which themselves are the records of how the business operates over time.

The deviation analysis compares actual performance to projected or budgeted performance on a monthly basis. As a guard against runaway expenses or destroyed budgets, it's unbeatable. You should compare both income statement and cash flow projections against actual performance. Most business experts will agree that more businesses are destroyed by the cumulative effects of a lot of small, sloppy errors (which deviation analysis highlights and helps you correct) than by large, powerful, obvious mismanagement.

Together, the income statement, cash flow, breakeven, deviation analysis, and balance sheet afford a comprehensive model of the operations, liquidity, and the past and near future of your business. If you have a computer and spreadsheet software, the information can be easily manipulated to give you answers to many revealing what-if questions: What if we raised prices 5 percent? What if we lose 15 percent of our customer base? Would it make sense to add these fixed expenses to obtain 10 percent greater productivity? And so on.

The value of such an interactive model of your business is hard to overstate. If you are not familiar with computerized financial models, check with the nearest business school (or your accountant). Just being able to trace out the short-term financial implications of a business decision can make a big difference in the quality of your judgments, to say nothing of your profits.

If there is only a single statement that is available, let it be your cash flow.

If there is only a single statement that is available, let it be your cash flow. A business that can't pay its bills can't stay in business for long even though the business may be operating at a profit. A schematic model of the cash flow is shown on page 82. Remember: Cash inflows must be greater than or equal to cash outflows.

Projections are an integral part of the Financial Data section and are critical to accurately evaluating the feasibility of your deal and to planning just how large an investment is required to get your business to a stable level of operation. Your assumptions must be carefully thought out and explained. Be honest here for your own benefit: Too much optimism can accelerate failure.

The following items should appear in the Financial Data section:

A. Sources and Applications of Funding
B. Capital Equipment List
C. Balance Sheet
D. Breakeven Analysis
E. Income Statement Projections
F. Cash Flow Projections
G. Deviation Analysis
H. Historical Records (for an existing business)

A. SOURCES AND APPLICATIONS OF FUNDING

This subsection is needed for financing proposals but also is handy for you as the owner. It's a restatement of the information in Section 1-H: Application and Expected Effect of Loan on page 49. Major anticipated expenditures should be supported by copies of contracts, lease or purchase agreements, or other relevant documents.

The information presented here will show up in the cash flow projections, as the timing of the funds' flow is particularly important to maintaining liquidity.

B. CAPITAL EQUIPMENT LIST

Capital equipment is equipment that you will use and wear out or consume as you do business.

Your business plan should contain a capital equipment list: to help maintain control over depreciable assets, for insurance purposes, to insure against letting your reserve for replacement of capital equipment become too low (or be used as a slush fund), and to assist in the creation of a cost budget.

Capital equipment is equipment that you use to manufacture a product, provide a service, or use to sell, store, and deliver merchandise. It is not equipment you will sell in the normal course of business but rather is equipment that you will use and wear out or consume as you do business. This does not include items that are expected to need replacement annually or more frequently.

A Sample Description of Sources and Applications of Funding

Finestkind Seafoods, Inc.

Sources

1. Mortgage loan	$ 75,000
2. Term loan	30,000
3. Reserved loan	15,000
4. New investment from Gosling and Swan	30,000
Total	**$150,000**

Applications

1. Purchase 123 Main Street property	$105,000
2. Equipment	4,650
3. Renovations	12,500
4. Inventory	1,500
5. Working capital	12,000
6. Cash reserve for contingencies	14,350
Total	**$150,000**

To be secured by the assets of the business and personal guarantees of the principals, Mike Gosling and Mike Swan.

Examples of capital equipment are office furniture and business machines (desks, typewriters, computers, adding machines), store fixtures (display cases, refrigeration units, permanent fixtures such as air conditioning and lighting fixtures), machinery used to make products or deliver services (lathes, medical equipment), and delivery vehicles. None of these types of equipment is expected to wear out before a period of years. These goods are depreciable. Depreciation, the writing off of fixed assets over a period of years, is expressed as "depreciation expense" on the income statement, and serves to shelter income against taxes so you can replace the equipment as needed.

A sample capital equipment list for Finestkind appears on page 60. No allowance for depreciation has been made because it is a new business. Otherwise, a column for accumulated depreciation would be shown so the depreciated value of the capital equipment could be displayed.

A cost budget is another useful control document that, due to the scope of this handbook, has been omitted. Its function is to allocate indirect expenses (overhead, interest on loans, office salaries, etc.) to separate operations of the business on a pro rata basis. Such allocations are especially important for a business that submits bids on contract. The SBA has an excellent booklet on this topic: SBA Management Aid No. 221, Business Plan for a Small Contractor.

A Sample Capital Equipment List

Finestkind Seafoods, Inc.

Major Equipment and Normal Accessories	Model	Cost or List Price (whichever is lower)
Storequip, Inc. display case, glass front, ice	handmade	$ 600
Storequip, Inc. display case, glass front, refrigerated	SST6-77K	1,700
Dayton air compressor	45-cah-990	365
Bendix standing freezer	3979-7584	350
GE standard freezer	—	50
Cleaning table, fiberglassed	handmade	200
Freezing locker and compressor	handmade	4,500
Total		**$ 7,765**
Minor Shop Equipment		
Miscellaneous knives, scalers, etc.	—	$ 500
Miscellaneous display trays, boxes	—	350
Total		**$ 850**
Other Equipment		
Pickup truck with insulated body	1983 Ford, Lo-bed	$ 4,000
Safe	1879 Diebold Mosler	200
Cash register	523 NCR	350
Calculator	TI-120	65
Computer and software	Super Clone	2,100
Light fixtures	custom	400
Total		**$ 7,115**
Capital Equipment Total		**$15,730**

If applicable, add sales tax and installation fees back onto the lower of cost or list price.

C. BALANCE SHEET

Balance sheets are designed to show how the assets, liabilities, and net worth of a company are distributed at a given point in time. The format is standardized to facilitate analysis and comparison—do not deviate from it.

Balance sheets for all companies, great and small, contain the same categories arranged in the same order. The difference is one of detail. Your balance sheet should be designed with your business information needs in mind. These will differ according to the kind of business you are in, the size of your business, and the amount of information your bookkeeping and accounting systems make available.

Current Assets: cash, government securities, marketable securities, notes receivable (other than from officers or employees), accounts receivable, inventories, prepaid expenses, any other item that will or could be converted to cash in the normal course of business within one year.

Fixed Assets: land, plant, equipment, leasehold improvements, other items that have an expected useful business life measured in years. Depreciation is applied to those fixed assets that (unlike land) will wear out. The fixed asset value of a depreciable item is shown as the net of cost minus accumulated depreciation.

Other Assets: intangible assets such as patents, copyrights, exclusive use contracts, notes receivable from officers and employees.

Long-Term Liabilities: mortgages, trust deeds, intermediate and long-term bank loans, equipment loans (all of these net of the current portion of long-term debt, which appears as a current liability).

Net Worth: owner's equity, retained earnings, other equity.

Footnotes: You should provide displays of any extraordinary item (for example, a schedule of payables). Contingent liabilities such as pending lawsuits should be included in the footnotes. Changes of accounting practices would also be mentioned here.

A Sample Balance Sheet Format

Name of Business
Date (month, day, year)
Balance Sheet

Assets

Current Assets		$_____
Fixed Assets	$_____	
Less Accumulated Depreciation	$_____	
Net Fixed Assets		$_____
Other Assets		$_____
Total Assets		$_____

Footnotes:

> **Current Liabilities:** accounts payable, notes payable, accrued expenses (wages, salaries, withholding tax, FICA), taxes payable, current portion of long-term debt, other obligations coming due within one year.

Liabilities

Current Liabilities	$_____
Long-Term Liabilities	$_____
Total Liabilities	$_____
Net Worth (total assets minus total liabilities) or **Owner's Equity**	$_____
Total Liabilities and Net Worth	$_____

Footnotes:

Finestkind Seafoods, Inc.
October 1,19—
Balance Sheet

Assets		Liabilities	
CURRENT ASSETS		**CURRENT LIABILITIES**	
Cash	$2,150	Accounts Payable	$8,077
Accounts Receivable (net)	1,700	Current Portion Long-Term Debt	1,440
Merchandise Inventory	3,900		
Supplies	450	**Total Current Liabilities**	**$9,517**
Prepaid Expenses	320		
		LONG-TERM LIABILITIES	
Total Current Assets	**$8,520**	Note Payable (a)	$535
		Bank Loan Payable (b)	1,360
FIXED ASSETS		Equity Loan Payable (c)	9,250
Fixtures and Leasehold Improvements (d)	$13,265	**Total Long-Term Liabilities**	**$11,145**
Building (freezer)	4,500		
Equipment	3,115	**Total Liabilities**	**$20,662**
Trucks	6,500		
		NET WORTH	
Total Fixed Assets	**$27,380**	Owners' Equity	$15,238
Total Assets	**$35,900**		
		Total Liabilities and Net Worth	**$35,900**

ACCOUNTS PAYABLE DISPLAY

Eldredge's Inc.	$3,700
Lesswing's	4,119
Paxstone	180
B&B Refrigeration	78
	$8,077

(a) Dave N. Hall for electrical work.

(b) Term loan secured by 1987 Jeep, 1992 Ford.

(c) S & C Finance Corp., Anytown, Maine.

(d) Includes $10,000 in improvements since June.

The categories can be defined more precisely. However, the order of the categories is important and you should follow it. They are arranged in order of decreasing liquidity (for assets) and decreasing immediacy (for liabilities). Examine the sample balance sheet for Finestkind, for example.

If you need to provide more detail, do so—but remember to follow the standard format. If your balance sheet is assembled by an accountant, the accountant will specify whether it is done with or without audit. If you do it yourself, it is without audit. The decision to use a CPA (Certified Public Accountant) should be made carefully for tax and other legal reasons.

The sample balance sheet for Finestkind is modestly detailed. No depreciation has been taken, for example, because the business has just been started. The net worth section could have been more complex. The important thing to notice is that it provides a level of detail appropriate for the purposes of the principals, who own all of the stock.

Some financing sources (banks or other investors) may want to see balance sheets projected for each quarter for the first year of operation and annually for the next two. This would quickly show changes in debt, net worth, and the general condition of the business, and could be another helpful control document. You may wish to have a monthly balance sheet (easily done with a microcomputer-powered accounting system), but for many businesses, a year-end balance sheet is all that is required.

> *The balance sheet for Finestkind provides a level of detail appropriate for the purposes of the principals, who own all of the stock.*

Preliminary Balance Sheet Analysis

1. *Working Capital.* Working capital is calculated by subtracting current liabilities from current assets. Cash is only a portion of working capital. Finestkind's working capital is negative [$8,520 − $9,517 = ($997)], a dangerous but not uncommon position for many small (and at times, large) businesses to be in.

A low or negative working capital position is a major danger signal. A firm with this working capital situation is said to be illiquid. Because owners' equity is less than the debt, the creditors in effect "own" the business, and bankers would be reluctant to extend further loans. Among possible solutions to this type of problem would be a working capital loan (long term, to be repaid from operating profits), sale of fixed assets, or financing accounts payable by arranging to spread payment over a longer term. The best solution (the one Finestkind chose) is to get new equity investment. (See Sources and Applications of Funding section on page 58.)

2. *Comparison.* Comparison of year-end balance sheets over a period of years will highlight trends and spotlight weak areas. Because Finestkind is new, this option is not open to them. However, they can compare their business to other, similar operations by ratio analysis.
3. *Ratio Analysis.* This technique permits comparison in terms of percentages rather than dollars, thus making comparisons with other companies more accurate and informative. Among the more useful ratios are:

A. *Current Ratio.* This measures the liquidity of the company, its ability to meet current obligations (those coming due during the current year). It is calculated by dividing current assets by current liabilities. For Finestkind, divide $8,520 by $9,517. This yields a current ratio of 0.89, which is well below the current ratio of 2.0 some analysts would like to see. Finestkind is mildly illiquid. However, you need to know exactly what is represented by the figures to make a meaningful analysis. Inventory composition, quality of receivables, time of year, and position in the sales cycle are all possible factors affecting the current ratio.

B. *Acid Test.* This is another measure of liquidity (sometimes called the quick ratio), and it is calculated by dividing the most liquid assets (cash, securities, and possibly current accounts receivable) by current liabilities. For Finestkind, $3,850/$9,517 = 0.40. The rule-of-thumb ratio should be 1.0.

> *The rule-of-thumb ratios are far from infallible because the date on which the balance sheet is drawn and the kind of business will affect the ratios you come up with.*

A word of caution: The rule-of-thumb ratios are far from infallible because the date on which the balance sheet is drawn and the kind of business will affect the ratios you come up with. Some companies need a current ratio of 2.7 to be considered liquid, others can get by with 1.5 or less (such as department stores just prior to the Christmas rush when their inventories and payables are particularly high).

Try to get trade figures for your kind of business from the following:

- Trade associations. These are apt to be very specific—a good example would be the Hardware Association's annual figures. Check with *Ayer's Directory of Associations* in your library and call the appropriate association for more information.
- *Annual Statement Studies,* which your banker will usually have, is available from the Robert Morris Associates.
- Dun & Bradstreet publishes *Key Business Ratios, Cost of Doing Business: Partnerships & Proprietorships;* also available for corporations.
- Ask a friendly competitor, perhaps in a noncompeting location.
- Ask your banker and accountant for help finding current trade figures.
- Check your local library, business school, and chamber of commerce.

D. BREAKEVEN ANALYSIS

A breakeven analysis provides a sales objective expressed in either dollar or unit sales at which your business will be breaking even, that is, neither making a profit nor losing money. Once you know your breakeven point, you have an objective target that you can plan to reach by carefully reasoned steps.

It is essential to remember that increased sales do not necessarily mean increased profits.

More than one company has gone broke by ignoring the need for breakeven analysis, especially in those cases where variable costs (those directly related to sales levels) get out of hand as sales volume grows.

Calculating the breakeven point can be simple (for a one-product business) or very complex (for a multi-line business). Whatever the complexity, the basic technique is the same. Some of the figures you will need to calculate will have to be estimates. It is a good idea to make your estimates conservative by using somewhat pessimistic sales and margin figures and by slightly overstating your expected costs.

The basic breakeven formula is:

$$S = FC + VC$$
where
S = Breakeven level of sales in dollars,
FC = Fixed costs in dollars, and
VC = Variable costs in dollars

Fixed costs are those costs that remain constant no matter what your sales volume may be*, those costs that must be met even if you make no sales at all. These include overhead costs (rent, office and administrative costs, salaries, benefits, FICA, etc.) interest charges on term loans and mortgages, and "hidden costs" such as depreciation, amortization, and interest.

Variable costs are those costs associated with sales including cost of goods sold, variable labor costs, and sales commissions. These cost figures are further elaborated in the next section, Projected Income Statement.

When you want to calculate a projected breakeven and you therefore do not know what your total variable costs will be, you have to use a variation of the basic "$S = FC + VC$" formula. If you know what gross margin (profit on sales) to expect as a percent of sales, use the following formula:

$$S = FC / GM$$
where
GM = Gross margin expressed as a percentage of sales

If instead of calculating a dollar breakeven you want to determine how many units you need to sell to break even, simply divide the breakeven derived above in dollars by the unit price to get the number of units to be sold.

Because sales are projected at a total of $216,000 for the first year, Finestkind doesn't expect to make a profit—but because they know what they are apt to face, they will be able to plan ahead to finance their business properly.

---

* These costs remain constant only in a relevant range. Your sales could rise dramatically—for example, you may need a new building, some new administrative employees, and new equipment—and drive your fixed costs up disproportionately. Fixed costs tend to move up in chunks, not smoothly, if sales rise quickly. For Finestkind's experience, look at the three-year projections on page 73. "F" and "V" (on the extreme left-hand margin) denote fixed and variable cost allocations respectively. Note how the totals change over three years.

A Sample Breakeven Analysis

Projected figures from Finestkind's Three-Year Income Projection

Fixed costs $FC = \$62{,}220$

Gross margin $GM = (57{,}680/216{,}000) = 26.7\%$

Thus, breakeven sales $= S =$ $FC\ /\ GM$

$= (\$62{,}220/.267)$

$= \$233{,}033/\text{year}$

On a monthly basis, $S =$ $\$19{,}419/\text{month}$

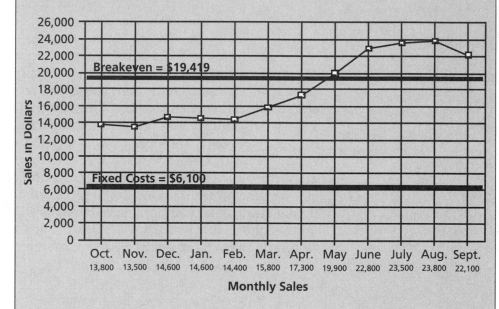

	Oct.	Nov.	Dec.	Jan.	Feb.	Mar.	Apr.	May	June	July	Aug.	Sept.
	13,800	13,500	14,600	14,600	14,400	15,800	17,300	19,900	22,800	23,500	23,800	22,100

Monthly Sales

This pictorial representation of breakeven points is a handy way to make objectives more tangible than the usual "$20,000 a month" kind of goal. It can be very illuminating (or daunting) to post your breakeven projections, then trace out—in some vivid color on a monthly basis—how near to the projection you have come.

You can also use breakeven charts to measure progress toward annual profit goals. Suppose Finestkind had aimed at a $12,000 profit the first year. What sales would be needed?

$$S = (FC + \text{Profit})\ /\ GM$$

where Profit = $12,000;

$S = (\$62{,}220 + 12{,}000)/.267 = (\$74{,}220)/.267 = \$277{,}977/\text{year}$ or $\$23{,}164/$ month.

Graphically,

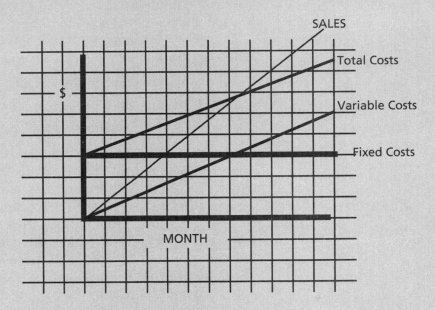

Any time you can help your employees visualize progress toward a goal, you benefit. Breakeven charts (again) are useful for more than financial planning purposes. Once you have calculated breakeven sales, you may find it very helpful to break the sales down in terms of customers needed—as a reality check, this can keep you from making overly optimistic projections.

Here is how Finestkind determined the number of customers needed per month at breakeven:

Assumptions:

1. They assumed that the proportions of retail and wholesale will remain the same as in the income projections.

2. Breakeven in sales   = $233,033

    Retail = (126/216) x 233,033   = $136,000/year

    Wholesale = (90/216) x 233,033   = $ 97,000/year

Experience has shown that the average retail customer spends $16 per visit to Finestkind and comes to the store (on average) twice a month.

Retail sales/month = $136,000/12 = around $11,000/month

$11,000/$16 (average sale) = approximately 700 transactions each month. Because Finestkind's retail clientele consists of both steady local customers and tourist (one-time, drop-in) business, they plan in terms of gross sales.

Finestkind has projected retail sales of $126,000 for the first year, or $10,500/month. If they add $500/month to their retail sales, they will hit (retail) breakeven projections. Finestkind currently has 17 wholesale customers who average 4 transactions per month at $60/transaction. To achieve breakeven as projected above,

Wholesale sales/month = $96,000/12 = around $8,000/month

$8,000/$60 (average sale) = approximately 130 transactions each month,

or 33 wholesale customers.

Finestkind has projected wholesale sales of $90,000 for the first year, or $7,500/month. They currently average about $4,000/month wholesale but view the wholesale market as ripe for expansion. They think they can add the necessary 16 new customers and/or increase the average sale. In fact, their marketing plans depend on being able to achieve a market penetration of better than 12 percent over the next 12 months (12 percent of 300 = 36 customers).

Breakeven analysis may also be represented pictorially. The diagramming helps establish forecasts, budgets, and projections. Using a chart lets you substitute different combinations of numbers to obtain a rough estimate of their effect on your business.

A helpful technique is to make worst case, best case, and most probable case assumptions, chart them to see how soon they cover fixed costs, and then derive more accurate figures by applying the various formulas and kinds of thinking displayed above. This is of particular value if you are thinking of making a capital investment and want a quick picture of the relative merits of buying or leasing.

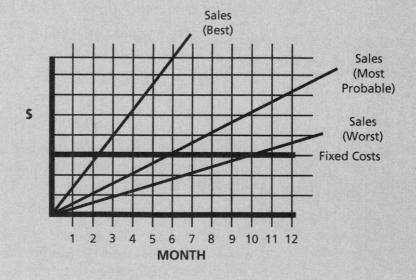

E. PROJECTED INCOME STATEMENT

Income statements, also called profit and loss statements, complement balance sheets. The balance sheet gives a static picture of the company at a given point in time. The income statement provides a moving picture of the company during a particular period of time.

Financial statements that depict a future period are called pro forma or projected financial statements. They represent what the company is expected to look like financially, based on a set of assumptions about the economy, market growth, and other factors.

Income projections are forecasting and budgeting tools.

Income projections are forecasting and budgeting tools estimating income and anticipating expenses in the near to mid-range future. For most businesses (and for most bankers) income projections covering one to three years are more than adequate. In some cases, a longer range projection may be called for, but in general, the longer the projection, the less accurate it will be as a guide to action.

You don't need a crystal ball to make your projection. While no set of projections will be 100 percent accurate, experience and practice tend to make the projections more precise. Even if your income projections are not accurate, they will provide you with a rough set of benchmarks to test your progress toward short-term goals. They become the base of your budgets.

There is nothing sacred about income projections. If they are wildly incorrect, correct them to make a more realistic guide. When you do this is a matter of judgment. A rule of thumb is that if they are more than 20 percent off for a quarter (three months), redo them. If they are less than 20 percent off, wait for another quarter. Do not change your projections more often. In a short period, certain trends will be magnified, and these distortions will usually be evened out over the long run. Of course, if you find you have omitted a major expense item or discover a significant new source of revenue, you will want to make immediate corrections. Use your common sense.

The reasoning behind income projection is: Because most expenses are predictable and income doesn't fluctuate too drastically, the future will be much like the past. For example, if your gross margin has historically been 30 percent of net sales, it will (barring strong evidence to the contrary) continue to be 30 percent of net sales. If you are in a startup situation, look for financial statement information and income ratios for businesses similar to yours. The Robert Morris Associates' *Annual Statement Studies* and trade association publications are two sources mentioned earlier. (See Resources at the back of the book.)

It is important to be systematic and thorough when you list your expenses. The expense that bleeds your business dry (makes it illiquid) is almost always one that was overlooked or seriously misjudged—and therefore unplanned for. There are some expenses that cannot be foreseen, and the best way to allow for them is to be conservative in your estimates and to document your assumptions.

Try to understate your expected sales and overstate expenses.

It is better to exceed a conservative budget than to fall below optimistic projections. However, being too far under can also create problems—such as not having enough capital to finance growth. Basing income projections on hopes or unjustified fears is hazardous to your business's health. Be realistic; your budget is an extension of your forecasts.

Income statements and projections are standardized to facilitate comparison and analysis. They must be dated to indicate the period of time they cover and also contain notes to explain any unusual items such as windfall profits, litigation expenses and judgments, changes in depreciation schedules, and other material information. Any assumptions should be footnoted—to help remind you of how the numbers were originally justified and to provide a boost up the learning curve when you review your projections before making new ones.

Detect deviations as soon as possible to correct problems before they become major and to seize opportunities while they are still fresh.

Income statements should be reviewed at least once a quarter to check their validity and, if necessary, to make adjustments or make changes in your business's operations. As a budget tool, the actual progress of your business should be compared against the projections every month. You have to detect deviations as soon as possible to correct problems before they become major and to seize opportunities while they are still fresh.

Suggested formats for an income statement and an income projection follow. The content as shown in the sample may have to be modified to fit your particular operation, but do not change the basic form.

Remember: The purpose of financial statements and forecasts is to provide you with the maximum amount of useful information and guidance, not to dazzle a prospective investor.

For the most useful projection, state your assumptions clearly. Do not put down numbers that you cannot rationally substantiate. Do not puff your gross sales projection to make the net profit positive. Give yourself conservative sales figures and pessimistic expense figures to make the success of your deal more probable. Be realistic.

You want your projections to reflect the realities of your business.

Income and Cash Flow Forecasting

Smaller businesses should make three-year projections for both planning purposes and loan proposals. The proper sequence for both income and cash flow projections is:

1. A three-year summary.
2. First year projected by month. If the business doesn't break even in the first year, you might want to continue the monthly projections until it does.
3. Years two and three by quarter.

If you are already in business or are considering taking over an existing business, historical financial statements should be included for two immediately previous years. Tax returns help to substantiate the validity of unaudited statements.

Net Sales: Gross sales less returns, allowances, and discounts.

Cost of Goods Sold: Includes cost of inventories.

Gross Margin: (1) Net Sales minus (2) Cost of Goods Sold. Represents the gross profit on sales without taking indirect costs into account.

Operating Expenses: These are the costs that, together with (5) Other Expenses, must be met no matter what the sales level may be. The order in which they are stated isn't important. Thoroughness is. If some costs are trivial, lump them together under a heading of "miscellaneous," but be prepared to break them out if the miscellaneous totals more than an arbitrary 1 percent of net sales.

Other Expenses: These are nonoperating expenses. The most common is interest expense. It is helpful to display your interest expense in some detail to both highlight the cost of money and to provide easy access to information used for ratio analysis.

Total Expenses: Sum of (4) Operating Expenses and (5) Other Expenses.

Profit (Loss) Pretax: (3) Gross Margin minus (6) Total Expenses. This is the tax base, the figure on which your tax will be calculated.

Taxes: Consult your accountant.

Net Profit (Loss): (7) minus (8). This represents the success or lack thereof for your business. There are three ways to make this figure more positive: increase gross margin, decrease total expenses, or both.

A Sample Income Statement Format

(1) **Net Sales**

(2) less **Cost of Goods Sold**

(3) equals **Gross Margin**

(4) **Operating Expenses**

    Salaries and Wages

    Payroll Taxes and Benefits

    Rent

    Utilities

    Maintenance

    Office Supplies

    Postage

    Automobile and Truck

    Insurance

    Legal and Accounting

    Depreciation

    Others:

    _____

    _____

    _____

(5) **Other Expenses**

    Interest

(6) **Total Expenses**

(7) **Profit (Loss) Pretax**

(8) **Taxes**

(9) **Net Profit (Loss)**

A Note on Sales Forecasts

Your sales forecasts are the basis for most of your financial planning.

Whether you've been in business for a while or are starting a business, your sales forecasts are the basis for most of your financial planning.

One helpful technique to use involves breaking your goods and services into several lines, then applying a three-column form to arrive at a "most likely" figure.

Begin by assuming the worst. In the column headed "low," put down the sales you expect if everything goes wrong—poor weather, loss of market share to a new competitor, new product competition that you can't match, and so on. Be gloomy. Assume your salespeople will be loutish, lazy and surly.

Then—this is more fun—assume everything works out the way you'd wish. In the column headed "high," put down your rosiest hopes. All your promotional efforts will succeed, markets will grow dynamically, your competition will stub their toes and slink away from the market, your suppliers will be able to instantaneously fulfill your stocking requirements.

Now look to a realistic scenario, where things work out in between the high and low estimates. The figures here will (usually) be more accurate than a one-time estimate can be, because more thought has gone into their preparation. Do this for the period you need to forecast.

You can apply the same process to forecasting expenses, even though most expenses are reasonably predictable once the sales forecasts have been established.

Finestkind broke sales into two categories, wholesale and retail. If they had had a third line, for example direct mail sales, they would have added a third sales forecast line to their planning.

Sales Forecast
for (month, year) to (month, year)

Sales	Low	Most Likely	High
Product/Service 1	_____	_____	_____
Product/Service 2	_____	_____	_____
Product/Service 3	_____	_____	_____
Product/Service 4	_____	_____	_____
Total Sales	_____	_____	

	A	B	C	D	E
		FINESTKIND SEAFOODS, INC.			
		Income Projection: Three-Year Summary			
1		Year 1	Year 2	Year 3	% of Sales
2					Year 1
3	Sales				
4	Wholesale	$90,000	$265,000	$325,000	60.75%
5	Retail	$126,000	$180,000	$210,000	39.25%
6	**Total Sales**	**$216,000**	**$445,000**	**$535,000**	**100.00%**
7					
8	*V Cost of Materials	$155,520	$320,400	$385,200	72.00%
9	V Variable Labor	$2,800	$2,800	$7,520	1.41%
10	Total Cost of Goods Sold	$158,320	$323,200	$392,720	73.41%
11					
12	**Gross Margin**	**$57,680**	**$121,800**	**$142,280**	**26.59%**
13					
14	Operating Expenses				
15	F Utilities	$2,160	$2,640	$2,880	0.54%
16	F Salaries	$22,800	$39,000	$46,800	8.75%
17	V/F Payroll Taxes and Benefits	$2,850	$4,875	$5,850	1.09%
18	F Advertising	$9,555	$11,125	$13,375	2.50%
19	F Office Supplies	$300	$360	$480	0.09%
20	F Insurance	$1,200	$3,800	$4,100	0.77%
21	F Maintenance and Cleaning	$300	$360	$420	0.08%
22	F Legal and Accounting	$1,500	$2,000	$2,500	0.47%
23	V/F Delivery Expenses	$1,800	$8,900	$9,095	1.70%
24	F Licenses	$115	$115	$115	0.02%
25	V/F Boxes, Paper, etc.	$400	$800	$1,200	0.22%
26	F Telephone	$1,020	$1,800	$2,400	0.45%
27	F Depreciation	$7,700	$12,500	$12,500	2.34%
28	F Miscellaneous	$480	$600	$720	0.13%
29	F Rent	$1,650	$0	$0	0.00%
30	**Total Operating Expenses**	**$53,830**	**$88,875**	**$102,435**	**19.15%**
31					
32	Other Expenses				
33	F Interest (Mortgage)	$6,258	$8,280	$8,052	1.51%
34	F Interest (Term Loan)	$1,632	$3,189	$2,900	0.54%
35	F Interest (Line of Credit)	$500	$500	$500	0.09%
36	Total Other Expenses	$8,390	$11,969	$11,452	2.14%
37					
38	**Total Expenses**	**$62,220**	**$100,844**	**$113,887**	**21.29%**
39					
40	**Net Profit (Loss) Pretax**	**($4,540)**	**$20,956**	**$28,393**	**5.31%**
41					
42	*V = Variable Cost, F = Fixed Cost				

FINESTKIND SEAFOODS, INC.
Income Projection by Month, Year One

	October	November	December	January	February	March	April	May	June	July	August	September	Total	% of Total Sales
Sales														
Wholesale	$4,000	$4,000	$5,200	$5,600	$6,000	$7,000	$7,000	$8,400	$10,600	$11,300	$11,300	$9,600	$90,000	41.67%
Retail	$9,730	$9,500	$9,500	$9,000	$8,400	$8,750	$10,300	$11,540	$12,165	$12,165	$12,475	$12,475	$126,000	58.33%
Total Sales	$13,730	$13,500	$14,700	$14,600	$14,400	$15,750	$17,300	$19,940	$22,765	$23,465	$23,775	$22,075	$216,000	100.00%
Cost of Materials	$9,886	$9,720	$10,584	$10,512	$10,368	$11,340	$12,456	$14,357	$16,391	$16,895	$17,118	$15,894	$155,520	72.00%
Variable Labor	$0	$0	$0	$0	$0	$0	$0	$0	$604	$796	$796	$604	$2,800	1.30%
Cost of Goods Sold	$9,886	$9,720	$10,584	$10,512	$10,368	$11,340	$12,456	$14,357	$16,995	$17,691	$17,914	$16,498	$158,320	73.30%
Gross Margin	$3,844	$3,780	$4,116	$4,088	$4,032	$4,410	$4,844	$5,583	$5,770	$5,774	$5,861	$5,577	$57,680	26.70%
Operating Expenses														
Utilities	$160	$165	$180	$200	$200	$180	$170	$165	$185	$185	$185	$185	$2,160	1.00%
Salaries	$1,900	$1,900	$1,900	$1,900	$1,900	$1,900	$1,900	$1,900	$1,900	$1,900	$1,900	$1,900	$22,800	10.56%
Payroll Taxes and Benefits	$237	$238	$237	$238	$237	$238	$237	$238	$237	$238	$237	$238	$2,850	1.32%
Advertising	$450	$450	$450	$450	$450	$450	$4,605	$450	$450	$450	$450	$450	$9,555	4.42%
Office Supplies	$25	$25	$25	$25	$25	$25	$25	$25	$25	$25	$25	$25	$300	0.14%
Insurance	$70	$70	$70	$110	$110	$110	$110	$110	$110	$110	$110	$110	$1,200	0.56%
Maintenance and Cleaning	$25	$25	$25	$25	$25	$25	$25	$25	$25	$25	$25	$25	$300	0.14%
Legal and Accounting	$125	$125	$125	$125	$125	$125	$125	$125	$125	$125	$125	$125	$1,500	0.69%
Delivery Expenses	$150	$150	$150	$150	$150	$150	$150	$150	$150	$150	$150	$150	$1,800	0.83%
Licenses	$9	$9	$9	$9	$9	$10	$10	$10	$10	$10	$10	$10	$115	0.05%
Boxes, Paper, etc.	$15	$15	$15	$15	$20	$35	$40	$45	$50	$50	$50	$50	$400	0.19%
Telephone	$85	$85	$85	$85	$85	$85	$85	$85	$85	$85	$85	$85	$1,020	0.47%
Depreciation	$0	$0	$0	$455	$460	$460	$1,050	$1,055	$1,055	$1,055	$1,055	$1,055	$7,700	3.56%
Miscellaneous	$40	$40	$40	$40	$40	$40	$40	$40	$40	$40	$40	$40	$480	0.22%
Rent	$550	$550	$550	$0	$0	$0	$0	$0	$0	$0	$0	$0	$1,650	0.76%
Total Operating Expenses	$3,841	$3,847	$3,861	$3,827	$3,836	$3,833	$8,572	$4,423	$4,447	$4,448	$4,447	$4,448	$53,830	24.92%
Other Expenses														
Interest (Mortgage)	$0	$0	$0	$695	$695	$696	$695	$695	$696	$695	$695	$696	$6,258	2.90%
Interest (Term Loan)	$0	$0	$0	$0	$0	$0	$272	$272	$272	$272	$272	$272	$1,632	0.76%
Interest (Credit Line)	$0	$85	$85	$0	$0	$0	$0	$0	$165	$165	$0	$0	$500	0.23%
Total Other Expenses	$0	$85	$85	$695	$695	$696	$967	$967	$1,133	$1,132	$967	$968	$8,390	3.88%
Total Expenses	$3,841	$3,932	$3,946	$4,522	$4,531	$4,529	$9,539	$5,390	$5,580	$5,580	$5,414	$5,416	$62,220	28.81%
Net Profit (Loss) Pretax	$3	($152)	$170	($434)	($499)	($119)	($4,695)	$193	$190	$194	$447	$161	($4,540)	
Cumulative Profit (Loss)	$3	($149)	$21	($413)	($912)	($1,031)	($5,726)	($5,533)	($5,343)	($5,149)	($4,702)	($4,540)		
						**Low Point								

FINESTKIND SEAFOODS, INC.

Income Projection by Quarter, Year Two

	A	B	C	D	E	F
		1st Qtr	2nd Qtr	3rd Qtr	4th Qtr	Total
1						
2						
3	Sales					
4	Wholesale	$38,900	$54,800	$76,500	$94,800	$265,000
5	Retail	$41,000	$37,400	$48,600	$53,000	$180,000
6	**Total Sales**	**$79,900**	**$92,200**	**$125,100**	**$147,800**	**$445,000**
7						
8	Cost of Materials	$57,528	$66,384	$90,072	$106,416	$320,400
9	Variable Labor	$0	$0	$604	$2,196	$2,800
10	Total Cost of Goods Sold	$57,528	$66,384	$90,676	$108,612	$323,200
11						
12	**Gross Margin**	**$22,372**	**$25,816**	**$34,424**	**$39,188**	**$121,800**
13						
14	Operating Expenses					
15	Utilities	$660	$660	$660	$660	$2,640
16	Salaries	$9,750	$9,750	$9,750	$9,750	$39,000
17	Payroll Taxes and Benefits	$1,219	$1,219	$1,219	$1,219	$4,875
18	Advertising	$1,998	$2,305	$3,128	$3,695	$11,125
19	Office Supplies	$90	$90	$90	$90	$360
20	Insurance	$950	$950	$950	$950	$3,800
21	Maintenance and Cleaning	$90	$90	$90	$90	$360
22	Legal and Accounting	$500	$500	$500	$500	$2,000
23	Delivery Expenses	$1,598	$1,844	$2,502	$2,956	$8,900
24	Licenses	$25	$30	$30	$30	$115
25	Boxes, Paper, etc.	$150	$175	$225	$250	$800
26	Telephone	$450	$450	$450	$450	$1,800
27	Depreciation	$3,125	$3,125	$3,125	$3,125	$12,500
28	Miscellaneous	$150	$150	$150	$150	$600
29	Rent	$0	$0	$0	$0	$0
30	**Total Operating Expenses**	**$20,754**	**$21,338**	**$22,868**	**$23,915**	**$88,875**
31						
32	Other Expenses					
33	Interest (Mortgage)	$2,070	$2,070	$2,070	$2,070	$8,280
34	Interest (Term Loan)	$798	$798	$797	$796	$3,189
35	Interest (Credit Line)	$0	$0	$140	$360	$500
36	Total Other Expenses	$2,868	$2,868	$3,007	$3,226	$11,969
37						
38	**Total Expenses**	**$23,622**	**$24,206**	**$25,875**	**$27,141**	**$100,844**
39						
40	**Net Profit (Loss) Pretax**	**($1,250)**	**$1,610**	**$8,549**	**$12,047**	**$20,956**

FINESTKIND SEAFOODS, INC

Income Projection by Quarter, Year Three

	A	B	C	D	E	F
1		**1st Qtr**	**2nd Qtr**	**3rd Qtr**	**4th Qtr**	**Total**
2						
3	Sales					
4	Wholesale	$58,750	$55,000	$97,500	$113,750	$325,000
5	Retail	$47,400	$43,600	$56,000	$63,000	$210,000
6	**Total Sales**	**$106,150**	**$98,600**	**$153,500**	**$176,750**	**$535,000**
7						
8	Cost of Materials	$76,428	$70,992	$110,520	$127,260	$385,200
9	Variable Labor	$0	$0	$1,622	$5,898	$7,520
10	Total Cost of Goods Sold	$76,428	$70,992	$112,142	$133,158	$392,720
11						
12	**Gross Margin**	**$29,722**	**$27,608**	**$41,358**	**$43,592**	**$142,280**
13						
14	Operating Expenses					
15	Utilities	$720	$720	$720	$720	$2,880
16	Salaries	$11,700	$11,700	$11,700	$11,700	$46,800
17	Payroll Taxes and Benefits	$1,463	$1,463	$1,463	$1,463	$5,850
18	Advertising	$2,654	$2,465	$3,838	$4,419	$13,375
19	Office Supplies	$120	$120	$120	$120	$480
20	Insurance	$1,025	$1,025	$1,025	$1,025	$4,100
21	Maintenance and Cleaning	$105	$105	$105	$105	$420
22	Legal and Accounting	$625	$625	$625	$625	$2,500
23	Delivery Expenses	$1,805	$1,676	$2,610	$3,005	$9,095
24	Licenses	$25	$30	$30	$30	$115
25	Boxes, Paper, etc.	$200	$200	$350	$450	$1,200
26	Telephone	$600	$600	$600	$600	$2,400
27	Depreciation	$3,125	$3,125	$3,125	$3,125	$12,500
28	Miscellaneous	$180	$180	$180	$180	$720
29	Rent	$0	$0	$0	$0	$0
30	**Total Operating Expenses**	**$24,346**	**$24,034**	**$26,490**	**$27,566**	**$102,435**
31						
32	Other Expenses					
33	Interest (Mortgage)	$2,013	$2,013	$2,013	$2,013	$8,052
34	Interest (Term Loan)	$725	$725	$725	$725	$2,900
35	Interest (Credit Line)	$0	$0	$140	$360	$500
36	Total Other Expenses	$2,738	$2,738	$2,878	$3,098	$11,452
37						
38	**Total Expenses**	**$27,084**	**$26,772**	**$29,368**	**$30,664**	**$113,887**
39						
40	**Net Profit Pretax**	**$2,638**	**$836**	**$11,991**	**$12,928**	**$28,393**

Explanation for Income Statement Projections

This section will:

- Explain how the figures on the projection were calculated. Note that Column O, percent of total sales, provides a way to compare this statement with trade averages as well as future projections and performance.
- Detail the assumptions that were made. Numerical references have been made by line—for example, (21) Maintenance and Cleaning.

(3) Sales include sales of seafood and ancillary products such as seasonings, sauces, baitbags, bait. In the future, some tourist items may be included.

(4) Wholesale and **(5) Retail.** Finestkind plans to service the wholesale trade more extensively than is shown here, although the trend has been built into the calculations. Due to a major marketing effort [see **(18) Advertising** below], wholesale sales should increase to 60 percent of gross sales within two years. Retail sales are expected to be more volatile than the wholesale business, leveling off around $20,000/month due to space restrictions. Volatility is seasonal, building from late March to a late summer peak. The increases shown in **(4) Wholesale** are based both on the greater number of restaurants open in the summer and the intense marketing efforts, planned for the winter months, to sell directly to the many restaurants that don't yet know Finestkind. Wholesale sales for September of the preceding year were $9,600, so these figures are perhaps more conservative than they need to be.

(4) Wholesale in Years Two and Three follow the same pattern as Year One (seasonality) but start at $10,000/October Year Two as the result of advertising and marketing efforts, longer experience with the wholesale market, and greater exposure to the market. Year Three is a bit more seasonal, reflecting a flattening out of the sales curve.

The degree of pessimism you should build into a projection is a matter of judgment.

The degree of pessimism you should build into a projection is a matter of judgment. Some is good; too much can be bad, as it will distort a reasonably good game plan and make a realistic deal look too risky.

(6) Total Sales. (4) plus (5).

(8) Cost of Materials. Finestkind's inventory has an average cost of 68 percent of sales (including a startup spoilage rate of 5 percent that has been reduced to under 1 percent of sales), and has been calculated as 72 percent of sales to allow for the fluctuation of dockside prices during the winter.

(9) Variable Labor. In Years One and Two, two part-time summer helpers will be needed: a counter person at $4/hour for 16 hours/week for 10 weeks, and a fish cutter at $6.75/hour for 20 hours/week for 16 weeks. In Year Three, two full-time counter helpers and a full-time cutter will be needed for 10 and 16 weeks, respectively.

(10) Cost of Goods Sold. (8) plus (9).

(12) Gross Margin. (6) minus (10).

(14) Operating Expenses. These are (by and large) the fixed expenses, those that don't vary directly with sales levels. Keeping control of operating expenses is immensely important and easily overlooked, perhaps because so much emphasis is placed on generating sales. A profitable business needs to control costs and maintain (or increase) sales.

(15) Utilities. Prorated by agreement with the utility companies. Goes from $165/month (Year One) to $220 to $240 in Year Three. It will probably change as new equipment and better insulation are installed.

(16) Salaries.

Year One: $950/month for Gosling and Swan
Year Two: $1,200/month for Gosling and Swan
            $850/month for a full-time employee
Year Three: $1,500/month for Gosling and Swan
            $900/month ($50/month raise) for employee

Salaries are lower than Finestkind would pay for a professional manager in order to preserve scarce capital (they are undercapitalized, and the salaries reflect "sweat equity"). As the business grows, they hope to take annual bonuses based on profits—after capital needs are met.

(17) Payroll Taxes and Benefits. 12.5 percent of (16). This is low; in many businesses fringe benefits alone are over 25 percent of salaries. In a small business, benefits are often skimpy.

(18) Advertising. Local newspaper and radio spots. This is an expense that Finestkind might profitably increase. They reason (correctly) that a consistent, though modest, campaign will be more productive than sporadic, intensive promotions. The advertising budget is 4.4 percent of (6) Total Sales. In Year One, a large one-time promotional blitz will be made in April to build off-season wholesale business.

(20) Insurance. Includes liability, workers compensation, vehicle, and other normal forms of insurance. As the business can afford it, they will add key-man disability to the life insurance coverage. Year Two reflects the increase in workers comp and the property insurance.

(21) Maintenance and Cleaning. Mainly supplies—a food market must meet stringent health codes.

(22) Legal and Accounting. Retainers to an attorney and an accountant, used to smooth out cash flow. Otherwise, occasional large bills would distort monthly income projection figures, even though the use of these services is spread evenly over the year.

(23) Delivery Expenses. Delivery of merchandise to restaurants and other markets. Year Two: 2 percent of total sales; Year Three: 1.7 percent. As the wholesale business increases, route efficiency should also increase, causing delivery expenses as a percentage of sales to decrease.

(24) Licenses. Required by state and local authorities.

(25) Boxes, Paper, etc. Packaging supplies, which are a semifixed expense.

(26) Telephone. Needed for sales, pricing, contacting suppliers and markets.

(27) Depreciation. Five-year, straight-line on equipment (beginning April, Year One); straight-line 19 years on building (beginning January, Year One). These are based on the assumption that $\frac{1}{5}$ and $\frac{1}{19}$ respectively will be "used up" in the normal course of doing business. Some businesses try to set this sum aside as a replacement fund.

(28) Miscellaneous. Operating expenses too small to be itemized. Some experts suggest to clients that this category be used as a contingency allocation of 15 percent of gross revenues for the first year, 10 percent for the second, and 5 percent for the third, on the expectation that in a startup there will always be cost overruns. Others suggest keeping it small, and establishing a contingency fund in some other way, usually on the balance sheet.

(29) Rent. Applicable for three months in Year One; will be replaced by (33) Interest (Mortgage) on the income statement. The principal payments show up on the cash flow projections as part of mortgage payments. (The $876/month includes both principal and interest. Principal payments on loans do not appear as income statement items.)

(30) Total Operating Expenses. Sum of (15) through (29).

(32) Other Expenses. Nonoperating costs are broken out to give them special prominence.

(33) Interest (Mortgage). $75,000 mortgage for 15 years at 11.5 percent. This is a normal term and interest rate for commercial buildings at this time. More than 15 years is rare.

(34) Interest (Term Loan). $30,000 loan for seven years at 12.25 percent. A rule of thumb: The longer the term, the higher the risk to the bank—so the higher the interest rate to you.

(35) Interest (Credit Line). Estimated use of line: average of $7,500 outstanding for six months a year at 13.5 percent. Lines of credit are not intended to replace permanent capital or long-term credit needs.

(36) Total Other Expenses. Sum of (33), (34), (35).

(38) Total Expenses. Sum of (30) and (36).

(40) Net Profit (Loss) Pretax. (12) Gross Margin minus (38) Total Expenses. On this statement (and the other projections) a tax liability should be imputed. We left that liability off as it will vary from one state to another and with the legal structure of your business. Make sure to check with your accountant to arrive at a true net profit (loss) figure. As one banker puts it, "There is no such thing as a pretax profit."

Finestkind does not expect to make much money for the first few years. This is no surprise for a business so thinly capitalized. Even if there were no debt at all, net profit would have been only $8,000 for the year, or less than 4 percent of sales.

This is a projection based on conservative figures. In their more optimistic moments, Gosling and Swan hope to hold fixed costs to $4,500/month, not the $5,200 projected, and increase sales 12.5 percent. Their budgeted net profit would be around $18,000, not the projected loss of $4,540. If their gross margin were to continue at 30 percent of sales, not the 27 percent projected, their net profit would be over $18,000, their "best-case" assumption.

One item that should be mentioned again is rent. The cost of space appears on the cash flow as mortgage ($876/month). Another is loan

As one banker puts it, "There is no such thing as a pretax profit."

amortization, which also appears on the cash flow as term loan ($534/month). These include interest and debt retirement, which are not expenses because they are for capital improvements that will be written off as "depreciation expense" over the course of several years. It is important not to double-deduct expenses: Such a practice is not only illegal but also obscures the information about your business.

Information is the most important result of financial statements. Accurate, timely information helps you run your business.

F. CASH FLOW PROJECTION

The cash flow projection can make the difference between success and failure, and between growth and stagnation.

The cash flow projection is the most important financial planning tool available to you. If you were limited to one financial statement (which fortunately isn't the case), the cash flow projection would be the one to choose.

For a new or growing business, the cash flow projection can make the difference between success and failure. For an ongoing business, it can make the difference between growth and stagnation.

Your cash flow analysis will:

- show you how much cash your business will need;
- when it will be needed;
- whether you should look for equity, debt, operating profits, or sale of fixed assets; and
- where the cash will come from.

The cash flow projection attempts to budget the cash needs of a business and shows how cash will flow in and out of the business over a stated period of time. Cash flows into the business from sales, collection of receivables, capital injections, and so forth, and flows out through cash payments for expenses of all kinds.

This financial tool emphasizes the points in your calendar when money will be coming into and going out of your business. The advantage of knowing when cash outlays must be made is the ability to plan for those outlays and not be forced to resort to unexpected borrowing to meet cash needs. Illiquidity is a killer, even for profitable businesses. Lack of profits won't kill a business (noncash expenses such as depreciation can make your profits look negative, while your cash flow is positive). Lack of cash to meet your trade and other payables will.

If you project your cash flow for the near to intermediate future, you can see the effect of a loan to your business far more clearly than from the income statement. You may be able to find ways to finance your business operations or minimize your credit needs to keep interest expense down. Many of the advantages of studying the cash flow projection stem from timing: More options are available to you, at lower costs, with less panic.

Cash is generated primarily by sales. However, not all sales are cash sales. Perhaps your business is all cash—but if you offer any credit (charge accounts, term payments, trade credit) to your customers, you need to have a means of telling when those credit sales will turn into cash-in-hand. This is blurred in the income statement but made very clear by the cash flow. Your business may be subject to seasonal bills, and again, a cash flow makes the liquidity problems attending such large, occasional expenses clear.

A cash flow deals only with actual cash transactions. Depreciation, a noncash expense, does not appear on a cash flow. Loan repayments (including interest), on the other hand, do, because they represent a cash disbursement.

After it has been developed, use your cash flow projections as a budget. If the cash outlays for a given item increase over the amount allotted for a given month, you should find out why and take corrective action as soon as possible. If the figure is lower, you should also find out why. If the cash outlay is lower than expected, it is not necessarily a good sign. Maybe a bill wasn't paid. By reviewing the movement of your cash position you can better control your business.

*D*iscrepancies between expected and actual cash flows are indicators of opportunities as well as problems.

On a more positive note, the savings may tip you off to a new way of economizing. Discrepancies between expected and actual cash flows are indicators of opportunities as well as problems. If the sales figures don't match the cash flow projections, look for the cause. Maybe projections were too low. Maybe you've opened a new market or introduced a new product that can be pushed even harder.

Use the Cash Flow Management Sketch on page 82 to make sure you don't omit any ordinary cash flow item. But be sure to add any items that are peculiar to your business.

The level of detail you wish to provide is another judgment call. You may want to provide much more detail than is shown in these examples— for example, you might benefit from breaking down your cash flow into a series of cash flows, each representing one profit center or other business unit. This can be particularly handy if you have more than one source of revenue or if you are a manufacturer and need to prepare numerous bids. The accumulated information gained by several projections can be very valuable.

Cash flow projections lend themselves to computerization. Spreadsheet programs such as Lotus 1-2-3™ or Microsoft Excel™ (among others) are made even more valuable because you can tie in graphic displays to your hard numbers, link together several different financial statements, or play "what-if" with much greater speed and accuracy than was possible when we were limited to pencils, adding machines, 13-column accounting paper, and erasers.

CASH FLOW MANAGEMENT SKETCH

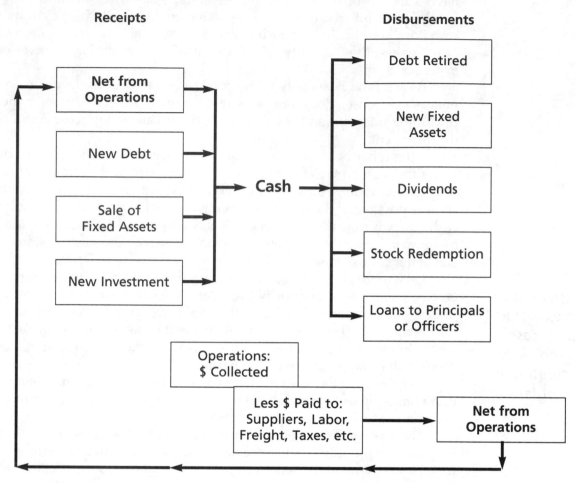

Cash Flow Sketch

1. Cash at Beginning of Period
   Add Revenues, etc.:
2. Sales of products (cash)
3. Sales of products (receivables collected)
4. Cash received from assets sold
5. Cash received from equity investment
6. Cash received from loans
7. Cash received from bad debt recovery
8. Miscellaneous cash received
   Total: Cash Received

   Subtract: Cash Disbursements
9. New inventory purchased for cash
10. Salaries/wages
11. FICA, federal and state withholding tax
12. Fringe benefits paid
13. New equipment to be purchased for cash
14. Processing
15. Office, sales equipment
16. Transportation equipment
17. Insurance premiums
18. Fees
19. Accounting
20. Legal
21. Utilities
22. Telephone
23. Heat, light, power
24. Advertising

25. Principal and interest on debt
26. Transportation
27. Oil, gas
28. Vehicle maintenance
29. Tires
30. Freight
31. Provision for bad debts (if funded with cash)
32. Taxes payable
33. Income (state, federal, other if applicable)
34. Property
35. Excise
36. Sales taxes (if applicable)
37. Dividends paid, cash withdrawal by partner, or contribution to profit-sharing plan
38. Provision for unforeseen circumstances (if funded)
39. Provision for replacement of depreciable assets (if funded)

Total Cash Received less Total Disbursements Equals Cash at End of Period

Note: Only cash disbursements are included. These are actual dollars that you pay out, not obligations that you incur now to be paid off at some future date. Those appear on the income projection and balance sheet.

FINESTKIND SEAFOODS, INC.
Cash Flow Projection by Month, Year One

	A	October	November	December	January	February	March	April	May	June	July	August	September	Total
1		October	November	December	January	February	March	April	May	June	July	August	September	Total
2	Cash Receipts													
3	Sales Receivables	$2,000	$1,333	$1,333	$1,733	$1,867	$2,000	$2,333	$2,333	$2,800	$3,533	$3,767	$3,767	$28,800
4	Wholesale	$2,667	$2,667	$3,467	$3,733	$4,000	$4,667	$4,667	$5,600	$7,067	$7,533	$7,533	$6,400	$60,000
5	Retail	$9,730	$9,500	$9,500	$9,000	$8,400	$8,750	$10,300	$11,540	$12,165	$12,165	$12,475	$12,475	$126,000
6	Other Sources (see notes)	$7,500	$7,500	$0	$105,000	$0	$0	$30,000	$0	$15,000	$0	$0	$0	$165,000
7	Total Cash Receipts	$21,897	$21,000	$14,300	$119,467	$14,267	$15,417	$47,300	$19,473	$37,032	$23,232	$23,775	$22,642	$379,800
8	Cash Disbursements													
9	Cost of Goods	$9,886	$9,720	$10,584	$10,512	$10,368	$11,340	$12,456	$14,357	$16,391	$16,895	$17,118	$15,894	$155,520
10	Variable Labor	$0	$0	$0	$0	$0	$0	$0	$0	$604	$796	$796	$604	$2,800
11	Advertising	$1,000	$400	$400	$400	$400	$400	$4,555	$400	$400	$400	$400	$400	$9,555
12	Insurance	$0	$300	$0	$0	$300	$0	$0	$300	$0	$0	$300	$0	$1,200
13	Legal and Accounting	$0	$0	$375	$0	$0	$375	$0	$0	$375	$0	$0	$375	$1,500
14	Delivery Expenses	$75	$75	$75	$100	$75	$100	$150	$200	$200	$250	$250	$250	$1,800
15	*Fixed Cash Disbursements	$2,535	$2,535	$2,535	$2,535	$2,535	$2,535	$2,535	$2,535	$2,535	$2,535	$2,535	$2,535	$30,425
16	Mortgage (rent)	$550	$550	$550	$876	$876	$876	$876	$876	$876	$876	$876	$876	$9,535
17	Term Loan	$0	$0	$0	$0	$0	$0	$534	$534	$534	$534	$534	$534	$3,202
18	Line of Credit	$0	$85	$15,085	$0	$0	$0	$0	$0	$165	$165	$15,000	$0	$30,500
19	Other Disbursements	$0	$0	$0	$105,000	$0	$30,000	$0	$0	$0	$0	$0	$0	$135,000
20	Total Cash Disbursements	$14,046	$13,665	$29,604	$119,424	$14,555	$45,627	$21,106	$19,202	$22,080	$22,451	$37,809	$21,468	$381,037
21														
22	Net Cash Flow	$7,851	$7,335	($15,304)	$43	($288)	($30,210)	$26,194	$271	$14,952	$781	($14,034)	$1,174	($1,237)
23														
24	Cumulative Cash Flow	$7,851	$15,185	($119)	($76)	($364)	($30,574)	($4,380)	($4,109)	$10,843	$11,624	($2,410)	($1,237)	
25														
26	*Fixed Cash Disbursements	(FCD)												
27	Utilities	$2,160												
28	Salaries	$22,800												
29	Payroll Taxes and Benefits	$2,850												
30	Office Supplies	$300												
31	Maintenance and Cleaning	$300												
32	Licenses	$115												
33	Boxes, Paper, etc.	$400												
34	Telephone	$1,020												
35	Miscellaneous	$480												
36	Total FCD/yr	$30,425												
37	Avg FCD per month	$2,535												
38														
39	Cash on Hand													
40	Opening Balance	$2,150	$10,001	$17,335	$2,031	$2,074	$1,786	($28,424)	($2,230)	($1,959)	$12,993	$13,774	($260)	
41	+Cash Receipts	$21,897	$21,000	$14,300	$119,467	$14,267	$15,417	$47,300	$19,473	$37,032	$23,232	$23,775	$22,642	$379,793
42	-Cash Disbursements	($14,046)	($13,665)	($29,604)	($119,424)	($14,555)	($45,627)	($21,106)	($19,202)	($22,080)	($22,451)	($37,809)	($21,468)	$381,037
43	Total = New Cash Balance	$10,001	$17,335	$2,031	$2,074	$1,786	($28,424)	($2,230)	($1,959)	$12,993	$13,774	($260)	$913	

FINESTKIND SEAFOODS, INC

Cash Flow Projection by Quarter, Year Two

	A	B	C	D	E	F
1		1st Qtr	2nd Qtr	3rd Qtr	4th Qtr	Total
2	Cash Receipts					
3	Sales Receivables	$3,200	$0	$0	$0	$3,200
4	Wholesale	$38,900	$54,800	$76,500	$94,800	$265,000
5	Retail	$41,000	$37,400	$48,600	$53,000	$180,000
6	Other Sources	$0	$0	$12,000	$15,000	$27,000
7	**Total Cash Receipts**	**$83,100**	**$92,200**	**$137,100**	**$162,800**	**$475,200**
8	Cash Disbursements					
9	Cost of Goods	$57,528	$66,384	$90,072	$106,416	$320,400
10	Variable Labor	$0	$0	$604	$2,196	$2,800
11	Advertising	$1,998	$2,305	$3,125	$3,695	$11,125
12	Insurance	$950	$950	$950	$950	$3,800
13	Legal and Accounting	$500	$500	$500	$500	$2,000
14	Delivery Expenses	$1,600	$1,844	$2,500	$2,956	$8,900
15	* Fixed Cash Disbursements	$12,630	$12,640	$12,640	$12,640	$50,550
16	Mortgage (rent)	$2,628	$2,628	$2,628	$2,628	$10,512
17	Term Loan	$1,602	$1,602	$1,602	$1,602	$6,408
18	Line of Credit	$0	$0	$12,140	$15,360	$27,500
19	Other Disbursements (see notes)	$0	$0	$0	$0	$0
20	**Total Cash Disbursements**	**$79,440**	**$88,850**	**$126,762**	**$148,940**	**$443,992**
21						
22	**Net Cash Flow**	**$3,660**	**$3,350**	**$10,338**	**$13,860**	**$31,208**
23						
24	**Cumulative Cash Flow**	**$3,662**	**$7,012**	**$17,350**	**$31,210**	
25						
26	***Fixed Cash Disbursements (FCD)**	Year Two				
27	Utilities	$2,640				
28	Salaries	$39,000				
29	Payroll Taxes and Benefits	$4,875				
30	Office Supplies	$360				
31	Maintenance and Cleaning	$360				
32	Licenses	$115				
33	Boxes, Paper, etc.	$800				
34	Telephone	$1,800				
35	Miscellaneous	$600				
36	Total FCD/yr	$50,550				
37	Avg FCD per quarter	$12,638				
38						
39	Note: Minor rounding errors have occurred. These are not sufficiently serious to cause alarm.					

FINESTKIND SEAFOODS, INC
Cash Flow Projection by Quarter, Year Three

	A	B	C	D	E	F
1		1st Qtr	2nd Qtr	3rd Qtr	4th Qtr	Total
2	Cash Receipts					
3	Sales Receivables	$0	$0	$0	$0	$0
4	Wholesale	$58,750	$55,000	$97,500	$113,750	$325,000
5	Retail	$47,400	$43,600	$56,000	$63,000	$210,000
6	Other Sources	$0	$0	$12,000	$15,000	$27,000
7	Total Cash Receipts	$106,150	$98,600	$165,500	$191,750	$562,000
8	Cash Disbursements					
9	Cost of Goods	$76,428	$70,992	$110,520	$127,260	$385,200
10	Variable Labor	$0	$0	$1,622	$5,898	$7,520
11	Advertising	$2,655	$2,465	$3,835	$4,420	$13,375
12	Insurance	$1,025	$1,025	$1,025	$1,025	$4,100
13	Legal and Accounting	$625	$625	$625	$625	$2,500
14	Delivery Expenses	$1,805	$1,675	$2,610	$3,010	$9,100
15	*Fixed Cash Disbursements	$15,216	$15,216	$15,216	$15,216	$60,865
16	Mortgage (rent)	$2,628	$2,628	$2,628	$2,628	$10,512
17	Term Loan	$1,602	$1,602	$1,602	$1,602	$6,408
18	Line of Credit	$0	$0	$12,140	$15,360	$27,500
19	Other Disbursements (see notes)	$0	$0	$0	$0	$0
20	Total Cash Disbursments	$101,984	$96,228	$151,823	$177,044	$527,080
21						
22	Net Cash Flow	$4,166	$2,372	$13,677	$14,706	$34,920
23						
24	Cumulative Cash Flow	$4,166	$6,538	$20,215	$34,920	
25						
26	*Fixed Cash Disbursements (FCD)	Year Three				
27	Utilities	$2,880				
28	Salaries	$46,800				
29	Payroll Taxes and Benefits	$5,850				
30	Office Supplies	$480				
31	Maintenance and Cleaning	$420				
32	Licenses	$115				
33	Boxes, Paper, etc.	$1,200				
34	Telephone	$2,400				
35	Miscellaneous	$720				
36	Total FCD/yr	$60,865				
37	Avg FCD per quarter	$15,216				

Explanation for Cash Flow Projections

The receipts shown on these cash flow projections include both sales and other cash sources to emphasize their impact on Finestkind. The cash flow projections show how business operations affect cash flow, so some people prefer to isolate "Other Sources" of cash receipts in the cash reconciliation section [lines (40)–(43) in the Year One Cash Flow Projection]. References are to line numbers on the accounting sheet unless otherwise noted.

(3) Sales Receivables. Sales are cash for retail, cash or 10-day net for wholesale accounts. If Finestkind provided longer terms, their cash flow could be significantly altered. As it is, the cash flow assumes a conservative 10-day lag on all wholesale sales. Because wholesale sales in September were $6,400, $2,000 (10/30 of September wholesale sales) turns to cash in October.

The same rationale applies to the rest of the year: One-third of wholesale receipts aren't collected until the following month.

The collection lag is not continued beyond the first quarter of Year Two. Experience will correct the cash flow, and new figures should be calculated for Year Two on a monthly basis for Year Two business planning.

(4) Wholesale. Note the total of $28,700 + 60,100 (Total Sales Receivable and Total Wholesale) = $88,800, which is $1,200 less than the projected sales of $90,000 shown on the income statement. To reconcile the difference between these figures, note that $2,000 in cash receipts come from September of the preceding year, while $3,200 of cash receipts are postponed for September of Year One. Sales figures are based on the Income Projections on pages 73 to 76.

(5) Retail. See Income Projections on pages 73 to 76.

(6) Other Sources.

October:	Inventory loan using credit line
November:	Closing costs, using credit line
January:	Purchase building; $30,000 from Gosling and Swan as new equity investment, along with a $75,000 mortgage
April:	Equipment and building improvements, from term loan
June:	Inventory loan, credit line

(7) Total Cash Receipts. The sum of (3) + (4) + (5) + (6). Note that the total is distorted by loans and new investment.

(8) Cash Disbursements. These are the disbursements that will be made in cash (including checks) during the normal course of business plus any major anticipated cash outlays.

(9) Cost of Goods. From Income Projection on page 73, line 10.

(10) Variable Labor. From Income Projection on page 73, line 9.

(11) Advertising. Budgeted at $400/month for the first year, plus an extra $600 in October for a tourist-oriented ad campaign and an extra $4,155 in April to an agency for the major wholesale marketing program, including implementation and execution.

(12) Insurance. Payable quarterly.

(13) Legal and Accounting. Payable quarterly.

(14) Delivery Expenses. Varies with volume of wholesale sales.

(15) Fixed Cash Disbursements. These are relatively independent of sales, so they are allocated evenly throughout the year. See display on lines (26) through (37) for details. If salaries fluctuate widely, break them out as a separate item with the other disbursements. For example, if you meet your payroll every other week, two months of the year will have three paydays rather than two, which can make those months look alarmingly costly.

(16) Mortgage (rent). Rent through December at $550/month, mortgage payments (principal and interest) at $876 thereafter.

(17) Term Loan. $534/month for seven years, which includes principal and interest.

(18) Line of Credit. Includes principal repayment and interest.

(19) Other Disbursements.

January:	Purchase building
March:	Equipment purchase and building improvements to be paid in full.

(20) Total Cash Disbursements. Sum of lines (9) through (19).

(22) Net Cash Flow. (7) minus (20).

(24) Cumulative Cash Flow. (22) + last month's (24). This sums up the net cash flow on a monthly basis, adding the present month's net cash flow to last month's cumulative cash flow. This is useful on a periodic basis (monthly or quarterly). Over a longer time, it's of academic interest only.

Some experts advise pushing a cash flow until the cumulative cash flow is consistently positive.

(39)–(43) Cash Balance Reconciliation. (40) + (41) − (42) = (43). This display (for Year One only) may be used as a quick check on how well the budget is doing. For Years Two and Three, it is not accurate enough to be useful.

Further explanation of these cash flow items appears on the notes supporting the income projections.

Samples of Notes and Explanations for a Cash Flow Projection

Notes and Explanations for Finestkind Seafoods, Inc.

Cash Flow Projection by Month, Year One

Further explanation of these cash flow items appears on the notes supporting the income projections on pages 77 through 80.

(3) Sales Receivables. Our terms are cash retail, net 10 for wholesale accounts. Assumes ⅓ wholesale will turn to cash in the following month.

(4) Wholesale. See income projections for derivation of these figures.

(5) Retail. See income projections for derivation.

(6) Other Sources. October, November credit line, $7,500; January $75,000 mortgage and $30,000 new equity from Swan and Gosling; April term loan for improvements and equipment, $30,000; June inventory buildup, $15,000 from credit line.

(9) Cost of Goods. 72 percent of current month sales [line (6) of income projections].

(10) Variable Labor. Part-time help from May to September to handle extra weekend tourist trade and extra seafood preparation.

(11) Advertising. $1,000 initial burst, $400/month thereafter. Add $4,155 to April for wholesale marketing program.

(16) Mortgage. $550/month rent to December, mortgage payments January on. Terms: $75,000, 15 year, 11.5 percent.

(17) Term Loan. $534/month payments scheduled for term loan. Terms: $30,000, 7 year, 12.25 percent.

Cash Flow Projection by Quarters for Years Two and Three

(3) Sales Receivables. Turn from September, Year One. Because this is a quarterly summary, no further allowance will be made for receivables turn.

(6) Other Sources. $12,000 for one month on line of credit third quarter, $15,000 for nine weeks on line of credit fourth quarter to meet inventory needs.

(15) Fixed Cash Disbursements. Could have included mortgage and term loan payments, but to preserve parity with detail of Year One, loan payments are displayed separately.

(24) Cumulative Cash Flow. Subtract $1,237 from net cash flow, first quarter Year Two, to reflect the total cumulative cash flow of Year One: ($1,237).

(26) Fixed Cash Disbursements. From income projections.

You should notice that only the most important cash flow items are annotated. Such annotation helps you remember your thinking at some later time—and helps avoid repeating errors. It also makes your projections much more believable because the numbers will be seen to have more foundation than guesswork.

Application of Funds Statement

This is a handy addition to your cash flow analysis. Your banker may be interested in a source and applications statement, which is a slightly more formal version—ask your CPA—but this is handy when you are looking at ways of financing major acquisitions.

Use of Funds	Total Amount Required	From Equity	From Loans	From Other
Acquire building	$105,000	$30,000	$75,000	
Improve building	24,000		20,000	$4,000
Equipment	10,000		10,000	

Section H. Deviation Analysis takes a more formal approach to using a budget. It uses the cash flow and income statements to set up a red-flag system. If over a three- or six-month time period your projections are seriously off, take the time to understand why the deviations have happened before changing your projections and your business operations. Then make the changes—based on informed knowledge rather than hunch, a major reason to document your assumptions in your financial statements.

G. HISTORICAL FINANCIAL REPORTS

A record of what happened in the past is an integral part of your business plan.

A record of what happened in the past is an integral part of your business plan. For most business deals, balance sheets and income statements for the past three years are sufficient.

The third major component of your past financial records is tax statements. Because they must be filed at least annually, they provide a summary of what you earned, how you earned it, and what your deductible expenses were. If you decide to sell your business, these tax statements will be the most important substantiation of your asking price, and will surely be requested and examined by prospective purchasers.

If you don't yet have an accountant, go directly to the nearest IRS office at a time well in advance of payment day and go over your business records with one of their representatives. By doing so, you gain the benefit of free advice from experts and get an insight into the best ways to handle your business taxes. The IRS will even help you set up your recordkeeping system to minimize the problems of preparing tax returns.

The IRS is more concerned with helping businesses properly handle their financial responsibilities (taxes) than you may have thought. It makes their job easier. They provide a number of free tax seminars for small businesses that can be useful, especially if you are trying to handle your own taxes.

Tax records can be used as an additional source of information. For example, copies of wage and deduction statements help in making projections. Payroll records can help settle unemployment claims; they have a certain legal weight, especially in situations where it's your word against that of a disgruntled former employee.

Most business owners know that it pays to hire a competent accountant to handle taxes. The tax code has something like 40,000 pages, changes frequently, and contains so many booby traps (for businesses as well as individuals) that it just doesn't make sense to try to do your returns yourself. Your job is making your business profitable. Your accountant's job is making sure that you don't pay more taxes than you are legally required to pay. And you can't do both jobs.

If you do not have clear, accurate, and well-substantiated historical financial records, or if you have lied to minimize your tax liabilities, you have only cheated yourself. In the first case, you've only demonstrated your incompetence. In the second case, you've simply lowered the performance level of the business, thus making it a worse risk for a lender. Either way, it just isn't worth it.

H. DEVIATION ANALYSIS

For most small businesses, the cash flow projection for one year provides an adequate operating budget. You may want to break down some of the cash flow items more finely to insure greater control, but in any case the cash flow projection is the basis for your budgets.

While anyone can learn to stay within a budget, only the best managers can draw up budgets worth staying within. While a well thought out cash flow projection doesn't guarantee a good budget, you can be sure that a budget drawn up without such projections won't be worth following.

Budget deviation analysis will help you hold down costs and increase profits.

Budget deviation analysis (BDA) is a direct control on your business operations. It will help you hold down costs and increase profits at a time cost of about one evening per month. It is an essential tool and should not be ignored even if everything is going well.

BDA must be performed periodically, at least monthly, if it is to be effective. If you are engaged in a business with several concurrent projects, it may be more helpful to devise separate budgets and deviation analyses for each project. BDA provides one of the best sources of current information available to you. Use it. Done properly, it will tell you at a glance which parts of your business are out of control and which ones are exceeding expectations.

Pages 92 to 95 are BDA forms that you should modify to suit the particular needs of your business. Columns C and D are derived from actual and budgeted figures. Experience will tell you which deviations—and of what magnitude—are significant. Any deviation, positive or negative, should be carefully examined and the reasons for its existence understood. Next, corrective action should be taken (if the deviation is working against you) or the serendipitous improvement in performance should be exploited (if the deviation is in your favor).

For example, suppose that utilities, budgeted for $200 in January, actually cost $340. Why? The weather was exceptionally cold, insulation was installed toward the end of the month, and a broken skylight was replaced on February 1. The indicated action was to cut utilities expense as soon as possible (which was done). If close attention had not been paid to the utility bill, that cost could easily have gotten out of hand. Again, suppose sales were $18,000 in January, not the anticipated (budgeted) $14,600. What went right? Careful attention to a positive deviation can pay off in greatly increased profits.

Year-to-date BDA is another good financial tool. If more expenditures fall in one month than were expected, you will find a corresponding lowering of expenditures the preceding or following month. The year-to-date BDA helps to level out these swings. Used with the monthly BDAs, this form will save you some unnecessary arithmetic and worry, as well as check the accuracy and effectiveness of your projections. With experience, your budgeting will become more exact, affording you greater control over your business and profits.

As with the other control documents, you should adapt the suggested formats that follow to fit your business needs. Your accountant should be helpful here—but you have to be the person who decides what information should be reflected by BDA.

For example, a manufacturer might want to have more control over inventories of work in progress, returns, and some quality control figures. These can be provided—but are not shown in the examples. Ask your accountant to help; you should only add information if you have a way to check it out against actual performance, and that will often call for professional expertise. You have a business to run, after all, which is why you hire accountants rather than become one yourself.

Small deviations can collectively become fairly large and have a devastating cumulative effect on profits.

You will also notice that "Column D: percent Deviation" will magnify small numbers. If maintenance and cleaning is budgeted at $25/month and comes in at $50, the percentage deviation is 100 percent. This is deliberate. Large dollar deviations show up clearly in "Column C: Deviation" but small deviations can collectively become fairly large and have a devastating cumulative effect on profits. This is another area where a bit of computer power takes the drudgery (and opportunities for error) out of repetitive monthly calculations. Set your tolerances. Then follow up on all significant deviations.

BUDGET DEVIATION ANALYSIS BY MONTH

**From the Income Statement
For the Month of _____**

	A Actual for Month	B Budget for Month	C Deviation (B – A)	D % Deviation (C/B x 100)
Sales				
Less Cost of Goods				
Gross Profit on Sales				
Operating Expenses:				
Variable Expenses Sales Salaries (commissions) Advertising Miscellaneous Variable				
Total Variable Expenses				
Fixed Expenses Utilities Salaries Payroll Taxes and Benefits Office Supplies Insurance Maintenance and Cleaning Legal and Accounting Delivery Licenses Boxes, Paper, etc. Telephone Miscellaneous Depreciation Interest				
Total Fixed Expenses				
Total Operating Expenses				
Net Profit (Gross Profit on Sales Less Total Operating Expenses)				
Tax Expense				
Net Profit after Taxes				

BUDGET DEVIATION ANALYSIS YEAR-TO-DATE

From the Income Statement
Year-to-Date _____

	A Actual for Year-to-Date	B Budget for Year-to-Date	C Deviation (B – A)	D % Deviation (C/B x 100)
Sales				
Less Cost of Goods				
Gross Profit on Sales				
Operating Expenses:				

Variable Expenses
    Sales Salaries (commissions)
    Advertising
    Miscellaneous Variable				

Total Variable Expenses				

Fixed Expenses
    Utilities
    Salaries
    Payroll Taxes and Benefits
    Office Supplies
    Insurance
    Maintenance and Cleaning
    Legal and Accounting
    Delivery
    Licenses
    Boxes, Paper, etc.
    Telephone
    Miscellaneous
    Depreciation
    Interest				

Total Fixed Expenses				
Total Operating Expenses				
Net Profit (Gross Profit on Sales Less Total Operating Expenses)				
Tax Expense				
Net Profit after Taxes				

Calculations: A. Add current month actual to last month's year-to-date analysis.
*   B. Add current month budget to last month's year-to-date analysis.*

BUDGET DEVIATION ANALYSIS BY MONTH

From the Cash Flow Statement
For the Month of _____

	A Actual for Month	B Budget for Month	C Deviation (B – A)	D % Deviation (C/B x 100)
Beginning Cash Balance				
Add:				
Cash Sales				
Accounts Receivable that Have Turned to Cash				
Other Cash Inflows				
Total Available Cash				
Deduct Estimated Disbursements:				
Cost of Materials Variable Labor Advertising Insurance Legal and Accounting Delivery Equipment* Loan Payments Mortgage Payment Property Tax Expense				
Deduct Fixed Cash Disbursements:				
Utilities Salaries Payroll Taxes and Benefits Office Supplies Maintenance and Cleaning Licenses Boxes, Paper, etc. Telephone Miscellaneous				
Total Disbursements				
Ending Cash Balance				

Equipment expense represents actual expenditures made for purchase of equipment.

BUDGET DEVIATION ANALYSIS YEAR-TO-DATE

From the Cash Flow Statement
Year-to-Date _____

	A Actual for Year-to-Date	B Budget for Year-to-Date	C Deviation (B – A)	D % Deviation (C/B x 100)
Beginning Cash Balance				
Add:				
Sales Revenue				
Other Revenue				
Total Available Cash				
Deduct Estimated Disbursements:				
Cost of Materials Variable Labor Advertising Insurance Legal and Accounting Delivery Equipment* Loan Payments Mortgage Payment Property Tax Expense				
Deduct Fixed Cash Disbursements:				
Utilities Salaries Payroll Taxes and Benefits Office Supplies Maintenance and Cleaning Licenses Boxes, Paper, etc. Telephone Miscellaneous				
Total Disbursements				
Ending Cash Balance				

Calculations: A. Add current month actual to last month's year-to-date analysis.
                B. Add current month budget to last month's year-to-date analysis.

*Equipment expense represents actual expenditures made for purchase of equipment.

I. SUMMARY

Budgeting, balancing objectives with reality, then guiding your business to achieve your goals within the budget constraints is a hard test of managerial ability.

With the exception of the historical financial reports, which reflect past management decisions, the Financial Data section stresses the importance of making and documenting careful assumptions about the objectives of your business as the first step in preparing financial projections.

Your income and cash flow projections are the basis of your planning efforts. They help set up a series of objectives: At what level do you hit break even? What are the budget items to monitor closely—monthly or more often? What profit levels do you want to achieve, and what sales levels are needed to reach those profit goals?

Planning is the key to business success.

Deviation analysis puts the controls more directly to work by providing an early-warning system pinpointing trouble before it gets out of hand. By measuring progress toward the goals set in your income and cash flow projections, and clamping down on costs with deviation analysis, your management workload will be greatly reduced.

The financial statements are not intended to be straitjackets. They should instead free you from the most pressing problem most small business owners/managers face: How do you find time for managing when there are so many brush fires to be put out? Your single most important asset is your time. To make effective use of your time, early planning is not a luxury. It is a necessity.

The financial statements are the easiest part of the business plan. The hard part, the thinking that goes into establishing the goals and strategies of your business and the effort that goes into staffing and managing people, has to be done before your financial projections can make sense. Your financial projections are a model of your business, based on your assumptions and experience and perceptions of your markets.

This model can provide the most effective control over your business available—or it can degenerate into a "fun with numbers" game. The choice is yours. You must take the time to think through your assumptions and objectives. You must make your assumptions as clear and as well defined as you can. And you must be prepared to continually review and reevaluate those assumptions and objectives.

Set aside time to review the information your financial statements provide. An excellent practice followed by many managers is to set aside an afternoon or evening each week away from the telephone and other interruptions for planning and review. If you feel you cannot afford the time, you have the clearest indication that you must plan, that you must take the time now.

Remember: Planning is the key to business success.

The Financing Proposal

*T*he purpose of this section is to help you turn your business plan into a financing proposal that fits your business needs and capital constraints.

Financing your venture begins with the capital you can invest, augmented in most cases by equity raised from friends and family. These investments should be treated formally. If the investment from your friends and family is a subordinated loan, make sure you have a loan agreement stating interest rate and the terms of the loan. If they invest in ownership of a portion of the business, make sure you both have a legal document that states the terms of the investment and how it might be withdrawn at a later time.

Keep the arrangement businesslike, with proper documentation to protect all parties. Your banker will provide legal forms covering almost all forms of capital investment. Have your accountant spell out the plusses and minuses of the financing arrangements, because these will depend on the people and form of investment involved.

The financing proposal in *The Business Planning Guide* is strongly slanted toward a banker's needs. In a very few situations, other capital sources should be approached—venture capital firms or investment bankers, for example. If your deal is large enough and the anticipated payoff is sufficiently high (financing needs of over $1 million, with an anticipated payout rate greater than 40 percent annually are two rough measures), your banker and other advisers will steer you to the right people. Otherwise, don't waste your time or theirs. Most deals never get beyond the first screening (1 percent or so make it through) and only a handful of those get venture capital or go public. If your deal is attractive enough to warrant attention, you will want to tailor your proposal to the needs of your intended audience, a process well beyond the scope of this handbook and one that requires detailed knowledge of the players involved.

For the rest of you with more modest deals, turn to your banker first. Your banker may refer you to a local venture capital club or other source of equity—but start with your banker. If you need more equity than you have available, check with your accountant and lawyer, who may be in touch with individuals who invest in local or startup deals. If you don't have a banker and an accountant, you surely will have no need for specialized financing.

The business plan you have developed throughout the preceding pages needs little alteration to become a first-rate financing proposal. Some areas of the plan will be of little use to your banker (personal histories can be replaced by résumés, deviation analysis won't be needed). The difference between a business plan and a financing proposal is one of emphasis rather than design: The main function of your plan is to enable you to understand and master the complexities of your business while the function of the financing proposal is to show your prospective backers that you not only know what you are doing but will also make their investment as risk-free as possible.

Most bankers deal with small business owners who don't understand the differences between types of financing, the importance of those distinctions to a business, and the banker's point of view. By showing some familiarity with how a business financing package looks from the banker's viewpoint, you will be on guard against two severe problems:

1. The banker who can't say "no" but who can't or won't provide adequate financing
2. The banker who gives the wrong loan for the wrong reasons

You will also better understand the role of a bank in the financing process: Banks are not venture capitalists, not risk takers, not gamblers. They shouldn't be. Their business is investing other people's money, and they have to be cautious.

Although the greatest dollar amounts of credit for businesses of all sizes is trade credit (money owed to suppliers), your single most important financing source is your local bank. Such esoteric financing tools as factoring, warehouse loans, and the many forms of stocks, bonds, and debt instruments just don't apply to most businesses. If you need them, your banker will help you find the right professionals.

DEBT VERSUS EQUITY

When you go to your bank for a loan, you are seeking debt money, which you will repay over a period of time at an additional cost (interest). The money you invest in your business is ordinarily equity, that is, money that will not be repaid to you unless you sell a portion of your ownership. Debt financing doesn't lead to sharing ownership of your business with the financier. Equity financing does.

The function of the financing proposal is to show your prospective backers that you not only know what you are doing but will also make their investment as risk-free as possible.

Presentation Skills

If you haven't had the experience of making presentations to a banker, you may well view asking a banker for money with alarm—or worse, feel that it will be so easy that no preparation is necessary.

Many courses require students to make presentations to a panel in a safe, controlled environment so they can learn to handle the kind of searching questions that bankers ask. If you have this option, avail yourself of it. At the very least, it will give you practice in responding to searching questions. Some small business owners join groups such as Toastmasters to get the same kind of experience. Making presentations is a learned skill, not something that you are born knowing how to do. So:

Rehearse your presentation. Have a financial person (your accountant or a banker to whom you won't be making the presentation) take the role of devil's advocate and grill you about your numbers. Because all financing proposals are basically optimistic, bankers have learned to be very skeptical. In particular, they will challenge you in two areas: pro formas and marketing plans, including the real level of competition you will face when you implement your plans.

You—not your accountant—have to explain the pro formas. You will be the person responsible for repayment of the loan. Bankers typically look first at the level of gross profit, second at margins, third at gross revenues. If your justification for these major financial elements isn't compelling, then the details will be examined. Your income pro formas and balance sheet should be reasonably close to trade averages. If there are substantial deviations, be prepared to explain why your figures are different. Your cash flow projections should clearly substantiate the need for a loan and give a hint at the probability of repayment.

Where will your revenues come from? If your numbers stand up to this first burst of questioning, interest will shift to how the revenues will be generated and the expenses held in check. All of the work you put into your market research comes in useful at this point. Bankers are increasingly interested in where you will fit in a competitive economy. Because you don't know what your banker knows and what she doesn't, ask your rehearsal coach to pepper you with questions, no matter how obvious the answers seem to you.

Then rehearse your presentation again. The aim of these rehearsals is to make you feel sufficiently at ease to respond to any reasonable question, and not get frozen in an overrehearsed spiel. You are trying to establish credibility as a knowledgeable person in your line of business. If your audience drums their fingers and asks out of nowhere what your contingency plans are, or if you have secured sufficient capital, or how their investment will be repaid if things go wrong, you must be prepared to answer without looking confused. And that takes rehearsing.

Appeal to more than the banker's cold sense of fiscal sobriety. Have supplemental information, just in case. If you are going to produce a product, show a sample. It's desirable for a chocolatier to bring a few of his truffles to a presentation, or a boatbuilder photos or models of her latest boat. People like to touch, see, taste, smell—so oblige them. Make your service visual by showing a report or demonstrating a technique. For example, if you plan to offer horticultural therapy to shut-ins, demonstrate what you will be doing by assembling a small container garden in front of the audience. Demonstrations go a long way to establishing understanding.

Dress appropriately. This may seem simplistic, but remember that bankers are conservative. You don't have to put on a bankerly black suit with white shirt, but do be neat, clean, and presentable. It's part of the image that you are endeavoring to project.

Rehearse once more. If you will be using a computer or other equipment to make the presentation, make sure that the overhead projector has a bulb, or the computer a power source. A presentation that relies on the zip and flash of presentation software can look mighty silly if the equipment breaks down. Keep Murphy's Law (Whatever can go wrong, will!) in mind.

Time your presentation. Keep it short, consistent with presenting the level of detail needed to make your proposal understood by the banker. More deals get turned down because the presenter drones on than you might expect. If the bankers want more information from you, they'll ask.

Good luck with your presentation. The fear of public speaking is allegedly as great as the fear of death for some people, but unlike death, you get many chances to rehearse presentations and develop your skills.

Control is another matter. Your banker may exert substantial control over your business through a legal loan document or through suggestions—but he or she doesn't own your business. Debt pays interest, usually for a finite time. Equity pays profits forever.

The distinction between debt and equity is important to your banker because the more debt there is in relation to equity, the higher the risk. A high debt-to-worth ratio (worth being roughly equivalent to equity but may include some kinds of subordinated debt) indicates high risk—and high risk costs high interest if you can find new debt money at all. Why? Because debt money is rented money, and the rent must be paid no matter what the business is doing. If you can't meet your debt payments, you go out of business.

Not only that, but a highly leveraged business (higher than normal debt-to-worth ratio for that kind of business) must earn more money. Sometimes it's possible to find so much debt money that the business never can get ahead. Without capital (permanent nonrepayable money invested in the business), you can spin your wheels forever, a problem called overtrading. Sales-to-worth ratios are guidelines to this and can help you pinpoint your capital needs relative to projected sales.

From a banker's viewpoint, the higher the debt, the riskier the deal. The longer the term, the riskier the deal. Short-term loans are less hazardous than long-term (with some exceptions) because if the loan goes sour, it does so in a hurry and can be easily detected, while a long-term decline can be almost imperceptible. The underlying issue—performance in the near term—can be predicted with much greater certainty than longer times allow.

Risk, the odds against an expected happening in the future, is just one of the elements in a credit decision.

The "Four C's of Credit": Character, Capacity, Contingency, and Capital.

Most bankers have been trained in the "Four C's of Credit": Character, Capacity, Contingency, and Capital. Character reflects the willingness to pay (a record of nonpayment or a prior personal bankruptcy, for example, might cause a banker to view a person's character as too risky). Capacity and capital reflect ability to carry out the intent to pay. Experience is a factor here: Your experience in a given business affects your banker's perception of your ability to successfully run this business. Contingency refers to the dangers inherent in any business's future and to your ability to present a backup or contingency plan just in case things go wrong. Capital is obvious: A well-capitalized business is inherently less risky than an undercapitalized business. Costs will be lower, for example, and a capital cushion makes for sounder decisions.

Two other C's are often cited: Condition (of the economy and of the business) and Collateral. If the economy in your area is rolling off a cliff, the risk of your deal will be magnified. Collateral is useful as a means of tying you to the deal. Experience has shown that people who have their own assets on the line fight harder to make a deal work than people who are working with little of their own money at risk—and collateral also serves as a comfort factor for the banker. Bankers have no desire to be secondhand equipment dealers or to sell out your stocks and bonds. But they like to have some recourse just in case your business fails.

That's as it should be. Bankers are not in business to take risks or shoot for a long shot. (Nor should you be. Most studies of successful business owners show a profile of moderate risk taking. Not too conservative, but certainly not too eager to run unjustified risks.)

Another way that bankers and other financiers look at a deal is to consider the personal, financial, and economic factors that are involved. The personal factors include many intangibles (integrity, for example; try to define it) but your personal track record provides a clue. This is why a full résumé has to be part of your financing proposal. If your banker has known you forever, fine—put it in anyway. Other bankers may not know you as well. Your education, experience, and history are important: The saying that "there are no small business loans; just loans to small business owners" is true. You'll probably have to sign personally for a loan while your business is small.

Financial factors will have been covered in some detail in your financial statements, and if they are based on clearly spelled-out, rational assumptions (which they will be if you have followed *The Business Planning Guide* to this point), will provide additional evidence of your personal commitment as well. Financial factors include product/service, marketing, competition, personnel, and management elements, so all the work of Section 1: The Business comes into play once more.

Economic factors may be beyond your control but, once again, will affect your banker's decision. Your business idea might be poor today but wonderful tomorrow—and no banker would do you a favor by launching you into business at the wrong time. If times are tight, think carefully about a new venture (that doesn't mean not to pursue it, just to think it through especially carefully).

Assuming that you pass these rough sorting criteria, what comes next? Your business plan, tailored to the banker as a financing proposal, gains added credibility if you ask for the appropriate financing to fit your needs. You can research this ahead of time by involving your banker in your planning (never a bad idea anyway) and by asking your accountant.

Fit the financing to the need.

The key here: Fit the financing to the need.

When you projected your cash flow, you did two things that help determine the right financing mix for your business. The deepest negative cash flows, both in net cash flow and cumulative cash flow, indicate how much money you need and when you need it. Projected cash receipts give you an inkling of how you will generate money to repay the loan or make good the investment. If you don't arrange for enough financing (of whatever kind), your deal will be dead. If you borrow more than you can service, your deal will also be dead. If you borrow at the wrong time, or for the wrong reasons, you aggravate the risks of being in business, risks that are already high.

Finestkind projected a worst negative cumulative cash flow in March of Year One (see page 83) due to a timing problem. The solution: a term loan for equipment and renovation. Protecting liquidity and ensuring adequate working capital are legitimate reasons to borrow—if you fit the financing to the need. The April Year One shortfall is marked to show a need for the line of credit if needed, another legitimate financing purpose and one their banker looked favorably on.

KINDS OF BANK FINANCING

Bankers customarily divide loans into three general categories:

1. *Short-term financing* is usually provided through notes to be paid within one year, usually in one sum. These notes are repaid

through inventory turn or by converting receivables to cash within the time frame of the note.

2. *Intermediate-term financing* ranges from one to five years and is usually repaid in fixed monthly payments or fixed principal payments plus interest. These loans are repaid from operating profits.

3. *Long-term financing* is provided for periods longer than five years. The most common example is real estate financing, where repayment is made on a prearranged schedule over many years.

These loans may be secured or unsecured. A secured loan is backed by collateral (liens against your property, savings account, or certificate of deposit, perhaps cosigned by someone with more assets) that would be applied to recover the loan in the event of default.

An unsecured loan (sometimes called a signature or character loan) is one not backed by any collateral. These are almost always short-term loans and available only to the most creditworthy individuals and companies. The loan is backed up by your banker's faith in your character, capability, and capital.

It helps to remember that bankers are in the business of investing money that isn't theirs, money that mustn't be subject to unusual risks. Banks do not and should not gamble with their depositors' money, and as a borrower you should understand this.

From a banker's viewpoint, a loan should be repaid as soon as possible.

Your banker will lend your business money if he or she feels comfortable with the risk. They are under no obligation to lend money to a business that doesn't fit their risk tolerance—a frequent source of anger to credit seekers. Help your banker decide in your favor: Lower the risk by keeping a low debt-to-worth ratio, make sure to have enough working capital to cover current liabilities, and match the financing request to your real needs. Note that from a banker's viewpoint, a loan should be repaid as soon as possible.

Long-term debt is for long-term needs: fixed assets that will be used and paid for over the long haul. It is a mistake to pay this kind of debt off too fast unless you are extremely well capitalized, in which case check with your banker and accountant first. They'll tell you.

Short-term debt is for short-term needs: seasonal inventory loans, short-run production or construction loans, short-term liquidity problems. These are repaid from the returns on specific transactions or series of transactions in a short period of time. If these are financed over a longer time span, the result is almost always deepening debt and the erosion of business assets. Even though your cash flow will look good by spreading the cost over a longer period, you would be violating a cardinal rule of borrowing: paying for a benefit after it has been exhausted. One reason bankers are hesitant to bail small businesses out of chronic trade debts is that those unpaid debts are evidence that the business is seriously mismanaged. Paying for a dead horse is bad business.

The line of credit (revolving or nonrevolving) is a short-term tool that works like a credit card: You arrange before the need arises to have so much credit to draw against; then you pay it off (or renew it). The main thing to avoid is to get used to paying for last year's short-term needs with new debt—bad enough for an individual but worse for a small business.

Intermediate-term debt is for those needs that last between one and five years. Most common are equipment loans and working capital loans for businesses undergoing rapid growth. By converting debt to earnings, and then retaining a portion of the earnings as capital, it is possible to grow using debt money. Don't plan on this, though, as it requires a far-sighted banker, considerable risk, and profits high enough to handle the added interest costs.

For any kind of financing, a final word may be helpful: Friday night financing never works.

Planning is the key to success.

Always make sure your banker knows your needs well in advance. Then you won't get caught in a cash squeeze. Borrowing in a panic is outrageously dangerous. Don't do it.

Earlier in this section, we mentioned the problem of the banker who can't say no but won't provide the right amount of financing. If you have thought through your business plan, you will know how much you need and when you'll need it. Make sure to get the right financing; less will only complicate matters. If your banker can give you good reasons to borrow less, pay attention—but think it through. Don't settle for enough money to get you into trouble but not enough to see you through.

Tell your banker what you need the money for, how it will be repaid—and why the deal makes good business sense. Your financing proposal does just that, and if based on your business plan and careful analysis, you should get the right financing.

A final reminder: Planning is the key to success.

Supporting Documents

You will want to include any documents that lend support to statements you have made in the body of the business plan. Items included here will vary according to the needs and stage of development of your particular business. The following list suggests some things that might be included:

- Résumé: very important—see Appendix 1: Additional Supporting Documents
- Credit information: forms included in Appendix 4: Worksheets
- Quotes or estimates
- Letters of intent from prospective customers
- Letters of support from credible people who know you
- Leases or buy/sell agreements
- Legal documents relevant to the business
- Census/demographic data

Sample Résumé

Mike Swan

March 19— to June 19—: Line Foreman, Fatback Fishfoods, East Machias, Maine. Responsible for hiring, training, and directing operations of 15 people in Frozen Food Filleting Department. Rescheduled work flow with resultant 30 percent increase in output per worker. Implemented new purchasing system that reduced spoilage 8 percent. Reduced personnel turnovers by working with local union for revision of company contract policy and by shifting from production line to team task approach. Received Grandiose Foodstuff, Inc. award for line management and was given special assignment in September, 19— to explain these changes to other line foremen at all 22 Fatback Fishfoods plants in New England and the Middle Atlantic states.

Mike Gosling

August 19— to September 19—: Self-employed carpenter. Responsibilities included cash flow forecasting, budgeting, and various other management functions needed in the operation of a single-employee business. Night courses have been taken concurrently in small business management and sales at the University of Maine. Currently serving on the Anytown Zoning Board. Prior experience included a three-year term in the U.S. Navy. Married, two children.

THE HOUSEHOLD CENSUS SURVEY

Most municipalities will have a census survey similar to Portsmouth's. You use these surveys to identify demographic characteristics of the local market. You can find income and educational levels, some indicators of local employment, and other key factors in making marketing decisions.

HOUSEHOLD CENSUS SURVEY

City of Portsmouth,

New Hampshire

June, 1995

TABLE OF CONTENTS

ME License 1000 NH License 2000

Johnson's Plumbing, Inc.
1327 Varnum Street,
Anytown, ME 04112
Phone: 332-2222

September 18, 19—

Finestkind Seafoods, Inc.
123 Main Street
Anytown, ME 04112
Attn.: Mr. Mike Gosling

Dear Mr. Gosling:

For the sum of $4,000, we propose to furnish and install the plumbing and heat work as shown on your outline sketch.

All work will be guaranteed and serviced for one year from the date of completion.

We would require a down payment of $1,150 and another payment of $1,150 when the rough plumbing and heating is completed, with the balance due upon final completion.

If the above meets with your approval, please sign and return one copy.

Signed by: _____

Date: _____

Thank you,

Derek LaMont Johnson

SAMPLE LETTER OF REFERENCE

Nightlife Clambakes
222 Rural Lane
Anytown, ME 04112

September 10, 19—

Gentlemen:

It is a pleasure to write this letter of recommendation for Finestkind Seafoods, Inc. Our dealings with Messrs. Gosling and Swan have been completely satisfactory. Our business requires a dependable supply of fresh fish, clams and lobsters of first quality. We have consistently received seafood products from Finestkind that meet these standards.

Our business is growing and we look forward to an ongoing relationship with Finestkind to satisfy our needs and customers.

Yours,

Alessandro Tetrazini

SAMPLE FLOOR PLAN

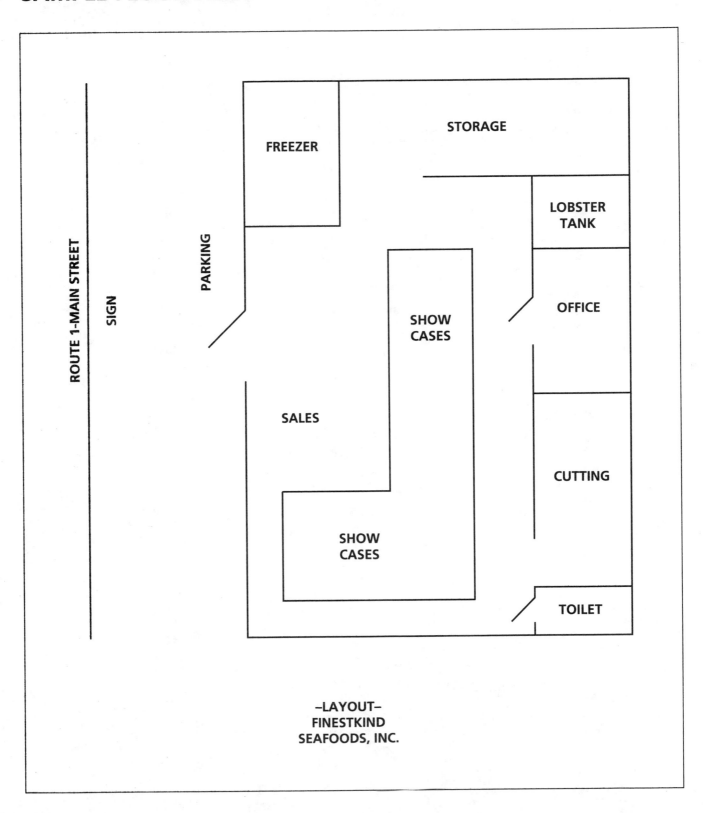

–LAYOUT–
FINESTKIND
SEAFOODS, INC.

Additional
Supporting
Documents

*T*hese forms have been made available to Upstart Publishing Company, Inc. by General Business Services, Inc. of Waco, Texas. GBS is a nationwide company providing tax and business counseling services to small businesses.

We have modified the forms. To obtain originals, ask your local GBS representative for GBS form 89927: Partnership Agreement, or GBS form 89929: Corporate Checklist. Call 817-745-2498 to find the GBS office nearest to you.

A SAMPLE PARTNERSHIP AGREEMENT

Agreement made _____, 19___, between _____,
City of _____, County of _____,
State of _____, and _____
of _____ (address),
City of _____, County of _____,
State of _____, hereinafter referred to as partners.

Item One

NAME, PURPOSE AND DOMICILE

The name of the partnership shall be _____. The partnership shall be conducted for the purposes of _____
_____. The principal place of business shall be
at _____ unless relocated by majority consent of
the partners.

Item Two

DURATION OF AGREEMENT

The term of this agreement shall be for _____ years, commencing
on _____, 19__, and terminating on _____, 19__,
unless sooner terminated by mutual consent of the parties or by operation
of the provisions of this agreement.

Item Three

CONTRIBUTION

Each partner shall contribute _____ dollars ($_____) on
or before _____, 19__, to be used by the partnership to establish
its capital position. Any additional contribution required of partners shall
only be determined and established in accordance with Item Seventeen.

Item Four

BOOKS AND RECORDS

Books of accounts shall be maintained by the partners, and proper entries
made therein of all sales, purchases, receipts, payments, transactions, and
property of the partnership, and the books of accounts and all records of
the partnership shall be retained at the principal place of business as spec-
ified in Item One herein. Each partner shall have free access at all times to
all books and records maintained relative to the partnership business.

Item Five

DIVISION OF PROFITS AND LOSSES

Each partner shall be entitled to _____ percent (____%) of the net profits of the business and all losses occurring in the course of the business
shall be borne in the same proportion, unless the losses are occasioned by

the willful neglect or default, and not mere mistake or error, of any of the partners, in which case the losses so incurred shall be made good by the partner through whose neglect or default the losses shall arise. Distribution of profits shall be made on the _____ day of _____ each year.

Item Six
PERFORMANCE

Each partner shall apply all of his or her experience, training, and ability in discharging his or her assigned functions in the partnership and in the performance of all work that may be necessary or advantageous to further business interests of the partnership.

Item Seven
BUSINESS EXPENSES

The rent of the buildings where the partnership business shall be carried on, and the cost of repairs and alterations, all rates, taxes, payments for insurance, and other expenses in respect to the buildings used by the partnership, and the wages for all persons employed by the partnership are all to become payable on the account of the partnership. All losses incurred shall be paid out of the capital of the partnership or the profits arising from the partnership business, or, if both shall be deficient, by the partners on a pro rata basis, in proportion to their original contribution.

Item Eight
ACCOUNTING

The fiscal year of the partnership shall be from _____ to _____ of each year. On the _____ day of _____, commencing in 19__, and on the _____ day of _____ in each succeeding year, a general accounting shall be made and taken by the partners of all sales, purchases, receipts, payments, and transactions of the partnership during the preceding fiscal year, and of all the capital property and current liabilities of the partnership. The general accounting shall be written in the partnership account books and signed in each book by each partner immediately after it is completed. After the signature of each partner is entered, each partner shall keep one of the books and shall be bound by every account, except that if any manifest error is found therein by any partner and shown to the other partners within _____ months after the error shall have been noted by all of them, the error shall be rectified.

Item Nine
SEPARATE DEBTS

No partner shall enter into any bond or become surety, security, bail, or cosigner for any person, partnership, or corporation, or knowingly condone anything whereby the partnership property may be attached or be taken in execution, without the written consent of the other partners.

Each partner shall punctually pay his or her separate debts and indemnify the other partners and the capital and property of the partnership against his or her separate debts and all expenses relating thereto.

Item Ten
AUTHORITY

No partner shall buy goods or articles into any contract exceeding the value _____ dollars ($_____) without the prior consent in writing of the other partners; or the other partners shall have the option to take the goods or accept the contract on account of the partnership or let the goods remain the sole property of the partner who shall have obligated himself or herself.

Item Eleven
EMPLOYEE MANAGEMENT

No partner shall hire or dismiss any person in the employment of the partnership without the consent of the other partners, except in cases of gross misconduct by the employee.

Item Twelve
SALARY

No partner shall receive any salary from the partnership, and the only compensation to be paid shall be as provided in Items Five and Fourteen herein.

Item Thirteen
DEATH OF A PARTNER

In the event of the death of one partner, the legal representative of the deceased partner shall remain as a partner in the firm, except that the exercising of the right on the part of the representative of the deceased partner shall not continue for a period in excess of _____ months, even though under the terms hereof a greater period of time is provided before the termination of this agreement. The original rights of the partners herein shall accrue to their heirs, executors, or assigns.

Item Fourteen
ADVANCE DRAWS

Each partner shall be at liberty to draw out of the business in anticipation of the expected profits any sums that may be mutually agreed on, and the sums are to be drawn only after there has been entered in the books of the partnership the terms of agreement, giving the date, the amount to be drawn by the respective partners, the time at which the sums shall be drawn, and any other conditions or matters mutually agreed on. The signatures of each partner shall be affixed thereon. The total sum of the advance draw for each partner shall be deducted from the sum that partner is entitled to under the distribution of profits as provided for in Item Five of this agreement.

Item Fifteen

RETIREMENT

In the event any partner shall desire to retire from the partnership, he or she shall give _____ months notice in writing to the other partners and the continuing partners shall pay to the retiring partner at the termination of the _____ months notice the value of the interest of the retiring partner in the partnership. The value shall be determined by a closing of the books and a rendition of the appropriate profit and loss, trial balance, and balance sheet statements. All disputes arising therefrom shall be determined as provided in Item Eighteen.

Item Sixteen

RIGHTS OF CONTINUING PARTNERS

On the retirement of any partner, the continuing partners shall be at liberty, if they so desire, to retain all trade names designating the firm name used, and each of the partners shall sign and execute assignments, instruments, or papers that shall be reasonably required for effectuating an amicable retirement.

Item Seventeen

ADDITIONAL CONTRIBUTIONS

The partners shall not have to contribute any additional capital to the partnership to that required under Item Three herein, except as follows: (1) each partner shall be required to contribute a proportionate share in additional contributions if the fiscal year closes with an insufficiency in the capital account of profits of the partnership to meet current expenses, or (2) the capital account falls below _____ dollars ($_____) for a period of _____ months.

Item Eighteen

ARBITRATION

If any differences shall arise between or among partners as to their rights or liabilities under this agreement, or under any instrument made in furtherance of the partnership business, the difference shall be determined and the instrument shall be settled by _____, acting as arbitrator, and his or her decision shall be final as to the contents and interpretations of the instrument and as to the proper mode of carrying the provision into effect.

Item Nineteen

RELEASE OF DEBTS

No partner shall compound, release, or discharge any debt that shall be due or owing to the partnership, without receiving the full amount thereof, unless that partner obtains the prior written consent of the other partners to the discharge of the indebtedness.

Item Twenty

ADDITIONS, ALTERATIONS, OR MODIFICATIONS

Where it shall appear to the partners that this agreement, or any terms and conditions contained herein, are in any way ineffective or deficient, or not expressed as originally intended, and any alteration or addition shall be deemed necessary, the partners will enter into, execute, and perform all further deeds and instruments as their counsel shall advise. Any addition, alteration, or modification shall be in writing, and no oral agreement shall be effective.

In witness whereof, the parties have executed this agreement on _____ the day and year first above written.

Courtesy of General Business Forms, Inc.

CORPORATE CHECKLIST

A. The formation of a corporation constitutes the formation of a separate legal entity under state law. It is essential that the services of a competent local attorney be obtained to help the client file the Articles of Incorporation and meet the terms of the state law.

B. Below is a sample election for the corporation to be treated as a Section 1244 Small Business Corporation. This is included so that the client may have it available to discuss with his or her attorney.

C. Following is a list of steps that will be necessary for a new corporation. It should not be deemed to be all-inclusive. It is not intended to be used as substitution to the client of a competent attorney.

1. *Incorporators.* Have a meeting of the incorporators and determine the following:

   a. The corporate name
   b. The classes and number of shares to authorize
   c. Business purpose for which the corporation is formed
   d. Initial capital needed
   e. The directors
   f. Location of business
   g. The corporate officers and their salaries
   h. Check on thin incorporation

2. *Determine startup date.* If the corporation is to take over a going business, a startup date should be set at some time in the future, so that all steps can be taken without unnecessary haste.

3. *Research the corporate name.* Check at once with the Secretary of State to see if the corporate name is available.

4. *Notify the following:*

   a. Insurance company—have policies changed. May also be necessary to increase coverage.
   b. Creditors—inform all creditors of former business.
   c. Customers—inform all customers of former business.
   d. State and local authorities—such as the state unemployment and disability department and county assessor.

5. *Transfer assets and liabilities.* If the corporation is to take over a going business, determine what assets and liabilities are to be turned over to the corporation, and shares or notes to be issued in exchange. Determine whether it qualifies as a tax-free exchange under IRC Sec. 3.

6. *Select banks.* Select bank or banks and furnish resolution authorizing who is to sign checks and negotiate loans.

7. *Obtain identification number.* File application for an identification number, Federal Form SS-4.

8. *File for workers' compensation coverage.*

9. *File for unemployment insurance coverage.*

10. *Obtain any special licenses.* Check on transfer of new license such as food, drug, cigarette, liquor, and so forth.

11. *File final returns.* If the new corporation is taking over a going business, file sales tax, FICA tax, unemployment tax, and workers' compensation final returns for the old business after the corporation takes over the operation of the new business.

12. *Determine federal unemployment requirements.* Determine if final Form 940, Employer's Annual Federal Unemployment Tax return is to be filed on old business.

13. *Sales tax.* Obtain a new sales tax vendor's license on the first day of business. Do not use any tax stamps purchased by the former business and do not use the plate from the former business.

14. *Tax elections:*

    a. Election under Subchapter S—Determine if the corporation is going to elect to be taxed as a partnership under Subchapter S. If so, prepare and file Form 2553, Election by Small Business Corporation, within 30 days after the first day of fiscal year of date new corporation commences to "do business."

    b. Section 1244 stock—If the corporation is eligible, issue stock in accordance with a written plan included in the minutes.

    c. Year ending—Determine the date the corporation's year will end.

    d. Accounting—Determine the method of accounting the corporation will use.

FUNCTIONAL RÉSUMÉS

Functional résumés are designed to provide financing agencies with the information needed to make decisions on managerial competence and experience. Ordinary résumés (such as the SBA Personal Information Sheet) can and do provide information such as job titles, dates, and salaries, but they do not answer such questions as: Did you have hiring and firing authority? Could you redesign work flow? And so forth.

A functional résumé is usually self-designed because most jobs are not standard. The objective of this section is to help you design a functional résumé that displays your experience and competence. Treat the following as suggestions, not ironclad rules.

Items 4 and 5 are those that make a functional résumé different from an ordinary, fact-oriented résumé. They should describe jobs, education, and interests in functional terms. For example:

A Suggested Format

Résumé of
YOUR NAME

1. Business address   2. Home address
   Telephone number   Telephone number

Business Experience

3. Most recent job first (include military experience).

Education

4. Most recent grade or diploma completed first.

Special Abilities and Interests

5. Hobbies, clubs, civic activities, etc.

Personal Information

6. Age, marital status, number of children.

References

7. Names and addresses of references (preferably businesspeople).

Standard Résumé

March 19— to June 19—: Foreman, Fatback Fishfoods, Machias, Maine. Beginning salary $160/week. Final salary $205/week.

Notice how the "standard" form is composed of brief detail. Contrast this with:

Functional Résumé

March 19— to June 19—: Line Foreman, Fatback Fishfoods, East Machias, Maine. Responsible for hiring, training, and directing operations of 15 persons in Frozen Food Filleting Department. Rescheduled work flow with resultant 30 percent increase in output per worker. Implemented new purchasing system that reduced spoilage 8 percent. Reduced personnel turnovers by working with local union for revision of company contract policy and by shifting from production line to team task approach. Received Grandiose Foodstuff, Inc. award for line management and was given special assignment in September, 19— to explain these changes to other line foremen at all 22 Fatback Fishfoods plants in New England and the Middle Atlantic states.

Two final points: First, a good résumé (functional or otherwise) should have no sizable time gaps (more than a month). Longer gaps create a credibility problem. Second, a good résumé will do more than inform the reader of what you have done. It will also give the reader an understanding of what you *can* do, and this understanding, based on demonstrated performance, can make the difference between a positive response to a financing proposal and a negative one.

Your objective in Items 4 and 5 is to show what you have accomplished and what abilities you have demonstrated. Item 5, "Special Abilities and Interests," can be used to cover nonjob achievements, interests, and skills that may or may not be directly relevant to your employment. For instance, this is where off-the-job managerial experience would be stressed (e.g., local politics, coaching, leadership of clubs).

Alternate Business Plan Outlines

*T*here is no one "correct" business plan format. Depending on the size and scope of your business, and on the audience, you might find one of these formats more helpful than another. They all contain the same basic parts, but are organized and named a bit differently.

THE BURCH OUTLINE

This outline is from *Entrepreneurship,* by John G. Burch, © 1986 John Wiley & Sons, Inc., pp. 397–398. Reprinted by permission of John Wiley & Sons, Inc.

I. Summary

    A. Summary format
    B. Added comments (not part of the business plan)

II. Business Description

    A. Name of business
    B. General business description
    C. History of the business
    D. Business goals and milestones
    E. Uniqueness of the business
    F. The industry
    G. The product or service

III. Market Research and Analysis

    A. Target market and customers
    B. Market survey
    C. Market position
    D. Market size and share
    E. The competition

IV. The Marketing Plan

    A. Sales and distribution
    B. Advertising and public relations
    C. Pricing

V. Research and Development Plan

VI. Manufacturing and Operations

    A. Production characteristics
    B. Labor force
    C. Suppliers
    D. Equipment
    E. Property and facilities
    F. Manufacturing cost data

VII. The Key People

    A. Description of management team and directors
    B. Remuneration
    C. Shareholders
    D. Consultants

VIII. Overall Schedule, Major Events, and Risks

IX. The Financing Program

    A. Reason for financing
    B. Sources of financing
    C. Financial package
    D. Timing and stages of financing
    E. Equity, control, and valuation-pricing

X. Financial Plan and Projections

A. The budget
B. Key assumptions and estimates

XI. Appendixes

XII. Bibliography (if applicable)

THE AMERICAN INSTITUTE OF SMALL BUSINESS OUTLINE

The following outline is from the American Institute of Small Business's, Minneapolis, MN 55426 "How to Write a Business Plan" software package, © 1994, pp. 13–17. Used by kind permission.

Summary of the Plan

Mission statement
Description of the business
    Overall purpose of the business
    Specific purpose of the business
Marketing strategy
Production process
Management team
Objectives of the management team
Financial considerations

Products and Services

Initial products and services
Proprietary features
Future Products and Services

Industry

What is the industry (definition)
Market definition
Competition
Major influences on the business and the industry

Marketing Plan

Marketing overview
Marketing objectives
Strategy—advertising, promotion, and public relations
How will sales be made
    Channels of distribution
    Special service situations

The Production Plan

Facility requirements
Equipment requirements
Labor
Production process and capacity
Subcontracting

Company Structure

How company will be structured
Business advisers
Management team

The Financial Plan

Location

Personal Financial Statements

Biographies of the Principals

A COMPUTERIZED BUSINESS PLANNING OUTLINE

The following is a shareware computerized business planning program from the Internet.

Objectives
Mission

Company

Company ownership
Company products
Company locations and facilities

Products and Services

Product and service description
Important features and comparison
Sales literature

Market Analysis

Industry analysis
Keys to success

Business Strategy and Implementation

Marketing strategy
    Target markets and market segments
    Pricing
    Promotion
    Marketing programs
    Sales strategy
    Strategic alliances

Management Summary

Management team
Other management team considerations

Financial Analysis

Financial plan

ADDITIONAL OUTLINE

This outline is from New Mexico State University. This was a result of a student's effort in Professor Stuart Devlin's small business management course. Used by kind permission.

Cover Sheet

Contact
Type of business
Company summary
Management
Product and competition
Funds required
Collateral
Use of funds
Exit strategy

Executive Summary

Current position
Goals
Strategy
Business description
Schedule
Financing required
Evaluation methods

Description of Business

History
Product(s)
Geographical area
Ownership structure
Major customers
Financial performance
Facilities and equipment
Organization

Market Analysis

Supply and demand
Marketing process
Customers

Operations and Management

Key individuals

Financial Components

Cash flow projections
Financial pro formas
>   Income statements for five years
>   Balance sheets

Sample
Business
Plans

**Financing Proposal for
Finestkind Seafoods, Inc.**

To be Submitted to
The Great Bay Bank and Trust Co.

Mike Gosling
Mike Swan
Finestkind Seafoods, Inc.
123 Main Street
Anytown, ME 04112
207/432-1111
October 31, 19—

SECTION ONE: THE BUSINESS

Statement of Purpose

Finestkind Seafoods, Inc. seeks loans totaling $120,000 to purchase equipment and inventory; purchase property and buildings at 123 Main Street, Anytown, Maine; perform necessary renovations and improvements; and maintain sufficient cash reserves to provide adequate working capital to successfully expand an existing wholesale/retail seafood market. This sum, together with an additional $30,000 equity investment by the principals, will finance transition through the expansion phase so that our business can operate at a higher level of profitability.

Table of Contents

Description of Business

Finestkind Seafoods, Inc. is a fish market specializing in selling extremely fresh (no more than one day from the boat) seafood to local retail and wholesale customers. At present, about 60 percent of sales are retail. Finestkind plans to concentrate more heavily on the wholesale trade (restaurants and grocery chains) in the future. Although margins are lower in the wholesale trade, profits are higher due to lower personnel costs and faster inventory turnover.

Finestkind began business in September 19—. The store is open seven days a week from 10:00 AM to 8:30 PM (6:00 PM in the winter) for retail business and from 6:30 AM to 8:30 PM year-round for wholesale.

The retail demand is seasonal and fluctuates according to weather (the store is located on a tourist route). The wholesale demand is constant and increasing. We feel that the latter can be improved by more direct selling efforts. Our customers agree (see letter from Nightlife Clambakes in Supporting Documents). The quality of our seafood is exceptional, and because Mr. Swan is a former fisherman with many personal friends in the fishing industry, we do not anticipate trouble maintaining good relations with our suppliers. We have made a policy of paying premium prices in cash at dockside for the best, freshest seafood.

Description of the Market

Finestkind will continue to provide premium-quality seafoods to both wholesale and retail customers. We plan to switch the balance from 60 percent retail/40 percent wholesale to 40 percent retail/60 percent wholesale as we grow. Retail business should grow over the next few years, but the greatest growth will be in wholesale accounts.

Our goal is to provide the freshest seafood at competitive prices to customers within 25 miles of York. This market has a total population of over 100,000 people and a potential of over 300 commercial wholesale accounts.

Customers will be attracted by:

- Direct approach to local restaurants, groceries, and other potential wholesale accounts

- A local radio and newspaper advertising campaign

- Word-of-mouth advertising from our present customer base

- Our location and signs on Route 1, a heavily traveled tourist route

As a footnote: In the past month distributors from four countries (Turkey, Germany, Poland, and Belgium) have purchased significant amounts of fresh and frozen lobsters from us. This may represent a low-risk growth opportunity because these accounts pay in advance of shipment. While we came across these accounts by a fluke, we think they could be an entry into a wider market. We are currently exploring this opportunity with our advisers and exporters recommended by the SBA.

3

Description of the Location

Finestkind is currently leasing a one-story, wooden frame building with cement floor (2,000 square feet) at 123 Main Street, Anytown, Maine, for $550/month with an option (in writing) to buy for $105,000. The area is zoned for commercial use. Main Street is part of U.S. Route 1, a heavily traveled tourist route with most nearby businesses catering to the tourist trade. Finestkind has performed major leasehold improvements, such as installing rough-sawed pine board walls and a walk-in freezer. The building is divided into (1) a sales/counter area (1,200 square feet); (2) a cutting area (100 square feet); (3) a multipurpose area, including toilet with separate entry, storage space, and room for some expansion of the freezer and processing areas (700 square feet in all). See the diagram in Supporting Documents.

Description of the Competition

There are three seafood operations competing directly with Finestkind:

1. **Ferd's Fish**—a scattered operation with one truck making the rounds and a small counter leased from a supermarket in Anytown. We have cut into their sales by making promised deliveries on time and at the agreed price. As a result, their operation has become marginal.

2. **Kingfisher**—a clean, three-man operation in Rye specializing in cheaper fish. Kingfisher has trouble with their suppliers because they aren't willing to pay top dockside prices in cash—the owner likes to haggle over price. The operation is well financed and managed, has modern equipment, and sells directly to homes from a fleet of three trucks (very convenient). They have some wholesale business that they want to expand. Their sales are apparently growing because they have been serving the same routes for five years and have an excellent reputation. Rumor has it that Kingfisher is interested in buying Ferd's Fish or adding another delivery truck or two.

3. **Job's Seafoods**—currently rebuilding because of a disastrous fire but will be our most serious competitor when their new store opens. Job's has been in business for 25 years in Anytown and has a good location on a scenic bridge two miles south of Finestkind. Job's has good relations with suppliers and serves most of the supermarkets. Currently, they have no retail business but plan to open a retail store in their new building. However, the owner needs a major eye operation and may be willing to part with some of his wholesale business because he is getting on in years.

Indirect competition is from major processors in Portland (45 miles east) and Boston (60 miles south). Because we fall between their primary market areas we can purchase from both on consignment basis.

Description of Management

Mr. Gosling was born in Anytown, Maine, and has lived there all his life. After graduating from local schools and serving in the U.S. Navy for three years, he became a self-employed carpenter, taking night courses in small business management and sales at the University of Maine, with the aim of owning and managing a retail store. He currently serves on the local zoning board. He and his wife (a medical secretary) live in Anytown with their two children.

Mr. Swan was born in Wisconsin, attended schools in Utah, Alaska, and Florida, and served four years in the Marines (rank upon separation: E-3). He test-drove motorcycles for a year, then served as parts manager for Wheely Cycles, Inc. before joining the Fatback Fish Division of Tasty Foods as a packer in March 1989 in their East Machias, Maine, plant. In June 1991 he resigned as line foreman of the Frozen Food Filleting Department to join Mr. Gosling in Finestkind. He is unmarried and lives in Anytown.

Both men are healthy and energetic. They believe their energies complement each other and will help them make Finestkind a success. In particular, Mr. Swan knows all of the fishermen while Mr. Gosling is a well-known member of the community. Because Mr. Swan has had experience in cost control and line management, he will be responsible for the store and inventory control. Mr. Gosling will be primarily responsible for developing the wholesale business. They will set policies together. Personnel decisions will be made jointly.

Salaries will be $950/month for the first year to enable the business to pay off startup costs. Mr. Gosling's wife earns enough to support their family; Mr. Swan's personal expenditures are low because he shares a house with five other men. In the second year they will earn $1,200/month; in the third year $1,500/month with any profits returned to the business.

In order to augment their skills, they have enlisted the help of Smith & Farley (CPAs), Dewey Cheatham & Howe (attorneys), and Halsey Johnson, a retired banker who will be on their advisory board. Other advisory board members are Andrew O'Bangfo, business consultant; the University of Maine's Venture Incubator Division's Etienne LeBlanc; and Gene Brudleigh of FROG (Fish Retailers Organized for Growth). This board will provide ongoing management review.

Description of Personnel

Finestkind will hire one part-time salesperson within six months to sell seafoods over the counter to the retail customers. He or she will be paid $4.00/hour for weekend work; no fringe benefits or overtime are anticipated. We will also employ, on an as-needed basis, one cutter at $6.75/hour to help process seafood for the wholesale trade. We think the counter help will be needed for 10 weeks during the summer and the cutter will be needed for about 20 hours/week for 16 weeks. (This should take care of the second summer as well. For the third year, we plan on two counter helpers plus a full-time summer cutter.) In the second year we'll add one full-time employee at $850/month, with a raise to $900/month in the third year.

No further employees are planned for unless business grows more rapidly than we have forecast.

Application and Expected Effect of Loan or Investment

The $120,000 will be used as follows:

Purchase of Main Street property	$75,000
Equipment	
Used Ford pickup with insulated body	3,885
Dayton compressor (used, serial #45-cah-990)	365
Sharp slicer (used, Speedy model)	400
Renovations (see contractor's letter in Supporting Documents)	12,500
Working capital	12,000
Inventory	1,500
Cash reserve	14,350
Total	**$120,000**

Finestkind can purchase the 123 Main Street property at a substantial savings under the terms of a lease/purchase agreement. An independent appraiser has calculated the value of the property, including leasehold improvements already done by Finestkind, at $135,000. The monthly payment for a 15-year mortgage ($75,000 at 11.5 percent interest) will be $875/month, a net increase of $325/month over the current rent. See the Financial Data section for the effect on the business.

The truck will be used to deliver merchandise to our wholesale customers, retard spoilage, and maintain the quality of the seafood.

The compressor will replace the one now used for the freezer and will lower electrical costs and provide a measure of insurance against loss of refrigeration. (We'll keep the old compressor as a spare.)

The slicer will save four man-hours of work daily. The time released will be used for soliciting more business and processing a greater volume of whole fish. With the slicer, relatively untrained help can fillet flounder with minimal waste.

The renovations are: a deep-water well required by the state, a toilet and wash sink separate from the work area, and replacement of the current obsolete heating system to reduce fuel expenses.

The working capital will enable Finestkind to meet current expenses, offset negative seasonal cash flow as shown in the Cash Flow Projection in the Financial Data section, and ensure the continued growth of the business.

The inventory is to take advantage of bulk rates on certain fresh-frozen packaged goods such as red snapper or South American spiny lobster.

The bank will hold the reserve as a line of credit. It will be used to take advantage of special opportunities or to meet emergencies.

Summary

Finestkind Seafoods, Inc. is a fish market serving retail and wholesale markets in and around Anytown, Maine. Mike Gosling and Mike Swan, the owners, are seeking $120,000 to purchase the 123 Main Street property, perform necessary renovations and improvements to the property, maintain a cash reserve, and provide adequate working capital for anticipated expansion of the business. This amount will be sufficient to finance transition through a planned expansion phase so the business can operate as an ongoing, profitable venture.

Careful analysis of the potential market shows an unfilled demand for exceptionally fresh seafood. Mr. Gosling's local reputation will help secure a sizable portion of the wholesale market, while Mr. Swan's managerial experience assures that the entire operation will be carefully controlled. Mr. Gosling's current studies at the University of Maine will provide even more control over the projected growth of Finestkind and complement the advice of a thoughtfully selected advisory board.

The funds sought will result in a greater increase in fixed assets than may be shown, as Mr. Gosling will be performing much additional renovation and improvements himself. The additional reserve and working capital will enable Finestkind to increase their sales substantially while maintaining profitability.

SECTION TWO: FINANCIAL DATA

Description of Sources and Applications of Funding

Finestkind Seafoods, Inc.

Sources

1.	Mortgage loan	$ 75,000
2.	Term loan	30,000
3.	Reserved loan	15,000
4.	New investment from Gosling and Swan	30,000

Total   **$150,000**

Applications

1.	Purchase 123 Main Street property	$105,000
2.	Equipment	4,650
3.	Renovations	12,500
4.	Inventory	1,500
5.	Working capital	12,000
6.	Cash reserve for contingencies	14,350

Total   **$150,000**

To be secured by the assets of the business and personal guarantees of the principals, Mike Gosling and Mike Swan.

Capital Equipment List

Finestkind Seafoods, Inc.

Major Equipment and Normal Accessories	Model	Cost or List Price (whichever is lower)
Storequip, Inc. display case, glass front, ice	handmade	$ 600
Storequip, Inc. display case, glass front, refrigerated	SST6-77K	1,700
Dayton air compressor	45-cah-990	365
Bendix standing freezer	3979-7584	350
GE standard freezer	—	50
Cleaning table, fiberglassed	handmade	200
Freezing locker and compressor	handmade	4,500
Total		**$ 7,765**

Minor Shop Equipment

Miscellaneous knives, scalers, etc.	—	$ 500
Miscellaneous display trays, boxes	—	350
Total		**$ 850**

Other Equipment

Pickup truck with insulated body	1983 Ford, Lo-bed	$ 4,000
Safe	1879 Diebold Mosler	200
Cash register	523 NCR	350
Calculator	TI-120	65
Computer and software	Super Clone	2,100
Light fixtures	custom	400
Total		**$ 7,115**
Capital Equipment Total		**$15,730**

9

Finestkind Seafoods, Inc.
October 1,19—
Balance Sheet

Assets		Liabilities	
CURRENT ASSETS		**CURRENT LIABILITIES**	
Cash	$ 2,150	Accounts Payable	$ 8,077
Accounts Receivable (net)	1,700	Current Portion Long-Term Debt	1,440
Merchandise Inventory	3,900		
Supplies	450	**Total Current Liabilities**	**$9,517**
Prepaid Expenses	320		
Total Current Assets	**$ 8,520**	**LONG-TERM LIABILITIES**	
		Note Payable (a)	$ 535
FIXED ASSETS		Bank Loan Payable (b)	1,360
Fixtures and Leasehold Improvements (d)	$13,265	Equity Loan Payable (c)	9,250
Building (freezer)	4,500	**Total Long-Term Liabilities**	**$11,145**
Equipment	3,115		
Trucks	6,500	**Total Liabilities**	**$20,662**
Total Fixed Assets	**$27,380**	**NET WORTH**	
		Owners' Equity	$15,238
Total Assets	**$35,900**		
		Total Liabilities and Net Worth	**$35,900**

ACCOUNTS PAYABLE DISPLAY

Eldredge's Inc.	$ 3,700
Lesswing's	4,119
Paxstone	180
B&B Refrigeration	78
	$ 8,077

(a) Dave N. Hall for electrical work.
(b) Term loan secured by 1987 Jeep, 1992 Ford.
(c) S & C Finance Corp., Anytown, Maine.
(d) Includes $10,000 in improvements since June.

10

Breakeven Analysis

Projected figures from Finestkind's Three-Year Income Projection

Fixed costs	$FC = \$62,220$
Gross margin	$GM = (57,680/216,000) = 26.7\%$

Thus, breakeven sales	$= S$	$=$	FC / GM
		$=$	$(\$62,220/.267)$
		$=$	$\$233,033/\text{year}$
On a monthly basis,	S	$=$	$\$19,419/\text{month}$

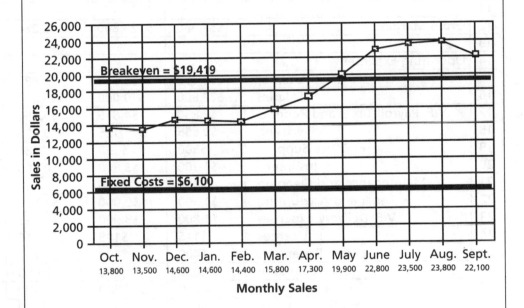

Breakeven = $19,419

Fixed Costs = $6,100

Sales in Dollars

Oct.	Nov.	Dec.	Jan.	Feb.	Mar.	Apr.	May	June	July	Aug.	Sept.
13,800	13,500	14,600	14,600	14,400	15,800	17,300	19,900	22,800	23,500	23,800	22,100

Monthly Sales

11

FINESTKIND SEAFOODS, INC.
Income Projection: Three-Year Summary

	A	B	C	D	E
1		Year 1	Year 2	Year 3	% of Sales
2					Year 1
3	Sales				
4	Wholesale	$90,000	$265,000	$325,000	60.75%
5	Retail	$126,000	$180,000	$210,000	39.25%
6	Total Sales	$216,000	$445,000	$535,000	100.00%
7					
8	*V Cost of Materials	$155,520	$320,400	$385,200	72.00%
9	V Variable Labor	$2,800	$2,800	$7,520	1.41%
10	Total Cost of Goods Sold	$158,320	$323,200	$392,720	73.41%
11					
12	Gross Margin	$57,680	$121,800	$142,280	26.59%
13					
14	Operating Expenses				
15	F Utilities	$2,160	$2,640	$2,880	0.54%
16	F Salaries	$22,800	$39,000	$46,800	8.75%
17	V/F Payroll Taxes and Benefits	$2,850	$4,875	$5,850	1.09%
18	F Advertising	$9,555	$11,125	$13,375	2.50%
19	F Office Supplies	$300	$360	$480	0.09%
20	F Insurance	$1,200	$3,800	$4,100	0.77%
21	F Maintenance and Cleaning	$300	$360	$420	0.08%
22	F Legal and Accounting	$1,500	$2,000	$2,500	0.47%
23	V/F Delivery Expenses	$1,800	$8,900	$9,095	1.70%
24	F Licenses	$115	$115	$115	0.02%
25	V/F Boxes, Paper, etc.	$400	$800	$1,200	0.22%
26	F Telephone	$1,020	$1,800	$2,400	0.45%
27	F Depreciation	$7,700	$12,500	$12,500	2.34%
28	F Miscellaneous	$480	$600	$720	0.13%
29	F Rent	$1,650	$0	$0	0.00%
30	Total Operating Expenses	$53,830	$88,875	$102,435	19.15%
31					
32	Other Expenses				
33	F Interest (Mortgage)	$6,258	$8,280	$8,052	1.51%
34	F Interest (Term Loan)	$1,632	$3,189	$2,900	0.54%
35	F Interest (Line of Credit)	$500	$500	$500	0.09%
36	Total Other Expenses	$8,390	$11,969	$11,452	2.14%
37					
38	Total Expenses	$62,220	$100,844	$113,887	21.29%
39					
40	Net Profit (Loss) Pretax	($4,540)	$20,956	$28,393	5.31%
41					
42	*V = Variable Cost, F = Fixed Cost				

FINESTKIND SEAFOODS, INC.
Income Projection by Month, Year One

	October	November	December	January	February	March	April	May	June	July	August	September	Total	% of Total Sales
Sales														
Wholesale	$4,000	$4,000	$5,200	$5,600	$6,000	$7,000	$7,000	$8,400	$10,600	$11,300	$11,300	$9,600	$90,000	41.67%
Retail	$9,730	$9,500	$9,500	$9,000	$8,400	$8,750	$10,300	$11,540	$12,165	$12,165	$12,475	$12,475	$126,000	58.33%
Total Sales	$13,730	$13,500	$14,700	$14,600	$14,400	$15,750	$17,300	$19,940	$22,765	$23,465	$23,775	$22,075	$216,000	100.00%
Cost of Materials	$9,886	$9,720	$10,584	$10,512	$10,368	$11,340	$12,456	$14,357	$16,391	$16,895	$17,118	$15,894	$155,520	72.00%
Variable Labor	$0	$0	$0	$0	$0	$0	$0	$0	$604	$796	$796	$604	$2,800	1.30%
Cost of Goods Sold	$9,886	$9,720	$10,584	$10,512	$10,368	$11,340	$12,456	$14,357	$16,995	$17,691	$17,914	$16,498	$158,320	73.30%
Gross Margin	$3,844	$3,780	$4,116	$4,088	$4,032	$4,410	$4,844	$5,583	$5,770	$5,774	$5,861	$5,577	$57,680	26.70%
Operating Expenses														
Utilities	$160	$165	$180	$200	$200	$180	$170	$165	$185	$185	$185	$185	$2,160	1.00%
Salaries	$1,900	$1,900	$1,900	$1,900	$1,900	$1,900	$1,900	$1,900	$1,900	$1,900	$1,900	$1,900	$22,800	10.56%
Payroll Taxes and Benefits	$237	$238	$237	$238	$237	$238	$237	$238	$237	$238	$237	$238	$2,850	1.32%
Advertising	$450	$450	$450	$450	$450	$450	$4,605	$450	$450	$450	$450	$450	$9,555	4.42%
Office Supplies	$25	$25	$25	$25	$25	$25	$25	$25	$25	$25	$25	$25	$300	0.14%
Insurance	$70	$70	$70	$110	$110	$110	$110	$110	$110	$110	$110	$110	$1,200	0.56%
Maintenance and Cleaning	$25	$25	$25	$25	$25	$25	$25	$25	$25	$25	$25	$25	$300	0.14%
Legal and Accounting	$125	$125	$125	$125	$125	$125	$125	$125	$125	$125	$125	$125	$1,500	0.69%
Delivery Expenses	$150	$150	$150	$150	$150	$150	$150	$150	$150	$150	$150	$150	$1,800	0.83%
Licenses	$9	$9	$9	$9	$9	$10	$10	$10	$10	$10	$10	$10	$115	0.05%
Boxes, Paper, etc.	$15	$15	$15	$15	$20	$35	$40	$45	$50	$50	$50	$50	$400	0.19%
Telephone	$85	$85	$85	$85	$85	$85	$85	$85	$85	$85	$85	$85	$1,020	0.47%
Depreciation	$0	$0	$0	$455	$460	$460	$1,050	$1,055	$1,055	$1,055	$1,055	$1,055	$7,700	3.56%
Miscellaneous	$40	$40	$40	$40	$40	$40	$40	$40	$40	$40	$40	$40	$480	0.22%
Rent	$550	$550	$550	$0	$0	$0	$0	$0	$0	$0	$0	$0	$1,650	0.76%
Total Operating Expenses	$3,841	$3,847	$3,861	$3,827	$3,836	$3,833	$8,572	$4,423	$4,447	$4,448	$4,447	$4,448	$53,830	24.92%
Other Expenses														
Interest (Mortgage)	$0	$0	$0	$695	$695	$696	$695	$695	$696	$695	$695	$696	$6,258	2.90%
Interest (Term Loan)	$0	$0	$0	$0	$0	$0	$272	$272	$272	$272	$272	$272	$1,632	0.76%
Interest (Credit Line)	$0	$85	$85	$0	$0	$0	$0	$0	$165	$165	$0	$0	$500	0.23%
Total Other Expenses	$0	$85	$85	$695	$695	$696	$967	$967	$1,133	$1,132	$967	$968	$8,390	3.88%
Total Expenses	$3,841	$3,932	$3,946	$4,522	$4,531	$4,529	$9,539	$5,390	$5,580	$5,580	$5,414	$5,416	$62,220	28.81%
Net Profit (Loss) Pretax	$3	($152)	$170	($434)	($499)	($119)	($4,695)	$193	$190	$194	$447	$161	($4,540)	
Cumulative Profit (Loss)	$3	($149)	$21	($413)	($912)	($1,031)	($5,726)	($5,533)	($5,343)	($5,149)	($4,702)	($4,540)		
							**Low Point							

FINESTKIND SEAFOODS, INC.

Income Projection by Quarter, Year Two

	A	B	C	D	E	F
		1st Qtr	2nd Qtr	3rd Qtr	4th Qtr	Total
1		1st Qtr	2nd Qtr	3rd Qtr	4th Qtr	Total
2						
3	Sales					
4	Wholesale	$38,900	$54,800	$76,500	$94,800	$265,000
5	Retail	$41,000	$37,400	$48,600	$53,000	$180,000
6	**Total Sales**	**$79,900**	**$92,200**	**$125,100**	**$147,800**	**$445,000**
7						
8	Cost of Materials	$57,528	$66,384	$90,072	$106,416	$320,400
9	Variable Labor	$0	$0	$604	$2,196	$2,800
10	Total Cost of Goods Sold	$57,528	$66,384	$90,676	$108,612	$323,200
11						
12	**Gross Margin**	**$22,372**	**$25,816**	**$34,424**	**$39,188**	**$121,800**
13						
14	Operating Expenses					
15	Utilities	$660	$660	$660	$660	$2,640
16	Salaries	$9,750	$9,750	$9,750	$9,750	$39,000
17	Payroll Taxes and Benefits	$1,219	$1,219	$1,219	$1,219	$4,875
18	Advertising	$1,998	$2,305	$3,128	$3,695	$11,125
19	Office Supplies	$90	$90	$90	$90	$360
20	Insurance	$950	$950	$950	$950	$3,800
21	Maintenance and Cleaning	$90	$90	$90	$90	$360
22	Legal and Accounting	$500	$500	$500	$500	$2,000
23	Delivery Expenses	$1,598	$1,844	$2,502	$2,956	$8,900
24	Licenses	$25	$30	$30	$30	$115
25	Boxes, Paper, etc.	$150	$175	$225	$250	$800
26	Telephone	$450	$450	$450	$450	$1,800
27	Depreciation	$3,125	$3,125	$3,125	$3,125	$12,500
28	Miscellaneous	$150	$150	$150	$150	$600
29	Rent	$0	$0	$0	$0	$0
30	**Total Operating Expenses**	**$20,754**	**$21,338**	**$22,868**	**$23,915**	**$88,875**
31						
32	Other Expenses					
33	Interest (Mortgage)	$2,070	$2,070	$2,070	$2,070	$8,280
34	Interest (Term Loan)	$798	$798	$797	$796	$3,189
35	Interest (Credit Line)	$0	$0	$140	$360	$500
36	Total Other Expenses	$2,868	$2,868	$3,007	$3,226	$11,969
37						
38	**Total Expenses**	**$23,622**	**$24,206**	**$25,875**	**$27,141**	**$100,844**
39						
40	**Net Profit (Loss) Pretax**	**($1,250)**	**$1,610**	**$8,549**	**$12,047**	**$20,956**

	A	B	C	D	E	F
	FINESTKIND SEAFOODS, INC					
	Income Projection by Quarter, Year Three					
		1st Qtr	2nd Qtr	3rd Qtr	4th Qtr	Total
1		**1st Qtr**	**2nd Qtr**	**3rd Qtr**	**4th Qtr**	**Total**
2						
3	Sales					
4	Wholesale	$58,750	$55,000	$97,500	$113,750	$325,000
5	Retail	$47,400	$43,600	$56,000	$63,000	$210,000
6	**Total Sales**	**$106,150**	**$98,600**	**$153,500**	**$176,750**	**$535,000**
7						
8	Cost of Materials	$76,428	$70,992	$110,520	$127,260	$385,200
9	Variable Labor	$0	$0	$1,622	$5,898	$7,520
10	Total Cost of Goods Sold	$76,428	$70,992	$112,142	$133,158	$392,720
11						
12	**Gross Margin**	**$29,722**	**$27,608**	**$41,358**	**$43,592**	**$142,280**
13						
14	Operating Expenses					
15	Utilities	$720	$720	$720	$720	$2,880
16	Salaries	$11,700	$11,700	$11,700	$11,700	$46,800
17	Payroll Taxes and Benefits	$1,463	$1,463	$1,463	$1,463	$5,850
18	Advertising	$2,654	$2,465	$3,838	$4,419	$13,375
19	Office Supplies	$120	$120	$120	$120	$480
20	Insurance	$1,025	$1,025	$1,025	$1,025	$4,100
21	Maintenance and Cleaning	$105	$105	$105	$105	$420
22	Legal and Accounting	$625	$625	$625	$625	$2,500
23	Delivery Expenses	$1,805	$1,676	$2,610	$3,005	$9,095
24	Licenses	$25	$30	$30	$30	$115
25	Boxes, Paper, etc.	$200	$200	$350	$450	$1,200
26	Telephone	$600	$600	$600	$600	$2,400
27	Depreciation	$3,125	$3,125	$3,125	$3,125	$12,500
28	Miscellaneous	$180	$180	$180	$180	$720
29	Rent	$0	$0	$0	$0	$0
30	**Total Operating Expenses**	**$24,346**	**$24,034**	**$26,490**	**$27,566**	**$102,435**
31						
32	Other Expenses					
33	Interest (Mortgage)	$2,013	$2,013	$2,013	$2,013	$8,052
34	Interest (Term Loan)	$725	$725	$725	$725	$2,900
35	Interest (Credit Line)	$0	$0	$140	$360	$500
36	Total Other Expenses	$2,738	$2,738	$2,878	$3,098	$11,452
37						
38	**Total Expenses**	**$27,084**	**$26,772**	**$29,368**	**$30,664**	**$113,887**
39						
40	**Net Profit Pretax**	**$2,638**	**$836**	**$11,991**	**$12,928**	**$28,393**

15

Explanation for Income Statement Projections

(4) Wholesale and **(5) Retail.** Due to a major marketing effort [see (18) Advertising below], wholesale sales should increase to 60 percent of gross sales within two years. Retail sales are expected to be more volatile than the wholesale business, leveling off around $20,000/month due to space restrictions. Volatility is seasonal, building from late March to a late summer peak. The increases shown in (4) Wholesale are based both on the greater number of restaurants open in the summer and the intense marketing efforts, planned for the winter months, to sell directly to the many restaurants that don't yet know Finestkind.

(4) Wholesale in Years Two and Three follow the same pattern as Year One (seasonally) but start at $10,000/October Year Two as the result of advertising and marketing efforts, longer experience with the wholesale market, and greater exposure to the market. Year Three is a bit more seasonal, reflecting a flattening out of the sales curve.

(8) Cost of Materials. Finestkind's inventory has an average cost of 68 percent of sales (including a startup spoilage rate of 5 percent that has been reduced to under 1 percent of sales), and has been calculated as 72 percent of sales to allow for the fluctuation of dockside prices during the winter.

(9) Variable Labor. In Years One and Two, two part-time summer helpers will be needed: a counter person at $4/hour for 16 hours/week for 10 weeks, and a fish cutter at $6.75/hour for 20 hours/week for 16 weeks. In Year Three, two full-time counter helpers and a full-time cutter will be needed for 10 and 16 weeks, respectively.

(15) Utilities. Prorated by agreement with the utility companies. Goes from $165/month (Year One) to $220 to $240 in Year Three.

(16) Salaries.

Year One:	$950/month for Gosling and Swan
Year Two:	$1,200/month for Gosling and Swan
	$850/month for a full-time employee
Year Three:	$1,500/month for Gosling and Swan
	$900/month ($50/month raise) for employee

(18) Advertising. Local newspaper and radio spots. The advertising budget is 4.4 percent of (6) Total Sales. In Year One, a large one-time promotional blitz will be made in April to build off-season wholesale business.

(23) Delivery Expenses. Delivery of merchandise to restaurants and other markets. Year Two: 2 percent of total sales; Year Three: 1.7 percent. As the wholesale business increases, route efficiency should also increase, causing delivery expenses as a percentage of sales to decrease.

(27) Depreciation. Five-year, straight-line on equipment (beginning April, Year One); straight-line 19 years on building (beginning January, Year One).

(29) Rent. Applicable for three months in Year One; will be replaced by (33) Interest (Mortgage) on the income statement.

(33) Interest (Mortgage). $75,000 mortgage for 15 years at 11.5 percent.

(34) Interest (Term Loan). $30,000 loan for seven years at 12.25 percent.

(35) Interest (Credit Line). Estimated use of line: average of $7,500 outstanding for six months a year at 13.5 percent.

16

FINESTKIND SEAFOODS, INC.
Cash Flow Projection by Month, Year One

	A	B	C	D	E	F	G	H	I	J	K	L	M	N
		October	November	December	January	February	March	April	May	June	July	August	September	Total
1														
2	Cash Receipts													
3	Sales Receivables	$2,000	$1,333	$1,333	$1,733	$1,867	$2,000	$2,333	$2,333	$2,800	$3,533	$3,767	$3,767	$28,800
4	Wholesale	$2,667	$2,667	$3,467	$3,733	$4,000	$4,667	$4,667	$5,600	$7,067	$7,533	$7,533	$6,400	$60,000
5	Retail	$9,730	$9,500	$9,500	$9,000	$8,400	$8,750	$10,300	$11,540	$12,165	$12,165	$12,475	$12,475	$126,000
6	Other Sources (see notes)	$7,500	$7,500	$0	$105,000	$0	$0	$30,000	$0	$15,000	$0	$0	$0	$165,000
7	Total Cash Receipts	$21,897	$21,000	$14,300	$119,467	$14,267	$15,417	$47,300	$19,473	$37,032	$23,232	$23,775	$22,642	$379,800
8	Cash Disbursements													
9	Cost of Goods	$9,886	$9,720	$10,584	$10,512	$10,368	$11,340	$12,456	$14,357	$16,391	$16,895	$17,118	$15,894	$155,520
10	Variable Labor	$0	$0	$0	$0	$0	$0	$0	$0	$604	$796	$796	$604	$2,800
11	Advertising	$1,000	$400	$400	$400	$400	$400	$4,555	$400	$400	$400	$400	$400	$9,555
12	Insurance	$0	$300	$0	$0	$300	$0	$0	$300	$0	$0	$300	$0	$1,200
13	Legal and Accounting	$0	$0	$375	$0	$0	$375	$0	$0	$375	$0	$0	$375	$1,500
14	Delivery Expenses	$75	$75	$75	$100	$75	$100	$150	$200	$200	$250	$250	$250	$1,800
15	*Fixed Cash Disbursements	$2,535	$2,535	$2,535	$2,535	$2,535	$2,535	$2,535	$2,535	$2,535	$2,535	$2,535	$2,535	$30,425
16	Mortgage (rent)	$550	$550	$550	$876	$876	$876	$876	$876	$876	$876	$876	$876	$9,535
17	Term Loan	$0	$0	$0	$0	$0	$0	$534	$534	$534	$534	$534	$534	$3,202
18	Line of Credit	$0	$85	$15,085	$0	$0	$0	$0	$0	$165	$165	$15,000	$0	$30,500
19	Other Disbursements	$0	$0	$0	$105,000	$0	$30,000	$0	$0	$0	$0	$0	$0	$135,000
20	Total Cash Disbursements	$14,046	$13,665	$29,604	$119,424	$14,555	$45,627	$21,106	$19,202	$22,080	$22,451	$37,809	$21,468	$381,037
21														
22	Net Cash Flow	$7,851	$7,335	($15,304)	$43	($288)	($30,210)	$26,194	$271	$14,952	$781	($14,034)	$1,174	($1,237)
23														
24	Cumulative Cash Flow	$7,851	$15,185	($119)	($76)	($364)	($30,574)	($4,380)	($4,109)	$10,843	$11,624	($2,410)	($1,237)	
25														
26	*Fixed Cash Disbursements	(FCD)												
27	Utilities	$2,160												
28	Salaries	$22,800												
29	Payroll Taxes and Benefits	$2,850												
30	Office Supplies	$300												
31	Maintenance and Cleaning	$300												
32	Licenses	$115												
33	Boxes, Paper, etc.	$400												
34	Telephone	$1,020												
35	Miscellaneous	$480												
36	Total FCD/yr	$30,425												
37	Avg FCD per month	$2,535												
38														
39	Cash on Hand													
40	Opening Balance	$2,150	$10,001	$17,335	$2,031	$2,074	$1,786	($28,424)	($2,230)	($1,959)	$12,993	$13,774	($260)	
41	+Cash Receipts	$21,897	$21,000	$14,300	$119,467	$14,267	$5,417	$47,300	$19,473	$37,032	$23,232	$23,775	$22,642	$379,793
42	- Cash Disbursements	($14,046)	($13,665)	($29,604)	($119,424)	($14,555)	($45,627)	($21,106)	($19,202)	($22,080)	($22,451)	($37,809)	($21,468)	($381,037)
43	Total = New Cash Balance	$10,001	$17,335	$2,031	$2,074	$1,786	($28,424)	($2,230)	($1,959)	$12,993	$13,774	($260)	$913	$381,037

FINESTKIND SEAFOODS, INC
Cash Flow Projection by Quarter, Year Two

	A	B	C	D	E	F
		1st Qtr	2nd Qtr	3rd Qtr	4th Qtr	Total
1						
2	Cash Receipts					
3	Sales Receivables	$3,200	$0	$0	$0	$3,200
4	Wholesale	$38,900	$54,800	$76,500	$94,800	$265,000
5	Retail	$41,000	$37,400	$48,600	$53,000	$180,000
6	Other Sources	$0	$0	$12,000	$15,000	$27,000
7	**Total Cash Receipts**	**$83,100**	**$92,200**	**$137,100**	**$162,800**	**$475,200**
8	Cash Disbursements					
9	Cost of Goods	$57,528	$66,384	$90,072	$106,416	$320,400
10	Variable Labor	$0	$0	$604	$2,196	$2,800
11	Advertising	$1,998	$2,305	$3,125	$3,695	$11,125
12	Insurance	$950	$950	$950	$950	$3,800
13	Legal and Accounting	$500	$500	$500	$500	$2,000
14	Delivery Expenses	$1,600	$1,844	$2,500	$2,956	$8,900
15	* Fixed Cash Disbursements	$12,630	$12,640	$12,640	$12,640	$50,550
16	Mortgage (rent)	$2,628	$2,628	$2,628	$2,628	$10,512
17	Term Loan	$1,602	$1,602	$1,602	$1,602	$6,408
18	Line of Credit	$0	$0	$12,140	$15,360	$27,500
19	Other Disbursements (see notes)	$0	$0	$0	$0	$0
20	**Total Cash Disbursements**	**$79,440**	**$88,850**	**$126,762**	**$148,940**	**$443,992**
21						
22	**Net Cash Flow**	**$3,660**	**$3,350**	**$10,338**	**$13,860**	**$31,208**
23						
24	**Cumulative Cash Flow**	**$3,662**	**$7,012**	**$17,350**	**$31,210**	
25						
26	***Fixed Cash Disbursements (FCD)**	Year Two				
27	Utilities	$2,640				
28	Salaries	$39,000				
29	Payroll Taxes and Benefits	$4,875				
30	Office Supplies	$360				
31	Maintenance and Cleaning	$360				
32	Licenses	$115				
33	Boxes, Paper, etc.	$800				
34	Telephone	$1,800				
35	Miscellaneous	$600				
36	Total FCD/yr	$50,550				
37	Avg FCD per quarter	$12,638				
38						
39	Note: Minor rounding errors have occurred. These are not sufficiently serious to cause alarm.					

	A	B	C	D	E	F
	FINESTKIND SEAFOODS, INC					
	Cash Flow Projection by Quarter, Year Three					
1		1st Qtr	2nd Qtr	3rd Qtr	4th Qtr	Total
2	Cash Receipts					
3	Sales Receivables	$0	$0	$0	$0	$0
4	Wholesale	$58,750	$55,000	$97,500	$113,750	$325,000
5	Retail	$47,400	$43,600	$56,000	$63,000	$210,000
6	Other Sources	$0	$0	$12,000	$15,000	$27,000
7	**Total Cash Receipts**	**$106,150**	**$98,600**	**$165,500**	**$191,750**	**$562,000**
8	Cash Disbursements					
9	Cost of Goods	$76,428	$70,992	$110,520	$127,260	$385,200
10	Variable Labor	$0	$0	$1,622	$5,898	$7,520
11	Advertising	$2,655	$2,465	$3,835	$4,420	$13,375
12	Insurance	$1,025	$1,025	$1,025	$1,025	$4,100
13	Legal and Accounting	$625	$625	$625	$625	$2,500
14	Delivery Expenses	$1,805	$1,675	$2,610	$3,010	$9,100
15	*Fixed Cash Disbursements	$15,216	$15,216	$15,216	$15,216	$60,865
16	Mortgage (rent)	$2,628	$2,628	$2,628	$2,628	$10,512
17	Term Loan	$1,602	$1,602	$1,602	$1,602	$6,408
18	Line of Credit	$0	$0	$12,140	$15,360	$27,500
19	Other Disbursements (see notes)	$0	$0	$0	$0	$0
20	**Total Cash Disbursments**	**$101,984**	**$96,228**	**$151,823**	**$177,044**	**$527,080**
21						
22	**Net Cash Flow**	**$4,166**	**$2,372**	**$13,677**	**$14,706**	**$34,920**
23						
24	**Cumulative Cash Flow**	**$4,166**	**$6,538**	**$20,215**	**$34,920**	
25						
26	***Fixed Cash Disbursements (FCD)**	**Year Three**				
27	Utilities	$2,880				
28	Salaries	$46,800				
29	Payroll Taxes and Benefits	$5,850				
30	Office Supplies	$480				
31	Maintenance and Cleaning	$420				
32	Licenses	$115				
33	Boxes, Paper, etc.	$1,200				
34	Telephone	$2,400				
35	Miscellaneous	$720				
36	Total FCD/yr	$60,865				
37	Avg FCD per quarter	$15,216				

19

Explanation for Cash Flow Projections

Cash Flow Projection by Month, Year One

(3) Sales Receivables. Our terms are cash retail, net 10 for wholesale accounts. Assumes 1/3 wholesale will turn to cash in the following month.

(6) Other Sources. October, November credit line, $7,500; January $75,000 mortgage and $30,000 new equity from Swan and Gosling; April term loan for improvements and equipment, $30,000; June inventory buildup, $15,000 from credit line.

(9) Cost of Goods. 72 percent of current month sales [line (6) of income projections].

(11) Advertising. $1,000 initial burst, $400/month thereafter. Add $4,155 to April for wholesale marketing program.

(16) Mortgage (rent). $550/month rent to December, mortgage payments January on. Terms: $75,000, 15 year, 11.5 percent.

(17) Term Loan. $534/month payments scheduled for term loan. Terms: $30,000, 7 year, 12.25 percent.

Cash Flow Projection by Quarters for Years Two and Three

(3) Sales Receivables. Turn from September, Year One. Because this is a quarterly summary, no further allowance will be made for receivables turn.

(6) Other Sources. $12,000 for one month on line of credit third quarter, $15,000 for nine weeks on line of credit fourth quarter to meet inventory needs.

(24) Cumulative Cash Flow. Subtract $1,237 from net cash flow, first quarter Year Two, to reflect the total cumulative cash flow of Year One: ($1,237).

SECTION THREE: SUPPORTING DOCUMENTS

Résumés

Mike Swan

March 19— to June 19—: Line Foreman, Fatback Fishfoods, East Machias, Maine. Responsible for hiring, training, and directing operations of 15 people in Frozen Food Filleting Department. Rescheduled work flow with resultant 30 percent increase in output per worker. Implemented new purchasing system that reduced spoilage 8 percent. Reduced personnel turnovers by working with local union for revision of company contract policy and by shifting from production line to team task approach. Received Grandiose Foodstuff, Inc. award for line management and was given special assignment in September, 19— to explain these changes to other line foremen at all 22 Fatback Fishfoods plants in New England and the Middle Atlantic states.

Mike Gosling

August 19— to September 19—: Self-employed carpenter. Responsibilities included cash flow forecasting, budgeting, and various other management functions needed in the operation of a single-employee business. Night courses have been taken concurrently in small business management and sales at the University of Maine. Currently serving on the Anytown Zoning Board. Prior experience included a three-year term in the U.S. Navy. Married, two children.

ME License 1000   NH License 2000

Johnson's Plumbing, Inc.
1327 Varnum Street,
Anytown, ME 04112
Phone: 332-2222

September 18, 19—

Finestkind Seafoods, Inc.
123 Main Street
Anytown, ME 04112
Attn.: Mr. Mike Gosling

Dear Mr. Gosling:

For the sum of $4,000, we propose to furnish and install the plumbing and heat work as shown on your outline sketch.

All work will be guaranteed and serviced for one year from the date of completion.

We would require a down payment of $1,150 and another payment of $1,150 when the rough plumbing and heating is completed, with the balance due upon final completion.

If the above meets with your approval, please sign and return one copy.

Signed by: _____

Date: _____

Thank you,

Derek LaMont Johnson

22

Nightlife Clambakes
222 Rural Lane
Anytown, ME 04112

September 10, 19—

Gentlemen:

It is a pleasure to write this letter of recommendation for Finestkind Seafoods, Inc. Our dealings with Messrs. Gosling and Swan have been completely satisfactory. Our business requires a dependable supply of fresh fish, clams and lobsters of first quality. We have consistently received seafood products from Finestkind that meet these standards.

Our business is growing and we look forward to an ongoing relationship with Finestkind to satisfy our needs and customers.

Yours,

Alessandro Tetrazini

23

Floor Plan

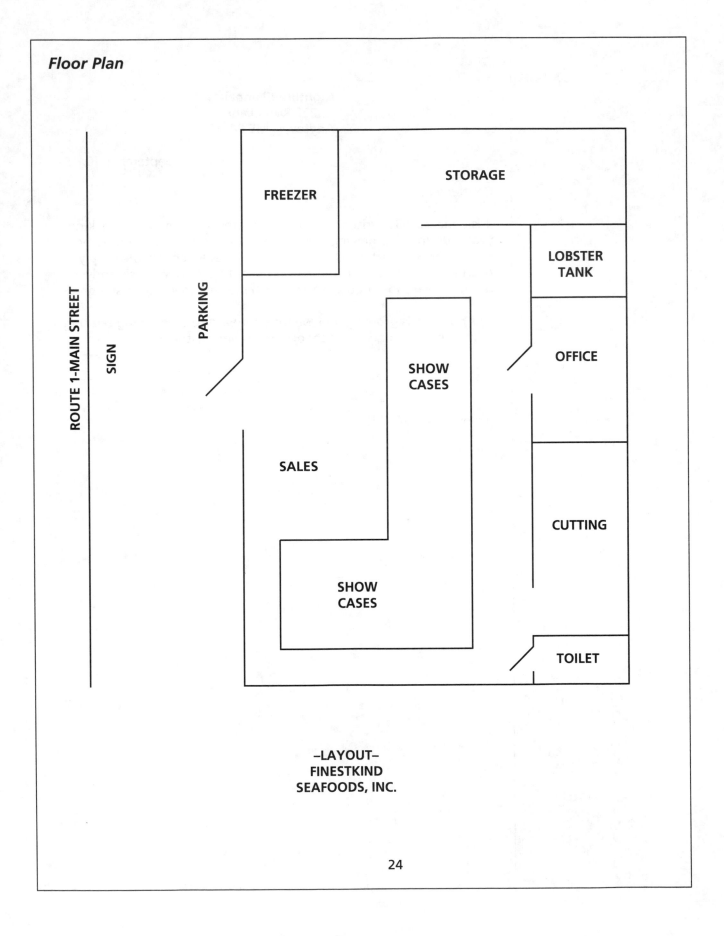

–LAYOUT–
FINESTKIND
SEAFOODS, INC.

24

WORLD BEAT TOURS BUSINESS PLAN

Christine Johnson's World Beat Tours business plan is an ongoing project. This draft was presented to a panel of bankers and consultants as part of a business planning seminar put on by the Women's Business Center, a nonprofit organization serving the needs of entrepreneurial women in New Hampshire.

There are a few areas that need to be worked on: the financials need to be made more explicit. The anticipated 2 percent buy response is optimistic for a $600 mailing list. Christine's personal investment in the business doesn't show—she has invested close to $8,000 in a variety of ways that her CPA suggests might be capitalized.

These kinds of improvements are only to be expected in a real business plan. Nobody sits down and writes a "perfect" plan. In fact, such a thing is impossible. Business plans are working documents, used for purposes ranging from feasibility studies to valuation of a prospective purchase to operating a business in a fluctuating environment.

The strengths of her plan are impressive: she gets straight to the point, seeks hard data, and has a workable marketing strategy that follows a proven model. She knows how much investment is needed and shows the impact of that investment on her income and cash flow projections. She adds a section on business risks that she feels makes her case stronger than it would have been without it. She has used *The Business Planning Guide* as a framework, not a rigid pattern. Given this, her next draft will be even stronger. Thanks, Christine!

World Beat Tours
Dance the world with us!

871 Islington Street, Suite 9
Portsmouth, NH 03801
603-430-6868

Business Plan by Christine Johnson

SECTION ONE: THE BUSINESS

Statement of Purpose

World Beat Music Tour seeks investments totaling $20,000 to purchase equipment; fund the initial marketing campaign; provide deposit monies for hotel and airline reservations; and maintain sufficient cash reserves to provide adequate working capital to successfully expand into a national tour operator. This sum will finance development through the expansion phase so that the company can operate at a high level of profitability. Initial investment plus a guaranteed 20 percent return will be repaid in full within 18 months of disbursement.

Description of the Business

World Beat Tours is an exciting new company that provides clients with a travel experience that engages body, mind, and spirit and enhances awareness of different cultures through music. Both international and domestic full-service music tours will be offered to individuals and groups from specialty markets across the United States. Products will include travel packages from major U.S. cities to events such as the following:

- Reggae Sunsplash—Montego Bay, Jamaica—February

- New Orleans Jazz Festival—New Orleans, Louisiana—May

- Telluride Bluegrass Festival—Telluride, Colorado—June

- Montreux Jazz Festival—Montreal, Switzerland—July

- Beatles Tour—London, England—August

- Bumbershoot—Seattle, Washington—Labor Day Weekend

World Beat Tours may also sell concert ticket/bus ride packages via radio promotions to clients locally who don't have access to major concert events in nearby cities (such as the recent Rolling Stones concert tour). This could provide a more immediate source of cash flow because the above tours have deposit schedules that span longer periods of time.

World Beat Tours began in September 1997 as a sole proprietorship (with plans to incorporate within two years). The office is located at 871 Islington Street, Portsmouth, New Hampshire. Hours are Monday through Friday, 10 AM to 6 PM. Because this is not a venture that anticipates walk-in clients (our customers will access us through a toll-free phone number), we currently share office space rent-free with a related business, Big World Productions. Big World is a concert production company whose owner, Joe Fletcher, is on our advisory board. Our office rental agreement is secure for one year, at which time we will negotiate a lease or choose another Portsmouth location. At that time, we may also consider the feasibility of opening a satellite office on the West Coast.

World Beat Tours has a high probability of success due to current favorable trends in adventure travel (see Attachment A) and to projected demographic trends (see Attachment B). Success will be realized through well-executed niche marketing. Our heaviest travel season will be from May to September annually, with the remainder of the year spent on marketing and preparation for upcoming seasons.

The Market

Our company is designed to cater to the needs of music lovers who are interested in incorporating their passion for music into a travel itinerary and have the means to do so. Through researching mailing lists companies, we have determined the potential client and market size to be as follows:

3

Customer Profile: Jazz music enthusiast, frequent traveler, income over $50,000 annually.

Metropolitan Area	# of Potential Clients
Boston	3,150
New York City	6,150
Seattle	1,950
Los Angeles	6,050
Total Sample Market	**17,300**

This is only a sample market size determined by selecting one musical genre preference and four major metropolitan areas. Market size can potentially be increased by thousands merely by adding other music preferences or cities. To keep growth manageable, only the above four cities will be initially targeted.

Marketing Plan

Our goal is to become the best music tour operator in the United States by providing a fully escorted adventure that will satiate all the senses and leave our clients feeling fulfilled, uplifted, and grateful for our services. We will offer this quality experience at an excellent value to our customers. The average price of a trip is $1,000. The customer benefits include adventure, relaxation, musical education, and peace of mind—a wonderful respite from the stresses of daily existence.

We will market to targeted individuals in choice metropolitan areas (Boston, New York, Los Angeles, Seattle) who have the desire and the means to travel to these events. Our main marketing vehicle will be our compelling brochure, which will drive a direct mail/telemarketing campaign. We will supplement the mailings with print advertising in high-profile music publications such as *Rolling Stone,* special radio promotions (offer stations a trip to give away), and an Internet presence. We will also market to the general public through an existing national sales force of travel agents who sell our packages on commission and are educated about our company through familiarization trips. We will focus special advertising efforts on group travelers such as student or college music groups, fan clubs of festival featured artists, and groups of music industry professionals (i.e., record label executives). Of course, we will also use publicity tools as a way to raise awareness and incur sales of our tours.

Competition

Currently, the biggest source of competition comes from two sources:

1. **Festival Organizers.** Individuals call the promoter's office directly and are given information on where to secure lodging, purchase festival tickets, and so forth. The disadvantage to clients is that they still have to go to a travel agency to purchase their airline ticket. Also, they have to spend time and

4

money on long distance phone calls and must work with more than one person. Unless they have personal experience with the area and the festival, they are relying on a promoter (not a travel professional) to make recommendations on lodging and transportation.

2. **Travel Agencies.** Individuals compelled to attend a world music festival who are not familiar with the promoter would likely visit their travel agent for more information. Their travel agent (trained only in general leisure travel) would then call festival organizers and put the trip together, adding the air service for the client. Again, the disadvantage to clients is not having an expert assisting them with their very specialized tour package.

Currently, we are not aware of existing tour operators that specialize in this category of travel.

Business Risks

Risk	Minimizing Strategy
Cancellation from client	Nonrefundable deposits required; cancellation insurance offered
Limited hotel space	Reserve space early; hold with deposits
Fluctuating foreign currency	Build extra percentage into cost of sales on all international trips; put currency clause into literature
General liability issues	Purchase professional liability insurance; require all participating vendors to provide certificates of insurance; require clients to sign liability waivers

Management

Christine Johnson is a 1989 Babson College graduate with a dual degree in entrepreneurial studies and marketing. Her passion for and industry experience in the areas of both music and travel make her uniquely qualified for this venture. She possesses excellent management and organizational skills as outlined in her résumé (see Attachment D). Of course, Christine has personal experience with all of the products she offers.

Professional Relationships

World Beat Tours is advised by the following professionals:

Cindy Vandewater, CPA
Foy Insurance Group
Lizabeth MacDonald, J.D.

Professional partnerships will be formed with a travel agency (to assist with airline ticketing) and a production/promotion company (to assist with ticket acquisition from festival promoters). These are:

Glen Fouers, Word Wide Travel
Joe Fletcher, Big World Productions

Summary

World Beat Tours is a specialty tour operator servicing the needs of travelers attending music festivals worldwide. Christine Johnson, the owner, is seeking $20,000 in outside investments to fund the startup phase. The majority of the funds will be used for marketing expenses and for deposits required by the hotels and airlines. This investment will provide ample working capital to carry World Beat Tours through the first four months of operation until positive cash flows begin.

Careful analysis of the market has revealed that the travel industry is undergoing significant changes that favor this type of venture. More and more tour operators and agencies are being forced to specialize within specific markets. Travel consumers are significantly more sophisticated and expect an expert to assist them with their plans. Statistics show that over 6 million Americans now book their travel direct with suppliers via the Internet (See Attachment C). World Beat Tours will capitalize on these trends with a well-executed niche marketing plan that focuses strictly on the music enthusiast who is in the $50,000+ annual income bracket and has a history of traveling more than three times a year.

Christine Johnson's knowledge and operational experience, combined with professional partnerships in both the music promotions and travel industries, will greatly increase the likelihood of success in this venture. The funds sought will result in a healthy financial beginning. An immediate client base will emerge as a direct result of initial expenditures on marketing. The remaining funds will be carried forward as reserve cash flow. Based on very conservative projections, the initial investment can be repaid during the 18th month of operations.

6

SECTION TWO: FINANCIAL DATA

Application and Expected Effect of Investment

The $20,000 investment will be used primarily to meet working capital needs until the first profits are realized. Each hotel property (one per tour) will require a minimum deposit of $2,000 to hold the necessary lodging space. These payments will be due early in 1998. We also require the following to kick off our marketing campaign:

Brochure design	$1,000
Mailing lists	600
Printing (brochures, business cards, letterhead)	2,340
Postage	625
Internet fees	150
Total Phase I marketing	**$4,715**

Equipment needs of $400 include a scanner (for Web site design) and a two-line telephone.

We also anticipate $2,000 in initial accounting and legal fees for basic accounting setup and trademark research.

Capital Equipment List

Item	Date of Purchase	Approximate Value

NEC 9733 166mhz 32 meg RAM computer with MMX technology with peripherals:
    NEC CS500 monitor
    Keyboard
    HP Desk Jet 820Cse color printer
	8/97	$2,500

Smith Corona x11800 typewriter	8/97	150
BellSouth 232x telephone	8/97	100
Sharp UX-106 fax machine	8/97	300
Canon NP2020 copier	used	500
Total		**$3,550**

**World Beat Tours
November 20,1997
Balance Sheet**

Assets		Liabilities and Equity	
CURRENT ASSETS		**CURRENT LIABILITIES**	
Cash	$ 300	Accounts Payable	$ 0
Accounts Receivable	0	Payroll Taxes Payable	0
Prepaid Expenses	0	Line of Credit	0
		Current Portion of Debt	0
Total Current Assets	**$ 300**	**Total Current Liabilities**	**$ 0**
FIXED ASSETS		**LONG-TERM LIABILITIES**	
Equipment	$3,550	Note Payable	$1,339
Vehicles	0	Equity Loan Payable	0
Real Estate	0		
Total Fixed Assets	**$3,550**	**Total Long-Term Liabilities**	**$1,339**
OTHER ASSETS		**Total Liabilities**	**$1,339**
Rental Deposit	$ 0		
Utility Deposit	0		
Other	0		
Total Other Assets	**$ 0**	**Owner's Equity**	**$2,511**
Total Assets	**$3,850**	**Total Liabilities and Owner's Equity**	**$3,850**

Breakeven Analysis

Year One

Total fixed costs of $24,300 ÷ $250 (per traveler gross profit margin) = 98 travelers.

Breakeven for the first year of operations will occur after the 98th client has paid for their travel with us. This should occur by July 1998.

Explanation for Income Statement and Cash Flow Projections

Year One Sales Assumptions

- A 7,500-piece direct mailer should yield a 2 percent buy response; this equals 150 travelers.

- 150 travelers spread out over 6 trips = 25 travelers per trip.

- Marketing in only 4 cities would require sales of only 6 people per trip from each city.

- This does not include sales derived from other advertising/marketing campaigns.

- This is a highly conservative estimate for first-year sales.

- Average sale = $1,000. Gross profit margin = 25 percent per sale = $250 gross profit margin per traveler.

Year Two Sales Assumptions

- A 15,000-piece direct mailer should yield a 2 percent buy response; this equals 300 travelers.

- This does not include sales derived from other advertising/marketing campaigns.

- Average gross profit margin per sales still equals $250.

Year Three Sales Assumptions

- A 25,000-piece direct mailer should yield a 2 percent buy response; this equals 500 travelers.

- This does not include sales derived from other advertising/marketing campaigns.

- Average gross profit margin per sales still estimated at $250.

9

	WORLD BEAT TOURS Income Projection: Three-Year Summary			
	A	B	C	D
1		1998	1999	2000
2	Projected Sales	$150,000	$300,000	$500,000
3	Cost of Sales (75%)	$112,500	$225,000	$375,000
4	**Gross Profit**	**$37,500**	**$75,000**	**$125,000**
5				
6	Operating Expenses			
7	Bad Debts	$0	$0	$0
8	Bank Charges	$120	$240	$360
9	Commissions	$0	$0	$0
10	Consumable Supplies	$0	$0	$0
11	Donations	$0	$0	$0
12	Employee Benefits	$0	$0	$0
13	Equipment Leases	$0	$0	$0
14	Equipment Maintenance	$0	$0	$0
15	Insurance	$1,500	$1,500	$2,000
16	Interest	$0	$0	$0
17	Legal and Accounting	$2,000	$2,000	$3,500
18	Marketing			
19	Advertising	$2,500	$3,500	$8,500
20	Brochure Design	$1,000	$1,250	$1,500
21	Internet Fees	$700	$600	$600
22	Mailing Lists	$600	$600	$600
23	Promotional Items	$1,500	$3,000	$5,000
24	Trade Shows	$0	$1,500	$2,000
25				
26	Memberships and Subscriptions	$195	$610	$610
27	Office Supplies	$300	$600	$900
28	Payroll Salaries	$0	$6,000	$12,000
29	Payroll Taxes	$0	$600	$1,200
30	Postage	$2,975	$4,850	$7,950
31	Printing	$2,340	$4,500	$7,000
32	Rent	$0	$6,000	$9,000
33	Repairs and Maintenance	$0	$0	$0
34	Taxes and Licenses	$0	$0	$0
35	Telephone			
36	Business Line	$535	$900	$1,200
37	Toll-Free 800 Number	$630	$1,500	$2,100
38				
39	Travel (contract negotiations)	$6,863	$6,000	$6,000
40	Uniforms	$500	$1,000	$1,000
41	Utilities	$0	$0	$0
42	**Total Operating Expenses**	**$24,258**	**$46,750**	**$73,020**
43				
44	Other Expenses			
45	Equipment Purchases	$400	$2,400	$1,000
46	Miscellaneous	$0	$1,000	$2,000
47	Total Other Expenses	$400	$3,400	$3,000
48				
49	**Total Expenses**	**$24,658**	**$50,150**	**$76,020**
50				
51	**Net Profit before Taxes**	**$12,842**	**$24,850**	**$48,980**

10

	WORLD BEAT TOURS Income Projection: Three-Year Summary (Investment Added)			
	A	**B**	**C**	**D**
1		1998	1999	2000
2	Projected Sales	$150,000	$300,000	$500,000
3	Cost of Sales (75%)	$112,500	$225,000	$375,000
4	**Gross Profit**	**$37,500**	**$75,000**	**$125,000**
5				
6	Operating Expenses			
7	Bad Debts	$0	$0	$0
8	Bank Charges	$120	$240	$360
9	Commissions	$0	$0	$0
10	Consumable Supplies	$0	$0	$0
11	Donations	$0	$0	$0
12	Employee Benefits	$0	$0	$0
13	Equipment Leases	$0	$0	$0
14	Equipment Maintenance	$0	$0	$0
15	Insurance	$1,500	$1,500	$2,000
16	Interest	$0	$4,000	$0
17	Legal and Accounting	$2,000	$2,000	$3,500
18	Marketing			
19	Advertising	$2,500	$3,500	$8,500
20	Brochure Design	$1,000	$1,250	$1,500
21	Internet Fees	$700	$600	$600
22	Mailing Lists	$600	$600	$600
23	Promotional Items	$1,500	$3,000	$5,000
24	Trade Shows	$0	$1,500	$2,000
25				
26	Memberships and Subscriptions	$195	$610	$610
27	Office Supplies	$300	$600	$900
28	Payroll Salaries	$0	$6,000	$12,000
29	Payroll Taxes	$0	$600	$1,200
30	Postage	$2,975	$4,850	$7,950
31	Printing	$2,340	$4,500	$7,000
32	Rent	$0	$6,000	$9,000
33	Repairs and Maintenance	$0	$0	$0
34	Taxes and Licenses	$0	$0	$0
35	Telephone			
36	Business Line	$535	$900	$1,200
37	Toll-Free 800 Number	$630	$1,500	$2,100
38				
39	Travel (contract negotiations)	$6,863	$6,000	$6,000
40	Uniforms	$500	$1,000	$1,000
41	Utilities	$0	$0	$0
42	**Total Operating Expenses**	**$24,258**	**$50,750**	**$73,020**
43				
44	Other Expenses			
45	Equipment Purchases	$400	$2,400	$1,000
46	Miscellaneous	$0	$1,000	$2,000
47	Total Other Expenses	$400	$3,400	$3,000
48				
49	**Total Expenses**	**$24,658**	**$54,150**	**$76,020**
50				
51	**Net Profit before Taxes**	**$12,842**	**$20,850**	**$48,980**

11

WORLD BEAT TOURS
Cash Flow Projection, Year One

#	A	B Nov. 1997	C Dec. 1997	D Jan. 1998	E Feb. 1998	F Mar. 1998	G Apr. 1998	H May 1998	I Jun. 1998	J Jul. 1998	K Aug. 1998	L Sept. 1998	M Oct. 1998	N Total Yr 1
2	Projected Sales	$0	$0	$25,000	$0	$25,000	$25,000	$25,000	$25,000	$25,000	$0	$0	$0	$150,000
3	Cost of Sales (75%)	$0	$2,000	$0	$16,750	$2,000	$2,000	$18,750	$18,750	$18,750	$16,750	$16,750	$0	$112,500
4	Gross Profit	$0	($2,000)	$25,000	($16,750)	$23,000	$23,000	$6,250	$6,250	$6,250	($16,750)	($16,750)	$0	$37,500
5														
6	Operating Expenses													
7	Bad Debts													
8	Bank Charges	$10	$10	$10	$10	$10	$10	$10	$10	$10	$10	$10	$10	$120
9	Commissions													$0
10	Consumable Supplies													$0
11	Donations													$0
12	Employee Benefits													$0
13	Equipment Leases													$0
14	Equipment Maintenance													$0
15	Insurance	$0	$0	$1,500	$0	$0	$0	$0	$0	$0	$0	$0	$0	$1,500
16	Interest													$0
17	Legal and Accounting	$0	$1,000	$1,000	$0	$0	$0	$0	$0	$0	$0	$0	$0	$2,000
18	Marketing													
19	Advertising	$0	$0	$500	$500	$500	$500	$500	$0	$0	$0	$0	$0	$2,500
20	Brochure Design	$0	$1,000	$0	$0	$0	$0	$0	$0	$0	$0	$0	$0	$1,000
21	Internet Fees	$0	$200	$50	$50	$50	$50	$50	$50	$50	$50	$50	$50	$700
22	Mailing Lists	$0	$600	$0	$0	$0	$0	$0	$0	$0	$0	$0	$0	$600
23	Promotional Items	$0	$0	$0	$0	$1,500	$0	$0	$0	$0	$0	$0	$0	$1,500
24	Trade Shows													$0
25														
26	Memberships and Subscriptions	$85	$10	$10	$10	$10	$10	$10	$10	$10	$10	$10	$10	$195
27	Office Supplies	$25	$25	$25	$25	$25	$25	$25	$25	$25	$25	$25	$25	$300
28	Payroll Salaries													$0
29	Payroll Taxes													$0
30	Postage	$100	$1,875	$100	$100	$100	$100	$100	$100	$100	$100	$100	$100	$2,975
31	Printing	$200	$2,140	$0	$0	$0	$0	$0	$0	$0	$0	$0	$0	$2,340
32	Rent													
33	Repairs and Maintenance													$0
34	Taxes and Licenses													$0
35	Telephone													
36	Business Line	$95	$40	$40	$40	$40	$40	$40	$40	$40	$40	$40	$40	$535
37	Toll-Free 800 Number	$0	$105	$0	$0	$0	$105	$105	$105	$105	$105	$0	$0	$630
38														
39	Travel (contract negotiations)	$363	$500	$0	$1,000	$0	$0	$1,000	$1,000	$1,000	$1,000	$1,000	$0	$6,863
40	Uniforms	$0	$0	$0	$500	$500	$0	$0	$0	$0	$0	$0	$0	$500
41	Utilities	$0	$0	$0	$0	$0	$0	$0	$0	$0	$0	$0	$0	$0
42	Total Operating Expenses	$878	$7,505	$3,235	$1,735	$2,735	$840	$1,840	$1,340	$1,340	$1,340	$1,235	$235	$24,258
43														
44	Net Income from Operations	($878)	($9,505)	$21,765	($18,485)	$20,265	$22,160	$4,410	$4,910	$4,910	($18,090)	($17,985)	($235)	$13,242
45														
46	Other Cash Disbursements													
47	Equipment Purchases	$400	$0	$0	$0	$0	$0	$0	$0	$0	$0	$0	$0	$400
48	Principal Payments													$0
49	Miscellaneous													$0
50	Total Other Disbursements	$400	$0	$0	$0	$0	$0	$0	$0	$0	$0	$0	$0	$400
51														
52	Other Cash Inflows													
53	Investors/Loans													$0
54														
55	Net Cash Flow	($1,278)	($9,505)	$21,765	($18,485)	$20,265	$22,160	$4,410	$4,910	$4,910	($18,090)	($17,985)	($235)	$12,842
56														
57	Beginning Cash Balance	$200	($1,078)	($10,583)	$11,182	($7,303)	$12,962	$35,122	$39,532	$44,442	$49,352	$31,262	$13,277	
58	Projected Ending Balance	($1,078)	($10,583)	$11,182	($7,303)	$12,962	$35,122	$39,532	$44,442	$49,352	$31,262	$13,277	$13,042	

WORLD BEAT TOURS
Cash Flow Projection, Year One (with Investment)

Row		Nov. 1997	Dec. 1997	Jan. 1998	Feb. 1998	Mar. 1998	Apr. 1998	May 1998	Jun. 1998	Jul. 1998	Aug. 1998	Sept. 1998	Oct. 1998	Total Yr 1
		B	C	D	E	F	G	H	I	J	K	L	M	N
2	Projected Sales	$0	$0	$25,000	$0	$25,000	$25,000	$25,000	$25,000	$25,000	$0	$0	$0	$150,000
3	Cost of Sales (75%)	$0	$2,000	$0	$16,750	$2,000	$2,000	$18,750	$18,750	$18,750	$16,750	$16,750	$0	$112,500
4	Gross Profit	$0	($2,000)	$25,000	($16,750)	$23,000	$23,000	$6,250	$6,250	$6,250	($16,750)	($16,750)	$0	$37,500
5														
6	Operating Expenses													
7	Bad Debts													$0
8	Bank Charges	$10	$10	$10	$10	$10	$10	$10	$10	$10	$10	$10	$10	$120
9	Commissions													$0
10	Consumable Supplies													$0
11	Donations													$0
12	Employee Benefits													$0
13	Equipment Leases													$0
14	Equipment Maintenance													$0
15	Insurance	$0	$0	$1,500	$0	$0	$0	$0	$0	$0	$0	$0	$0	$1,500
16	Interest													$0
17	Legal and Accounting	$0	$1,000	$1,000	$0	$0	$0	$0	$0	$0	$0	$0	$0	$2,000
18	Marketing													
19	Advertising	$0	$0	$500	$500	$500	$500	$500	$0	$0	$0	$0	$0	$2,500
20	Brochure Design	$0	$1,000	$0	$0	$0	$0	$0	$0	$0	$0	$0	$0	$1,000
21	Internet Fees	$0	$200	$50	$50	$50	$50	$50	$50	$50	$50	$50	$50	$700
22	Mailing Lists	$0	$600	$0	$0	$0	$0	$0	$0	$0	$0	$0	$0	$600
23	Promotional Items	$0	$0	$0	$0	$1,500	$0	$0	$0	$0	$0	$0	$0	$1,500
24	Trade Shows													$0
25														
26	Memberships and Subscriptions	$85	$10	$10	$10	$10	$10	$10	$10	$10	$10	$10	$10	$195
27	Office Supplies	$25	$25	$25	$25	$25	$25	$25	$25	$25	$25	$25	$25	$300
28	Payroll Salaries													
29	Payroll Taxes													
30	Postage	$100	$1,875	$100	$100	$100	$100	$100	$100	$100	$100	$100	$100	$2,975
31	Printing	$200	$2,140	$0	$0	$0	$0	$0	$0	$0	$0	$0	$0	$2,340
32	Rent													
33	Repairs and Maintenance													
34	Taxes and Licenses													
35	Telephone													
36	Business Line	$95	$40	$40	$40	$40	$40	$40	$40	$40	$40	$40	$40	$535
37	Toll-Free 800 Number	$0	$105	$0	$0	$0	$105	$105	$105	$105	$105	$0	$0	$630
38														
39	Travel (contract negotiations)	$363	$500	$0	$1,000	$0	$0	$1,000	$1,000	$1,000	$1,000	$1,000	$0	$6,863
40	Uniforms	$0	$0	$0	$0	$500	$0	$0	$0	$0	$0	$0	$0	$500
41	Utilities	$0	$0	$0	$0	$0	$0	$0	$0	$0	$0	$0	$0	$0
42	Total Operating Expenses	$878	$7,505	$3,235	$1,735	$2,735	$840	$1,840	$1,340	$1,340	$1,340	$1,235	$235	$24,258
43														
44	Net Income from Operations	($878)	($9,505)	$21,765	($18,485)	$20,265	$22,160	$4,410	$4,910	$4,910	($18,090)	($17,985)	($235)	$13,242
45														
46	Other Cash Disbursements													
47	Equipment Purchases	$400	$0	$0	$0	$0	$0	$0	$0	$0	$0	$0	$0	$400
48	Principal Payments													$0
49	Miscellaneous													$0
50	Total Other Disbursements	$400	$0	$0	$0	$0	$0	$0	$0	$0	$0	$0	$0	$400
51														
52	Other Cash Inflows													
53	Investors/Loans	$20,000	$0	$0	$0	$0	$0	$0	$0	$0	$0	$0	$0	$20,000
54														
55	Net Cash Flow	$18,722	($9,505)	$21,765	($18,485)	$20,265	$22,160	$4,410	$4,910	$4,910	($18,090)	($17,985)	($235)	$32,842
56														
57	Beginning Cash Balance	$200	$18,922	$9,417	$31,182	$12,697	$32,962	$55,122	$59,532	$64,442	$69,352	$51,262	$33,277	
58	Projected Ending Balance	$18,922	$9,417	$31,182	$12,697	$32,962	$55,122	$59,532	$64,442	$69,352	$51,262	$33,277	$33,042	

WORLD BEAT TOURS
Cash Flow Projection, Year Two

	A	B	C	D	E	F	G	H	I	J	K	L	M	N
1		Nov. 1998	Dec. 1998	Jan. 1999	Feb. 1999	Mar. 1999	Apr. 1999	May 1999	Jun. 1999	Jul. 1999	Aug. 1999	Sept. 1999	Oct. 1999	Total Yr 2
2	Projected Sales	$0	$0	$50,000	$0	$50,000	$50,000	$50,000	$50,000	$50,000	$0	$0	$0	$300,000
3	Cost of Sales (75%)	$0	$2,000	$0	$35,500	$2,000	$2,000	$37,500	$37,500	$37,500	$35,500	$35,500	$0	$225,000
4	Gross Profit	$0	($2,000)	$50,000	($35,500)	$48,000	$48,000	$12,500	$12,500	$12,500	($35,500)	($35,500)	$0	$75,000
5														
6	Operating Expenses													
7	Bad Debts													$0
8	Bank Charges	$20	$20	$20	$20	$20	$20	$20	$20	$20	$20	$20	$20	$240
9	Commissions													$0
10	Consumable Supplies													$0
11	Donations													$0
12	Employee Benefits													$0
13	Equipment Leases													$0
14	Equipment Maintenance													$0
15	Insurance	$0	$0	$1,500	$0	$0	$0	$0	$0	$0	$0	$0	$0	$1,500
16	Interest								$0					$0
17	Legal and Accounting	$0	$1,000	$1,000	$0	$0	$0	$0	$0	$0	$0	$0	$0	$2,000
18	Marketing													
19	Advertising	$500	$500	$500	$500	$500	$500	$500	$0	$0	$0	$0	$0	$3,500
20	Brochure Design	$1,250	$0	$0	$0	$0	$0	$0	$0	$0	$0	$0	$0	$1,250
21	Internet Fees	$50	$50	$50	$50	$50	$50	$50	$50	$50	$50	$50	$50	$600
22	Mailing Lists	$600	$600	$0	$0	$0	$0	$0	$0	$0	$0	$0	$0	$600
23	Promotional Items	$0	$0	$0	$0	$3,000	$0	$0	$0	$0	$0	$0	$0	$3,000
24	Trade Shows	$0	$0	$0	$1,500	$0	$0	$0	$0	$0	$0	$0	$0	$1,500
25														
26	Memberships and Subscriptions	$500	$10	$10	$10	$10	$10	$10	$10	$10	$10	$10	$10	$610
27	Office Supplies	$50	$50	$50	$50	$50	$50	$50	$50	$50	$50	$50	$50	$600
28	Payroll Salaries	$0	$0	$0	$1,000	$0	$0	$1,000	$1,000	$1,000	$1,000	$1,000	$0	$6,000
29	Payroll Taxes	$0	$0	$0	$100	$0	$0	$100	$100	$100	$100	$100	$0	$600
30	Postage	$100	$3,750	$100	$100	$100	$100	$100	$100	$100	$100	$100	$100	$4,850
31	Printing	$0	$4,500	$0	$0	$0	$0	$0	$0	$0	$0	$0	$0	$4,500
32	Rent	$500	$500	$500	$500	$500	$500	$500	$500	$500	$500	$500	$500	$6,000
33	Repairs and Maintenance													$0
34	Taxes and Licenses													$0
35	Telephone													
36	Business Line	$75	$75	$75	$75	$75	$75	$75	$75	$75	$75	$75	$75	$900
37	Toll-Free 800 Number	$50	$50	$200	$50	$50	$200	$200	$200	$200	$200	$50	$50	$1,500
38														
39	Travel (contract negotiations)	$0	$0	$1,000	$0	$0	$0	$1,000	$1,000	$1,000	$1,000	$1,000	$0	$6,000
40	Uniforms	$0	$0	$0	$0	$1,000	$0	$0	$0	$0	$0	$0	$0	$1,000
41	Utilities	$0	$0	$0	$0	$0	$0	$0	$0	$0	$0	$0	$0	$0
42	Total Operating Expenses	$4,095	$10,105	$5,005	$3,955	$5,355	$1,505	$3,605	$3,105	$3,105	$3,105	$2,955	$855	$46,750
43														
44	Net Income from Operations	($4,095)	($12,105)	$44,995	($39,455)	$42,645	$46,495	$8,895	$9,395	$9,395	($38,605)	($38,455)	($855)	$28,250
45	Other Cash Disbursements													
46														
47	Equipment Purchases													$0
48	Principal Payments													$0
49	Miscellaneous													$0
50	Total Other Disbursements	$0	$0	$0	$0	$0	$0	$0	$0	$0	$0	$0	$0	$0
51														
52	Other Cash Inflows													
53	Investors/Loans													$0
54														
55	Net Cash Flow	($4,095)	($12,105)	$44,995	($39,455)	$42,645	$46,495	$8,895	$9,395	$9,395	($38,605)	($38,455)	($855)	$28,250
56														
57	Beginning Cash Balance	$4,000	($95)	($12,200)	$32,795	($6,660)	$35,985	$82,480	$91,375	$100,770	$110,165	$71,560	$33,105	
58	Projected Ending Balance	($95)	($12,200)	$32,795	($6,660)	$35,985	$82,480	$91,375	$100,770	$110,165	$71,560	$33,105	$32,250	

14

WORLD BEAT TOURS
Cash Flow Projection, Year Two (with Investment)

	A	B Nov. 1998	C Dec. 1998	D Jan. 1999	E Feb. 1999	F Mar. 1999	G Apr. 1999	H May 1999	I Jun. 1999	J Jul. 1999	K Aug. 1999	L Sept. 1999	M Oct. 1999	N Total Yr 2
2	Projected Sales	$0	$0	$50,000	$0	$50,000	$50,000	$50,000	$50,000	$50,000	$0	$0	$0	$300,000
3	Cost of Sales (75%)	$0	$2,000	$0	$35,500	$2,000	$2,000	$37,500	$37,500	$37,500	$35,500	$35,500	$0	$225,000
4	**Gross Profit**	$0	($2,000)	$50,000	($35,500)	$48,000	$48,000	$12,500	$12,500	$12,500	($35,500)	($35,500)	$0	$75,000
5														
6	**Operating Expenses**													
7	Bad Debts													$0
8	Bank Charges	$20	$20	$20	$20	$20	$20	$20	$20	$20	$20	$20	$20	$240
9	Commissions													$0
10	Consumable Supplies													$0
11	Donations													$0
12	Employee Benefits													$0
13	Equipment Leases													$0
14	Equipment Maintenance													$0
15	Insurance	$0	$0	$1,500	$0	$0	$0	$0	$0	$0	$0	$0	$0	$1,500
16	Interest	$0	$0	$0	$0	$0	$4,000	$0	$0	$0	$0	$0	$0	$4,000
17	Legal and Accounting	$0	$1,000	$1,000	$0	$0	$0	$0	$0	$0	$0	$0	$0	$2,000
18	**Marketing**													
19	Advertising	$500	$500	$500	$500	$500	$500	$500	$0	$0	$0	$0	$0	$3,500
20	Brochure Design	$1,250	$0	$0	$0	$0	$0	$0	$0	$0	$0	$0	$0	$1,250
21	Internet Fees	$50	$50	$50	$50	$50	$50	$50	$50	$50	$50	$50	$50	$600
22	Mailing Lists	$0	$600	$0	$0	$0	$0	$0	$0	$0	$0	$0	$0	$600
23	Promotional Items	$0	$0	$0	$0	$3,000	$0	$0	$0	$0	$0	$0	$0	$3,000
24	Trade Shows	$0	$0	$0	$1,500	$0	$0	$0	$0	$0	$0	$0	$0	$1,500
25														
26	Memberships and Subscriptions	$500	$10	$10	$10	$10	$10	$10	$10	$10	$10	$10	$10	$610
27	Office Supplies	$50	$50	$50	$50	$50	$50	$50	$50	$50	$50	$50	$50	$600
28	Payroll Salaries	$0	$0	$0	$1,000	$0	$0	$1,000	$1,000	$1,000	$1,000	$1,000	$0	$6,000
29	Payroll Taxes	$0	$0	$0	$100	$0	$0	$100	$100	$100	$100	$100	$0	$600
30	Postage	$100	$3,750	$100	$100	$100	$100	$100	$100	$100	$100	$100	$100	$4,850
31	Printing	$1,000	$3,500	$0	$0	$0	$0	$0	$0	$0	$0	$0	$0	$4,500
32	Rent	$500	$500	$500	$500	$500	$500	$500	$500	$500	$500	$500	$500	$6,000
33	Repairs and Maintenance													$0
34	Taxes and Licenses													$0
35	**Telephone**													
36	Business Line	$75	$75	$75	$75	$75	$75	$75	$75	$75	$75	$75	$75	$900
37	Toll-Free 800 Number	$50	$50	$200	$50	$50	$200	$200	$200	$200	$200	$50	$50	$1,500
38														
39	Travel (contract negotiations)	$0	$0	$1,000	$0	$0	$0	$1,000	$1,000	$1,000	$1,000	$1,000	$0	$6,000
40	Uniforms	$0	$0	$0	$0	$1,000	$0	$0	$0	$0	$0	$0	$0	$1,000
41	Utilities	$0	$0	$0	$0	$0	$0	$0	$0	$0	$0	$0	$0	$0
42	**Total Operating Expenses**	$4,095	$10,105	$5,005	$3,955	$5,355	$5,505	$3,605	$3,105	$3,105	$3,105	$2,955	$855	$50,750
43														
44	**Net Income from Operations**	($4,095)	($12,105)	$44,995	($39,455)	$42,645	$42,495	$8,895	$9,395	$9,395	($38,605)	($38,455)	($855)	$24,250
45														
46	**Other Cash Disbursements**													
47	Equipment Purchases						$0							$0
48	Principal Payments	$0	$0	$0	$0	$0	$20,000	$0	$0	$0	$0	$0	$0	$20,000
49	Miscellaneous						$0							$0
50	**Total Other Disbursements**	$0	$0	$0	$0	$0	$20,000	$0	$0	$0	$0	$0	$0	$20,000
51														
52	**Other Cash Inflows**													
53	Investors/Loans													$0
54														
55	**Net Cash Flow**	($4,095)	($12,105)	$44,995	($39,455)	$42,645	$22,495	$8,895	$9,395	$9,395	($38,605)	($38,455)	($855)	$4,250
56														
57	Beginning Cash Balance	$24,000	$19,905	$7,800	$52,795	$13,340	$55,985	$78,480	$87,375	$96,770	$106,165	$67,560	$29,105	
58	Projected Ending Balance	$19,905	$7,800	$52,795	$13,340	$55,985	$78,480	$87,375	$96,770	$106,165	$67,560	$29,105	$28,250	

WORLD BEAT TOURS
Cash Flow Projection, Year Three

	A	B Nov. 1999	C Dec. 1999	D Jan. 2000	E Feb. 2000	F Mar. 2000	G Apr. 2000	H May 2000	I Jun. 2000	J Jul. 2000	K Aug. 2000	L Sept. 2000	M Oct. 2000	N Total Yr 3
2	Projected Sales	$0	$0	$83,333	$0	$83,333	$83,333	$83,333	$83,333	$83,333	$0	$0	$0	$499,998
3	Cost of Sales (75%)	$0	$2,000	$0	$60,500	$2,000	$2,000	$62,500	$62,500	$62,500	$60,500	$60,500	$0	$375,000
4	Gross Profit	$0	($2,000)	$83,333	($60,500)	$81,333	$81,333	$20,833	$20,833	$20,833	($60,500)	($60,500)	$0	$124,998
5	Operating Expenses													
7	Bad Debts													$0
8	Bank Charges	$30	$30	$30	$30	$30	$30	$30	$30	$30	$30	$30		$360
9	Commissions													$0
10	Consumable Supplies													$0
11	Donations													$0
12	Employee Benefits													$0
13	Equipment Leases													$0
14	Equipment Maintenance													$0
15	Insurance	$0	$0	$2,000	$0	$0	$0	$0	$0	$0	$0	$0	$0	$2,000
16	Interest													$0
17	Legal and Accounting	$1,500	$0	$2,000	$0	$0	$0	$0	$0	$0	$0	$0	$0	$3,500
18	Marketing													
19	Advertising	$500	$500	$1,000	$1,000	$1,000	$1,000	$1,000	$500	$500	$500	$500	$500	$8,500
20	Brochure Design	$1,500	$0	$0	$0	$0	$0	$0	$0	$0	$0	$0	$0	$1,500
21	Internet Fees	$50	$50	$50	$50	$50	$50	$50	$50	$50	$50	$50	$50	$600
22	Mailing Lists	$0	$600	$0	$0	$0	$0	$0	$0	$0	$0	$0	$0	$600
23	Promotional Items	$0	$0	$0	$0	$5,000	$0	$0	$0	$0	$0	$0	$0	$5,000
24	Trade Shows	$0	$0	$0	$2,000	$0	$0	$0	$0	$0	$0	$0	$0	$2,000
26	Memberships and Subscriptions	$500	$10	$10	$10	$10	$10	$10	$10	$10	$10	$10	$10	$610
27	Office Supplies	$75	$75	$75	$75	$75	$75	$75	$75	$75	$75	$75	$75	$900
28	Payroll Salaries	$1,000	$1,000	$1,000	$1,000	$1,000	$1,000	$1,000	$1,000	$1,000	$1,000	$1,000	$1,000	$12,000
29	Payroll Taxes	$100	$100	$100	$100	$100	$100	$100	$100	$100	$100	$100	$100	$1,200
30	Postage	$150	$6,300	$150	$150	$150	$150	$150	$150	$150	$150	$150	$150	$7,950
31	Printing	$0	$7,000	$0	$0	$0	$0	$0	$0	$0	$0	$0	$0	$7,000
32	Rent	$750	$750	$750	$750	$750	$750	$750	$750	$750	$750	$750	$750	$9,000
33	Repairs and Maintenance													$0
34	Taxes and Licenses													$0
35	Telephone													
36	Business Line	$100	$100	$100	$100	$100	$100	$100	$100	$100	$100	$100	$100	$1,200
37	Toll-Free 800 Number	$50	$50	$300	$50	$50	$300	$300	$300	$300	$300	$50	$50	$2,100
39	Travel (contract negotiations)	$0	$0	$1,000	$0	$0	$0	$1,000	$1,000	$1,000	$1,000	$1,000	$0	$6,000
40	Uniforms	$0	$0	$0	$0	$1,000	$0	$0	$0	$0	$0	$0	$0	$1,000
41	Utilities	$0	$0	$0	$0	$0	$0	$0	$0	$0	$0	$0	$0	$0
42	Total Operating Expenses	$6,305	$16,565	$8,565	$5,315	$9,315	$3,565	$4,565	$4,065	$4,065	$4,065	$3,815	$2,815	$73,020
44	Net Income from Operations	($6,305)	($18,565)	$74,768	($65,815)	$72,018	$77,768	$16,268	$16,768	$16,768	($64,565)	($64,315)	($2,815)	$51,978
45	Other Cash Disbursements													
47	Equipment Purchases													$0
48	Principal Payments													$0
49	Miscellaneous													$0
50	Total Other Disbursements	$0	$0	$0	$0	$0	$0	$0	$0	$0	$0	$0	$0	$0
52	Other Cash Inflows													
53	Investors/Loans													$0
55	Net Cash Flow	($6,305)	($18,565)	$74,768	($65,815)	$72,018	$77,768	$16,268	$16,768	$16,768	($64,565)	($64,315)	($2,815)	$51,978
57	Beginning Cash Balance	$8,000	$1,695	($16,870)	$57,898	($7,917)	$64,101	$141,869	$158,137	$174,905	$191,673	$127,108	$62,793	$51,978
58	Projected Ending Balance	$1,695	($16,870)	$57,898	($7,917)	$64,101	$141,869	$158,137	$174,905	$191,673	$127,108	$62,793	$59,978	

16

SECTION THREE: SUPPORTING DOCUMENTS

Attachment A

Adventure Tourism

. . . According to Mallett, almost 50 percent of the $400 billion U.S. travel industry is based on outdoor active recreation, with the driving force consisting of women, families, and people over 50 years old. . . . "We've made hard adventure safer and easier," says Mallett, "bringing it within reach of the general traveler." . . . In other words, travelers are swapping their rest and relaxation time for good old-fashioned thrill-seeking. Says Strader, "We're seeking something more than sitting around a pool with a piña colada."

Source: Dec. 1995 *Entrepreneur,* p. 111

Attachment B

Trends for the New Millennium

Clanning

The inclination to join up, belong to, hang out with groups of like kinds, providing a secure feeling that our own belief systems will somehow be validated by consensus.

Implications/Examples: Need for community; power of special interest groups (e.g., militia?). Products/services related to this trend might be clubby megabookstores, planned communities, 12-step programs, membership badges.

Fantasy Adventure

As a break from modern tensions, we actively seek excitement in basically risk-free adventures, whether it be via travel, food, or virtual reality.

Implications/Examples: Peterman Catalog (fantasy adventure/romance-oriented copy); eating exotic (buffalo steak) food; wearing military clothing; mountain bikes; wildering; fascination with aliens; "utility" vehicles that go anywhere.

Pleasure Revenge

Consumers tired of all the rules and regulations want to cut loose and have secret bacchanals with a bevy of forbidden fruits.

Implications/Examples: We are fed up with self-deprivation in the name of health and correct behavior. This trend is the pursuit of pleasure with a hint of anger—pleasure as a reward for all we have suffered. Butter sales are back up again!

Small Indulgences

Stressed out from ever increasing expenses, consumers are finding ways to reward themselves with affordable luxuries. One of the key words here is *small.*

Implications/Examples: This is an excellent area for small business to concentrate on—a good fit. When the economy is booming, a small indulgence might mean selecting a BMW convertible instead of a sedan. When the economy is down, a small indulgence might mean the occasional bouquet of flowers. The size of the indulgence will follow the economy. Small indulgences include indulging one's pets (witness the success of pet superstores). Products/services include fountain pens (at an all-time high) instead of ballpoints; mini trips; small but chic hotels; literally smaller size of regular items (palm-size color TV, mini-books).

Source: Popcorn, Faith and Marigold, Lys: *Clicking,* HarperCollins, Inc.; New York, NY; 1996; pp. 29–31.

Attachment C

Six million Americans will make travel arrangements over the Internet or an online service this year, according to the Travel Industry Association.

Source: TravelAge East, November 17, 1997.

Attachment D

Christine Johnson
30 Mill Street
Dover, NH 03820
603-749-2533

QUALIFICATIONS

Excel in human relations, able to deal gracefully with the public. Outstanding problem solver, work well independently. Strong leadership qualities. Highly motivated. Possesses a variety of computer skills, including Web master certification on Microsoft FrontPage.

EXPERIENCE
Sept. 1995–June 1997

SKI 93 TRIPS, INC., Exeter, New Hampshire
Account Executive

Built group tour business and maintained key relationships (including annual contract negotiations) with ski resorts and properties throughout Vermont, New York, and Western states. Serviced a base of over 2,000 skiers. Increased profit margin by 10 percent in a zero growth industry. Researched and assisted in the development of several travel programs including the South America Ski Division, the Western Ski Division, and the Adventure Travel Division. Attended industry conferences and trade shows regularly. Completely designed and created the Web page http://www.Ski93Trips.com.

June 1993–June 1995

KCMU 90.3 FM, Seattle, Washington
Public Relations Director and Promotions Coordinator

Initiated and implemented a complete redesign of the station's short- and long-term marketing strategies. Secured several key media sponsorships as a result of cultivating positive, professional relationships with the music, arts, and entertainment communities. Welcomed many sold-out performances such as the *Cranberries* concert. Supported the local music scene by originating and promoting KCMU New Night Music at one of the most frequented venues in town. Increased club card participation by 25 percent. Revived the station's ticket giveaway program and increased the number of free tickets available to listeners by 50 percent. Achieved all of the above in the first nine months of employment.

EDUCATION

Babson College, Wellesley, Massachusetts

Awarded Bachelor of Science in Marketing Communications and Entrepreneurial Studies, December 1989.

19

THE MEDIVERSE PRODUCTS, INC. (MPI) PLAN

The following is a plan for Mediverse Products, Inc. (MPI), a company distributing a series of products for the health care industry. This plan was created in order to attain additional financing for acquiring other, similar product lines and expanding the circle of distribution.

Mediverse Products, Inc. (MPI)

1. Executive Summary

    1.1 Objectives

    1.2 Mission

2. Company

    2.1 Company Ownership

    2.2 Company Products

    2.3 Company Locations and Facilities

3. Products and Services

    3.1 Product and Service Description

    3.2 Important Features and Comparison

    3.3 Sales Literature

4. Market Analysis

    4.1 Industry Analysis

        4.1.1 Participants

    4.2 Keys to Success

5. Business Strategy and Implementation

    5.1 Marketing Strategy

        5.1.1 Target Markets and Market Segments

        5.1.2 Pricing Strategy

        5.1.3 Promotion Strategy

        5.1.4 Marketing Programs

        5.1.5 Sales Strategy

        5.1.6 Strategic Alliances

6. Management Summary

    6.1 Management Team

    6.2 Other Management Team Considerations

7. Financial Analysis

    7.1 Financial Plan

1. EXECUTIVE SUMMARY

Mediverse Products, Inc. (MPI) distributes innovative, state-of-the art products in use in hospitals and laboratories. It has its head office in Seattle, Washington. Its products are sold through direct-response marketing and face-to-face contacts.

This business plan is the first in our business planning process. We plan to revise it every quarter.

In the next seven months we intend to be fully operational and to post revenues of $67,000.

Our keys to success and critical factors for the next year are, in order of importance:

- Meeting demands for high quality, innovative products in the health care and related industries

- Providing above average technical and customer service

- Financial control and cash flow planning

Mediverse Products, Inc. (MPI) is a relatively new company focused on establishing a niche in the health care industry. Based on projections of our future financial performance over the next three years, sales will increase to more than $372,000, while net profits will be $115,000.

1.1 Objectives

1. To introduce the line of Blue Protection Plus gloves to the Pacific Northwest area.

2. To maintain gross margin above 32 percent.

3. To grow sales to reach $15,000 monthly by the end of 1996 and $30,000 monthly by the end of 1997.

1.2 Mission

Mediverse Products, Inc. (MPI) is a distribution company whose mission is to introduce innovative products to the health care industry while steadily increasing its profitability and the value of the company.

2. COMPANY

Mediverse Products, Inc. (MPI) distributes innovative health care products to hospitals, laboratories, ambulance, and police departments in the Pacific Northwest area. Its customers include health care professionals such as physicians, nurses, laboratory technologists, emergency medical technicians, as well as police and fire departments and prison staff.

3

2.1 Company Ownership

Mediverse Products, Inc. (MPI) is a privately held Washington corporation. Chantal Lavalle, Mediverse Products, Inc. (MPI)'s president, is the majority owner. Marc J. Lavalle is the vice president and other shareholder. Both owners are also involved in the sales and marketing activities of the company.

Company History

Mediverse Products, Inc. (MPI) was founded in 1992 as a corporation in Canada where the operations were managed by the same owners. The product line at that time was limited to a few laboratory products.

In mid-1994, the owners relocated to Washington and continued to operate their Canadian company from the United States. Due to the nature of their business and the need for face-to-face contacts, the Canadian company did not flourish. At the end of 1994, Mediverse Products, Inc. (MPI) incorporated in the state of Washington and decided to seek out more innovative product lines such as the Blue Protection Plus gloves and other products. Plans are in the works to wind down the operation in Canada and to concentrate exclusively on the Pacific Northwest market in order to develop market share.

2.2 Company Products

Mediverse Products, Inc. (MPI)'s product line has grown out of a combination of existing market needs.

1. The health care industry's growing concern about the need to protect its workers' from infectious diseases such as HIV and hepatitis.

2. The reform of the health care industry and the need to provide alternative, high quality replacement parts for equipment at a fraction of the cost offered by the original equipment manufacturer.

3. The need in the market to seek out and offer products that are difficult to find in this country at an affordable price.

2.3 Company Locations and Facilities

Headquarters are located in Seattle, Washington. Mediverse Products, Inc. (MPI) is a home-based business.

As the business grows, we will need additional storage space for inventory and eventually we will also add employees.

3. PRODUCTS AND SERVICES

Mediverse Products, Inc. (MPI) distributes products in use in laboratories and hospitals in the Pacific Northwest area. It also services fire and police departments, emergency and ambulance services, and prisons.

3.1 Product and Service Description

As of January 1995, Mediverse Products, Inc. (MPI) has six product lines, some having a common customer base but not exclusively.

1. The Blue Protection Plus glove line is an exclusive line of latex gloves designed to provide extra protection to health care workers, emergency medical technicians, firefighters, and police in instances where heavy bleeding of victims occurs. The gloves are 10 grams heavier than ordinary latex gloves and provide better protection against HIV and hepatitis. They are also longer for added protection.

2. The Analyzer Parts product line is a line of replacement parts for blood analyzing instrumentation. The main focus of this product line is to offer high-quality replacement parts to hospitals and laboratories at a fraction of the cost offered by the original equipment manufacturer.

3. The VMA Kits product line is an exclusive line from Barcelona, Spain, which offers diagnostic kits for laboratory testing of special diseases. These products are relatively difficult to obtain in this country, thereby creating a need.

4. The Rheumatoid product line also comes from Spain. It offers easy-to-use diagnostic kits for the detection of rheumatoid arthritis and other serology tests to hospitals and laboratories.

5. The Quality Control Material product line is manufactured in Spain. It provides quality control to validate some of the diagnostic tests performed in laboratories. Due to the low manufacturing cost in Spain and the favorable transfer price, this is an extremely profitable product line.

6. The Instrumentation product line is a complement to the other products. It allows Mediverse Products, Inc. (MPI) to enter the capital equipment market segment with a low-end product. This product line is expandable.

3.2 Important Features and Comparison

Mediverse Products, Inc. (MPI) products include several important features that set them apart from other products that may be considered competitive:

1. The Blue Protection Plus gloves are unique in the sense that they are heavier than conventional latex gloves. With the

5

increasing need for protection in emergency situations, workers normally "double glove" in order to achieve extra protection. There is no need to do so with the Blue glove. Conventional gloves are also shorter than the Blue gloves, thereby exposing more of the forearm to contamination. The Blue gloves are also difficult to puncture, unlike standard latex gloves.

2. The Analyzer Parts offer substantial savings to the budget conscious hospital and laboratory. These replacement parts have the same warranty as the original equipment manufacturer and also tend to have a longer lifetime.

3. The other products from Spain offer the customer a source for difficult-to-find products at a low cost.

4. Mediverse Products, Inc. (MPI) offers technical assistance both on-site and via telephone.

3.3 Sales Literature

Copies of Mediverse Products, Inc. (MPI) advertisements and sales literature are attached in an appendix at the end of this document.

KEY OF PRODUCT LINES TO THE FOLLOWING GRAPHS

1 = Blue Protection Plus Gloves

2 = Analyzer Parts

3 = VMA Kits

4 = Rheumatoid Product

5 = Quality Control Material

6 = Instrumentation Product (N.A.)

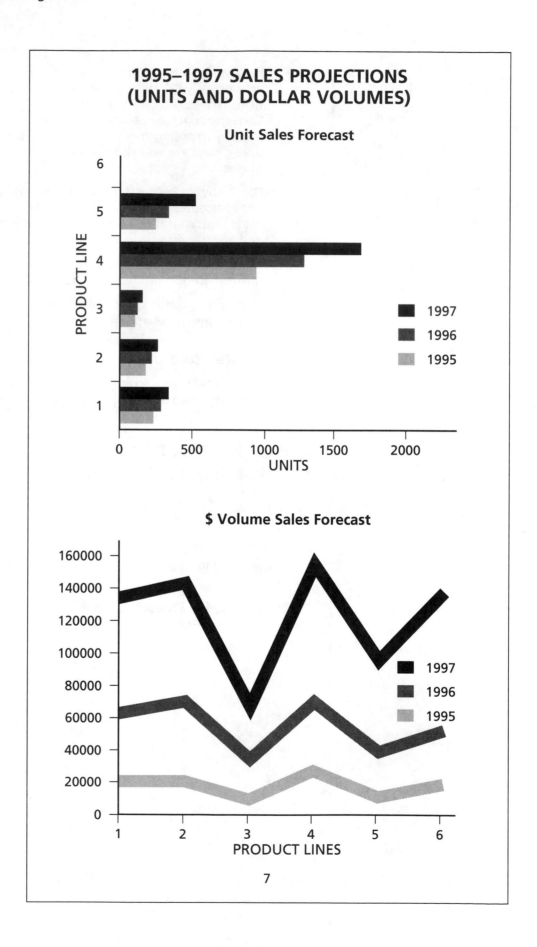

7

4. MARKET ANALYSIS

The market for latex gloves is worth an estimated $5 million at the end-user value in 1994, and is projected to maintain itself according to the Medical Devices News bulletin. Health care in general is in reorganization but sales to the diagnostics testing laboratories is estimated to be a $10 billion industry in the United States.

Market leaders in the latex glove business includes such giants and Johnson & Johnson and Baxter Health Care.

The market in diagnostic testing is extremely fragmented into several hundreds of manufacturers and distributors of various sizes.

4.1 Industry Analysis

The health care industry is a very concentrated market. Only a few major players remain in terms of services. The larger companies report revenues of only a few hundred million dollars per year, generally less than 1 percent of the total market, due to their high overheads and expenditures.

In order to survive in this industry it is necessary to position one's company as an innovative, reliable, and service-oriented company among a world of giants. It is less hazardous not to try to compete with the larger manufacturers and to offer products that are different and less of a competition to the larger companies.

4.1.1 Participants

In the diagnostics industry, several leaders have emerged:

- Boehringer Mannheim Corporation (Indianapolis, Ind.): manufacturer of diagnostic kits in use in laboratories worldwide. Due to an agreement with Hitachi instruments, they are also exclusive distributors of their blood chemistry analyzers.

- Beckman Instruments Inc. (Anaheim, Calif.): manufacturer of a variety of laboratory instrumentation and diagnostic kits.

- Johnson & Johnson (New York): pharmaceutical giant that has recently acquired Kodak instruments in order to enter the diagnostics race as well as diversify their product offering.

Market Segmentation

The market is generally segmented with approximately four to five large companies in leadership positions (70 percent of market share); five to seven medium-sized manufacturers and large distributors make up the next segment (20 percent of market share); and the remaining 10 percent is shared among small distributors such as Mediverse Products, Inc. (MPI)

8

4.2 Keys to Success

The keys to success in this business are:

- marketing via press releases on new products, trade shows, and customer mailings;

- product quality and affordability; and

- service that includes goods delivered on time, a knowledgeable staff, and a willingness to go the extra mile to ensure customer satisfaction and loyalty.

5. BUSINESS STRATEGY AND IMPLEMENTATION

Our strategy will be based on serving niche markets well. The diagnostics industry is full of me-too products; Mediverse Products, Inc. (MPI) wants to set itself apart from the pack by virtue of the uniqueness of its product mix and its services.

Also, what begins as a unique product in a segment of the market can eventually become a niche product that will fit the needs of customers across the country.

5.1 Marketing Strategy

We are focusing on a fairly narrow market in terms of the Blue Protection Plus gloves and also upon one department in the clinical laboratory or hospital.

Our customers are used to dealing with vendors that are highly qualified technically and expect the best. We can bring them practical solutions to their budget cutbacks and infection control issues.

5.1.1 Target Markets and Market Segments

As far as the glove market is concerned, we are concentrating on segments such as the police and fire departments, prisons, and emergency medical services where there is a need for this kind of product but the need has yet to be created because makeshift alternative solutions are in place, (i.e., double gloves).

As far as the analyzer parts market is concerned, there is a need already in terms of cost containment in the hospital and private laboratories is concerned. The quality of our service will be an issue here because the manufacturer is currently their benchmark.

The other diagnostics product lines appeal to customers because of their affordability and quality. This will be the emphasis taken in press releases and advertising.

The instrumentation product line will be essential if we want to enter the physician's office labs, which is a growing market.

5.1.2 Pricing Strategy

Pricing attempts to suggest quality and value at a reasonable price.

Pricing issues are of the utmost importance to Mediverse Products, Inc. (MPI). It is essential that we obtain the best transfer price from our vendors and that these prices be maintained. This is one of the key issues when we choose to carry a product line. Since we do import a good deal, it is essential that our landed costs be in line with our selling price. This allows us to keep our list prices reasonable while still allowing for an adequate gross margin.

5.1.3 Promotion Strategy

The short-term goal is enough visibility to generate enough leads. This will take place in the following way:

- Press releases in Clinical Lab Products, Clinical Laboratory News, and American Clinical Laboratory journals will expose the Diagnostic product line.

- Press releases in Physicians Market Place will introduce our Instrumentation line.

- Purchase of a mailing list ($200) will give us access to all physicians that operate a laboratory in the United States.

- Trade shows: The Washington Medical Show in October and the AACC regional show in November will contribute to our introduction in the Pacific Northwest area.

5.1.4 Marketing Programs

We are in the process of building our corporate identity. Our company colors are red, yellow, and black.

We also use "Affordable Technology" on our business cards as a trademark.

We are fortunate in that the manufacturer in Spain (BioSystems) supplies us with high quality brochures and technical documentation free of charge.

We plan to purchase one piece of direct mail per month to gain exposure.

5.1.5 Sales Strategy

The immediate goal is to get orders as quickly as possible.

The long-term goal is to expand into the Oregon, California, and Nevada areas through a commission-based sales force.

The three-year goal is to hire a telemarketing representative and one other technical sales representative.

5.1.6 Strategic Alliances

Our relationship with our manufacturers is crucial to our existence. It is important to communicate with them on a regular basis, obtain the latest product information, and meet with them at least once a year. It is also important to follow the FDA regulations on their behalf for those products requiring registration.

6. MANAGEMENT SUMMARY

Mediverse Products, Inc. (MPI) is a very lean organization at the moment, consisting of only two people.

Our personnel plan calls for increases from two people at the moment to three people three years from now.

6.1 Management Team

Chantal Lavalle, president and founder.

Mrs. Lavalle has worked in the diagnostics industry for the past 18 years. She originally founded Mediverse Products, Inc. (MPI) in Canada. She holds a B.Sc. in Biochemistry from Concordia University, Montreal. She has extensive experience in laboratory procedures as well as sales, marketing, and technical customer service.

Marc J. Lavalle, vice president and cofounder.

Mr. Lavalle has been in sales most of his adult life. His career spans 30 years with emphasis on transportation sales. He specializes in imports and is a key player in managing landed costs determinations.

Two more people have yet to be named to the board of directors in order to comply with Washington state requirements for a corporation.

6.2 Other Management Team Considerations

There are some gaps that have to be considered:

- The organization is extremely lean and this could affect the goals to be achieved.

- The present team has very good knowledge of the Canadian market and must stay focused on the much larger U.S. market in order to achieve the set goals.

- To a large extent, the success of Mediverse Products, Inc. (MPI) lies in retaining its innovative product lines and its continuing search for new products. This in itself can be viewed as a challenge.

11

7. FINANCIAL ANALYSIS

7.1 Financial Plan

All of the data regarding the financial analysis is included in the Appendix.

- Projected Profit and Loss (Pro Forma Income Statement)

- Cash Flow Analysis (Pro Forma Cash Flow)

- Projected Balance Sheet (Pro Forma Balance Sheet)

- Business Ratios, as projected through the next three years

MEDIVERSE PRODUCTS. INC. (MPI)
Pro Forma Income Statement

A	B	C	D	E	F	G	H	I	J	K	L	M	N	O	P
	1	2	3	4	5	6	7	8	9	10	11	12	1995	1996	1997
Sales	$0	$0	$0	$0	$2,600	$1,622	$4,970	$10,650	$16,060	$20,160	$31,520	$33,820	$121,402	$209,747	$372,353
Cost of Sales															
Cost of Unit Sales	$0	$0	$0	$0	$1,326	$1,025	$2,670	$5,385	$7,777	$9,345	$19,160	$20,340	$67,028	$90,534	$123,210
Total Cost of Sales	$0	$0	$0	$0	$1,326	$1,025	$2,670	$5,385	$7,777	$9,345	$19,160	$20,340	$67,028	$90,534	$123,210
Gross Margin	$0	$0	$0	$0	$1,274	$597	$2,300	$5,265	$8,283	$10,815	$12,360	$13,480	$54,374	$119,213	$249,143
Gross Margin Percent	0%	0%	0%	0%	49%	36.8%	46.28%	49.44%	51.58%	53.65%	39.21%	39.86%	44.79%	56.84%	66.91%
Sales & Marketing Expenses															
Sales & Marketing Salaries	$0	$0	$0	$0	$0	$0	$0	$0	$0	$1,000	$1,000	$2,000	$4,000	$30,000	$69,000
Advertising & Promotion	$0	$0	$0	$0	$150	$100	$150	$150	$150	$100	$100	$150	$1,050	$1,313	$1,641
Freight & Duty	$0	$0	$0	$0	$200	$50	$100	$100	$100	$200	$200	$300	$1,250	$1,875	$2,813
Commissions	$0	$0	$0	$0	$32	$15	$58	$132	$207	$270	$309	$337	$1,359	$2,980	$6,229
Travel Expenses	$0	$0	$0	$0	$100	$100	$100	$100	$150	$150	$150	$150	$1,000	$1,100	$3,000
Total Sales & Marketing Expenses	$0	$0	$0	$0	$482	$265	$408	$482	$607	$1,720	$1,759	$2,937	$8,659	$37,268	$82,683
Sales & Marketing Percent	0%	0%	0%	0%	18.5%	16.3%	8.2%	4.52%	3.78%	8.53%	5.58%	8.68%	7.13%	17.77%	22.21%
General & Administrative Expenses															
Leased Equipment	$0	$0	$0	$0	$0	$0	$0	$0	$0	$0	$50	$50	$50	$50	$2,000
Utilities	$30	$30	$30	$30	$30	$30	$30	$30	$30	$30	$30	$30	$360	$378	$1,000
Insurance	$20	$20	$20	$20	$20	$20	$20	$20	$20	$20	$20	$20	$240	$500	$1,000
Location	$0	$0	$0	$0	$0	$0	$0	$0	$0	$0	$0	$0	$0	$0	$6,000
Depreciation	$0	$0	$0	$0	$0	$0	$0	$0	$0	$0	$0	$0	$0	$2,500	$5,000
Payroll Burden	$0	$0	$0	$0	$0	$0	$0	$0	$0	$0	$0	$0	$0	$6,000	$7,000
Total General & Admin. Expenses	$50	$50	$50	$50	$50	$50	$50	$50	$50	$50	$100	$100	$650	$9,428	$22,000
General & Admin. Percent	0%	0%	0%	0%	1.92%	3.08%	1.01%	0.47%	0.31%	0.25%	0.32%	0.3%	0.54%	4.49%	5.91%
Total Operating Expenses	$50	$50	$50	$50	$532	$315	$458	$532	$657	$1,770	$1,859	$3,037	$9,309	$46,696	$104,683
Profit before Interest & Taxes	($50)	($50)	($50)	($50)	$742	$82	$1,843	$4,733	$7,626	$9,045	$10,501	$10,443	$45,065	$72,517	$144,460
Taxes Incurred	$0	$0	$0	$0	$0	$0	$0	$0	$0	$0	$0	$0	$0	$14,503	$28,892
Net Profit	($50)	($50)	($50)	($50)	$742	$82	$1,843	$4,733	$7,626	$9,045	$10,501	$10,443	$45,065	$58,013	$115,568
Net Profit Percent of Sales	0%	0%	0%	0%	28.5%	17.3%	37.08%	44.44%	47.48%	44.87%	33.32%	30.88%	37.12%	27.66%	31.04%

13

MEDIVERSE PRODUCTS. INC. (MPI)
Pro Forma Cash Flow Statement

	A	B	C	D	E	F	G	H	I	J	K	L	M	N	O	P
		1	2	3	4	5	6	7	8	9	10	11	12	1995	1996	1997
1																
2	Net Profit	($50)	($50)	($50)	($50)	$742	$82	$1,843	$4,733	$7,626	$9,045	$10,501	$10,443	$45,065	$58,013	$115,568
3	Plus:															
4	Depreciation	$0	$0	$0	$0	$0	$0	$0	$0	$0	$0	$0	$0	$0	$2,500	$5,000
5	Changes in Accounts Payable	$5	$0	$0	$0	$178	($51)	$176	$275	$248	$166	$977	$134	$2,108	$1,015	$1,505
6	Current Borrowing (repayment)	$0	$0	$0	$0	$0	$0	$0	$0	$0	$0	$0	$0	$0	$0	$0
7	Inc. (Dec.) Other Liabilities	$0	$0	$0	$0	$0	$0	$0	$0	$0	$0	$0	$0	$0	$0	$0
8	Long-Term Borrowing	$0	$0	$0	$0	$0	$0	$0	$0	$0	$0	$0	$0	$0	$0	$0
9	Capital Input	$100	$100	$200	$200	$200	$0	$0	$0	$0	$0	$0	$0	$800	$0	$0
10	Subtotal	$55	$50	$150	$150	$1,120	$231	$2,019	$5,008	$7,874	$9,211	$11,478	$10,577	$47,923	$61,528	$122,073
11																
12	Less:															
13	Changes in Accounts Receivable	$0	$0	$0	$0	$0	$0	$0	$0	$0	$0	$0	$0	$0	$0	$0
14	Changes in Inventory	$0	$0	$0	$0	$0	$0	$0	$0	$0	$0	$0	$0	$0	$0	$0
15	Changes in Other Short-Term Assets	$0	$0	$0	$0	$0	$0	$0	$0	$0	$0	$0	$0	$0	$0	$0
16	Capital Expenditures	$0	$0	$0	$0	$0	$0	$0	$0	$0	$0	$0	$0	$0	$0	$0
17	Dividends	$0	$0	$0	$0	$0	$0	$0	$0	$0	$0	$0	$0	$0	$8,000	$10,000
18	Subtotal	$0	$0	$0	$0	$0	$0	$0	$0	$0	$0	$0	$0	$0	$8,000	$10,000
19																
20	Net Cash Flow	$55	$50	$150	$150	$1,120	$231	$2,019	$5,008	$7,874	$9,211	$11,478	$10,577	$47,923	$53,528	$112,073

14

MEDIVERSE PRODUCTS. INC. (MPI)
Pro Forma Balance Sheet

	Starting Balances	1	2	3	4	5	6	7	8	9	10	11	12	1995	1996	1997
Short-Term Assets																
Cash	$1,000	$1,055	$1,105	$1,255	$1,405	$2,525	$2,756	$4,776	$9,784	$17,658	$26,869	$38,346	$48,923	$48,923	$102,451	$214,524
Accounts Receivable	$0	$0	$0	$0	$0	$0	$0	$0	$0	$0	$0	$0	$0	$0	$0	$0
Inventory	$0	$0	$0	$0	$0	$0	$0	$0	$0	$0	$0	$0	$0	$0	$0	$0
Other Short-Term Assets	$0	$0	$0	$0	$0	$0	$0	$0	$0	$0	$0	$0	$0	$0	$0	$0
Total Short-Term Assets	$1,000	$1,055	$1,105	$1,255	$1,405	$2,525	$2,756	$4,776	$9,784	$17,658	$26,869	$38,346	$48,923	$48,923	$102,451	$214,524
Long-Term Assets																
Capital Assets	$0	$0	$0	$0	$0	$0	$0	$0	$0	$0	$0	$0	$0	$0	$0	$0
Accumulated Depreciation	$0	$0	$0	$0	$0	$0	$0	$0	$0	$0	$0	$0	$0	$0	$2,500	$7,500
Total Long-Term Assets	$0	$0	$0	$0	$0	$0	$0	$0	$0	$0	$0	$0	$0	$0	($2,500)	($7,500)
Total Assets	$1,000	$1,055	$1,105	$1,255	$1,405	$2,525	$2,756	$4,776	$9,784	$17,658	$26,869	$38,346	$48,923	$48,923	$99,951	$207,024
DEBT and Equity																
Short-Term Liabilities																
Accounts Payable	$0	$5	$5	$5	$5	$183	$132	$309	$584	$832	$998	$1,974	$2,108	$2,108	$3,123	$4,628
Short-Term Notes	$0	$0	$0	$0	$0	$0	$0	$0	$0	$0	$0	$0	$0	$0	$0	$0
Other Short-Term Liabilities	$0	$0	$0	$0	$0	$0	$0	$0	$0	$0	$0	$0	$0	$0	$0	$0
Subtotal Short-Term Liabilities	$0	$5	$5	$5	$5	$183	$132	$309	$584	$832	$998	$1,974	$2,108	$2,108	$3,123	$4,628
Long-Term Liabilities	$0	$0	$0	$0	$0	$0	$0	$0	$0	$0	$0	$0	$0	$0	$0	$0
Total Liabilities	$0	$5	$5	$5	$5	$183	$132	$309	$584	$832	$998	$1,974	$2,108	$2,108	$3,123	$4,628
Paid-in Capital	$0	$100	$200	$400	$800	$800	$800	$800	$800	$800	$800	$800	$800	$800	$800	$800
Retained Earnings	$1,000	$1,000	$950	$900	$850	$800	$1,542	$1,824	$3,667	$8,400	$16,026	$25,071	$35,572	$35,572	$38,015	$86,028
Earnings	$0	($50)	($50)	($50)	($50)	$742	$282	$1,843	$4,733	$7,626	$9,045	$10,501	$10,443	$10,443	$58,013	$115,568
Total Equity	$1,000	$1,050	$1,100	$1,250	$1,400	$2,342	$2,624	$4,467	$9,200	$16,826	$25,871	$36,372	$46,815	$46,815	$96,828	$202,396
Total Debt and Equity	$1,000	$1,055	$1,105	$1,255	$1,405	$2,525	$2,756	$4,776	$9,784	$17,658	$26,869	$38,346	$48,923	$48,923	$99,951	$207,024
Net Worth	$1,000	$1,050	$1,100	$1,250	$1,400	$2,342	$2,624	$4,467	$9,200	$16,826	$25,871	$36,372	$46,815	$46,815	$96,828	$202,396

Mediverse Products, Inc. (MPI)
Ratio Analysis

Profitability Ratios	Last Year	1995	1996	1997
Gross Margin	0%	44.79%	56.84%	66.91%
Net Profit Margin	0%	37.12%	27.66%	31.04%
Return on Assets	0%	92.11%	58.04%	55.82%
Return on Equity	0%	96.26%	59.91%	57.1%

Activity Ratios	Last Year	1995	1996	1997
AR Turnover	0.00	0.00	0.00	0.00
Days Sales Outstanding	0	0	0	0
Inventory Turnover	0.00	0.00	0.00	0.00
Accts. Payable Turnover	n.a.	3.43	3.43	3.43
Total Asset Turnover	0.00	2.48	2.10	1.80

Debt Ratios	Last Year	1995	1996	1997
Debt to Net Worth	0.00	0.05	0.03	0.02
Debt to Net Worth Adj.	0.00	0.05	0.03	0.02
Short-Term Debt to Liab.	0.00	1.00	1.00	1.00

Liquidity Ratios	Last Year	1995	1996	1997
Current Ratio	0.00	23.20	32.80	46.35
Current Ratio Adj.	0.00	23.20	32.80	46.35
Quick Ratio	0.00	23.20	32.80	46.35
Quick Ratio Adj.	0.00	23.20	32.80	46.35
Net Working Capital	$1,000	$46,815	$99,328	$209,896
Net Working Capital Adj.	$1,000	$46,815	$99,328	$209,896
Interest Coverage		0.00	0.00	0.00

Additional Ratios		1995	1996	1997
Assets to Sales		0.40	0.48	0.56
Debt/Assets		4.31%	3.12%	2.24%
Total Assets/Current Debt		23.20	32.00	44.73
Acid Test		223.20	32.80	46.35
Asset Turnover		2.48	2.10	1.80
Sales/Net Worth		2.59	2.17	1.84
Dividend Payout		0.00	0.14	0.09

16

Worksheets

*T*hese blank forms and worksheets are for you to fill out and use. Upstart's *The Business Planning Guide: The Worksheets* may be ordered from Upstart Publishing Company, Inc. by calling 800-235-8866.

Personal Data Sheet

Name _____ Date of birth _____

Address _____

Telephone number _____ Years there _____

Marital status _____ Name of spouse _____ Dependents _____

Education

	Name and address	Grades completed/ diplomas/degrees obtained
High School		
Other		

Military service _____ Years _____

Highest rank obtained _____

Relevant training or work experience _____

_____

Work Experience

Business and address	Job title and duties	Supervisor	Dates

Trade, professional, or civic membership and activities _____

_____

Hobbies, interests, other relevant information _____

_____

Use another sheet if necessary.

Credit Inquiry

Name _____ Date of birth _____

Address _____

Telephone number _____ Years there _____

Former Address _____

_____ Years there _____

Marital Status _____ Name of Spouse _____ No. dependents _____

Employer _____ Years there _____

Address _____

Phone _____ Kind of business _____

Position _____ Net income $/ _____

Former employer and address _____ Years there _____

Spouse's employer and address _____

Net income $/ _____ Other income sources: $/month _____

Account	Bank	Acct. No.	Balance
Checking			
Savings			

Auto owned (year and make) _____ Purchased from _____ $ _____

Financed by _____ Balance owed $ _____ Monthly _____

Rent or mortgage payment/mo. $ _____ Paid to _____

Real estate owned in name of _____ Purchase price _____ Mtge. bal. _____

Credit references and all debts owing—other than above
(Bank, loan or finance companies., credit unions, budget)

Name	Address	Orig. amt.	Bal.	Mo. payment

Life insurance amount _____ Company _____

If co-maker for others, state where and for whom _____

Nearest relative or friend not living with you/relationship _____

Address _____

Cost of Living Budget

(Based on average month—does not cover purchase of any new items except emergency replacements)

Detailed Budget

Regular Monthly Payments

House payments
(principal, interest, taxes, insurance) or rent .... $ _____

Car payments (including insurance) .... $ _____

Appliance, TV payments .... $ _____

Home improvement loan payments .... $ _____

Personal loan, credit card payments .... $ _____

Health plan payments .... $ _____

Life insurance premiums .... $ _____

Other insurance premiums .... $ _____

Savings/investments .... $ _____

Total.. $ _____

Household Operating Expense

Telephone .... $ _____

Gas and electricity... $ _____

Water .... $ _____

Other household expenses, repairs, maintenance .... $ _____

Total.. $ _____

Personal Expense

Clothing, cleaning, laundry... $ _____

Prescription medications .... $ _____

Physicians, dentists.. $ _____

Education .... $ _____

Dues.. $ _____

Gifts and contributions... $ _____

(Continued)

Travel .... $ _____

Newspapers, magazines, books .... $ _____

Auto upkeep and gas .... $ _____

Spending money and allowances .... $ _____

Miscellaneous .... $ _____

Total .... $ _____

Food Expense

Food—at home .... $ _____

Food—away from home .... $ _____

Total .... $ _____

Tax Expense

Federal and state income taxes .... $ _____

Other taxes not included above .... $ _____

Total .... $ _____

Budget Summary

A. Income gross

    Monthly total .... $ _____

Less expense:

Regular monthly payments .... $ _____

Household operating expense .... $ _____

Personal expense .... $ _____

Food expense .... $ _____

Tax expense .... $ _____

Monthly total .... $ _____

B. Monthly total expenses .... $ _____

Savings (A − B) .... $ _____

R E S O U R C E S

Intellectual Property

Patent It Yourself, 6/e **by David Pressman, et al.**
(Nolo Press, 1997)

Marketing Your Invention, 2/e **by Tom Mosley**
(Upstart Publishing Co., 1997)

Copyrights, Patents, & Trademarks **by Hoyt L. Barber**
(McGraw-Hill, 1997)

Patent and Trademark Office
U.S. Department of Commerce
P.O. Box 9
Washington, DC 20231
703-308-HELP

Copyright Office
Library of Congress, Room 401
101 Independence Avenue SE
Washington, DC 20540
202-479-0700

National Technical Information Service Center
Center for the Utilization of Federal Technology
U.S. Department of Commerce
P.O. Box 1423
Springfield, VA 22151
707-487-4838

Legal Help

The Upstart Small Business Legal Guide, 2/e **by Robert Friedman**
(Dearborn Publishing Group, Inc., 1998)

The Complete Book of Business Forms and Agreements **by Cliff Roberson**
(McGraw-Hill, 1994)

Marketing

Guerrilla Marketing by Jay Conrad Levinson
(Houghton Mifflin Co., 1993)

The Market Planning Guide, 5/e by David H. Bangs, Jr.
(Upstart Publishing Co., 1998)

Target Marketing, 3/e by Linda Pinson and Jerry Jinnett
(Upstart Publishing Co., 1996)

Roger Parker's Guide to Web Content and Design: Eight Steps to Web Site Success by **Roger Parker**
(IDG Books, 1997)

Starting Your Business

The Start Up Guide, 2/e by David H. Bangs, Jr.
(Upstart Publishing Co., 1994)

Steps to Small Business Start-Up, 3/e by Linda Pinson and Jerry Jinnett
(Upstart Publishing Co., 1996)

Launching Your Home-Based Business by David H. Bangs, Jr. and Andi Axman
(Upstart Publishing Co., 1998)

Tax and Accounting

Financial Essentials for Small Business Success by Jeff Slater and Joe Tabet
(Upstart Publishing Co., 1994)

Keeping the Books, 4/e by Linda Pinson and Jerry Jinnett
(Upstart Publishing Co., 1998)

Periodicals

In Business.   A bimonthly magazine for small businesses, especially those with fewer than ten employees. J. G. Press, P.O. Box 323, Emmaus, PA 18049. $29.00/year.

Home Office Computing.   The best small business monthly these days, even if aimed primarily at home-based small businesses with a technological bent. Scholastic, Inc., 555 Broadway, New York, NY 10012 800-288-7812. $16.99/year.

Inc.   One of the leading small business magazines. 38 Commercial Wharf, Boston, MA 02110 617-248-8000. $19.00/year.

Accounting Software

QuickBooks
Intuit Software
P.O. Box 7850
Mountain View, CA 94039
650-944-6000
http://www.intuit.com

MYOB
Best!Ware, Inc.
300 Roundhill Dr.
Rockaway, NJ 07866
201-586-2200

Financing Your Business

Banks

Borrowing to Build Your Business by George M. Dawson
(Upstart Publishing Co., 1997)

Thomson Bank Directory
(U.S. and International Volumes)
(Thomson Financial Publishing Inc.)

Other Methods of Financing

Corporate Finance Sourcebook
(National Register Publishing Company)

Business Capital Sources
International Wealth Success, Inc.
24 Canterbury Road
Rockville Center, NY 11570
516-766-5850
$15.00/year

Preferred Lenders Hotline
800-368-5855

Financial Ratios

Annual Statement Studies
Robert Morris Associates
One Liberty Place, Suite 2300
1650 Market Street
Philadelphia, PA 19103
800-677-7621
(Annual)

Industry Norms and Key Business Ratios
(Annual)
(Dun & Bradstreet, 1982)

Almanac of Business and Industrial Ratios, 28/e by Leo Troy
(Annual)
(Prentice-Hall Trade, 1997)

Venture Capital

Pratt's Guide to Venture Capital Sources
Venture Economics
16 Laurel Avenue
P.O. Box 348
Wellesley Hills, MA 02181
617-431-8100

Venture Capital Journal
16 Laurel Avenue
P.O. Box 348
Wellesley Hills, MA 02181
617-431-8100

Demographics

Census Catalog & Guide
U.S. Government Printing Office
Washington, DC 20402
202-512-1800
(Annual) $21.00

Best 100 Sources for Market Information
American Demographics, Inc.
P.O. Box 68
Ithaca, NY 14851
800-828-1133

Statistical Abstract of the United States
U.S. Government Printing Office
Washington, DC 20402
202-512-1800
(Annual) $38.00

Industry Information

Standard & Poor's Register of Corporations, Directors, and Executives
Standard & Poor's Corporation
25 Broadway
New York, NY 10004
212-208-8000

Moody's Industrial Manual
Moody's Investors Service
99 Church Street
New York, NY 10007-0300
800-342-5647

U.S. Industrial Outlook
U.S. Government Printing Office
Washington, DC 20402
202-512-2250

Retailing

National Retail Federation
325 Seventh Street NW, Suite 300
Washington, DC 20004-2802

Franchising

What You Need to Know When You Buy a Franchise Directory
International Franchise Association
1350 New York Avenue NW, Suite 900
Washington, DC 20005
202-628-8000

Evaluating Franchise Opportunities
U.S. Small Business Administration
Office of Business Development
SBA Publications
P.O. Box 30
Denver, CO 80201-0030

Franchise Opportunities Handbook
U.S. Government Printing Office
Washington, DC 20402
202-512-2250

International Franchise Association
1350 New York Avenue NW, Suite 900
Washington, DC 20005
202-628-8000

Franchising 101: The Complete Guide to Evaluating, Buying, and Growing Your Franchise Business **[Association of Small Business Development Centers (ASBDC)] edited by Ann Dugan**
(Upstart Publishing Co., 1998)

Importing and Exporting

A Basic Guide to Exporting
U.S. Government Printing Office
Washington, DC 20402
202-512-2250

Customs Regulations
U.S. Government Printing Office
Washington, DC 20402
202-512-2250

Export Administration Regulations
U.S. Government Printing Office
Washington, DC 20402
202-512-2250

Export Profits **by Jack S. Wolf**
(Upstart Publishing Co., 1992)

Building an Import / Export Business, 2/e **by Kenneth D. Weiss**
(John Wiley & Sons, Inc., 1997)

Import and Export Business Guide
Entrepreneur, Inc.
2392 Morse Avenue
P.O. Box 19787
Irvine, CA 92713-9787
800-421-2300

American Export Register
(Thomas International Publishing Division, 1994)

Export / Import Procedures and Documentation
AMACOM Books
1601 Broadway
New York, NY 10019-7406
862-262-9699

Exporters' Encyclopedia
Dun & Bradstreet Information Services
Dun & Bradstreet Corporation
3 Sylvan Way
Parsippany, NJ 07054-3896
800-526-0651

Importing into the United States
U.S. Government Printing Office
Washington, DC 20402
202-512-2250

American Association of Exporters and Importers
11 West 42nd Street
New York, NY 10036
212-944-2230

International Trade Administration
U.S. Department of Commerce
14th Street and Constitution Avenue NW
Hoover Building, Room 3850
Washington, DC 20231
202-482-5933

U.S. Importers and Exporters
Journal of Commerce
445 Marshall Street
Phillipsburg, NJ 08865
800-222-0356

Home-Based Business

Launching Your Home-Based Business **by David H. Bangs, Jr. and Andi Axman**
(Upstart Publishing Co., 1998)

Working Solo **by Teri Lonier**
(Portico Press, 1994)

Surefire Strategies for Growing Your Home-Based Business **by David Schaefer**
(Upstart Publishing Co., 1998)

American Home Business Association
4505 S. Wasatah Blvd.
Salt Lake City, UT 84124
800-664-2422
http://www.homebusiness.com

Manufacturing

Business Plan for Small Manufacturers
U.S. Small Business Administration
Office of Business Development
SBA Publications
P.O. Box 30
Denver, CO 80201-0030
800-827-5722

Manufacturing USA: Industry Analyses, Statistics, and Leading Organizations
Gale Research Company
Book Tower
835 Penobscot Building
Detroit, MI 48226-4094
800-877-GALE

National Association of Manufacturers
1331 Pennsylvania Avenue NW, Suite 1500N
Washington, DC 20004
202-637-3000

Thomas Register of American Manufacturers, 88/e
(Thomas Register, 1998)

Manufacturers Representative / Agent Associations

Independent Manufacturers Representatives Forum
301 N. Fairfax Street
Alexandria, VA 22314
800-542-6672

Manufacturers Agents National Association
23016 Mill Creek Rd.
P.O. Box 3467
Laguna Hills, CA 92654
714-859-4040

Service Industry

Service Industries USA: Industry Analyses, Statistics,
And Leading Organizations
(Gale Research Company, 1996)

Sourcebooks

Business Information Sourcebook **by Gustav Berbe**
(John Wiley & Sons, Inc., 1991)

International Business Reference Sources **by Cynthia C. Ryan**
(Lexington Books, 1983)

Small Business Sourcebook, 12/e **by Robert J. Elster**
(Gale Research Company, 1998)

Encyclopedia of Business Information Sources, 12/e **by James Wolf**
(Gale Research Company, 1997)

Encyclopedia of Associations
(Gale Research Company, 1995)

Government and Miscellaneous Associations

U.S. Chamber of Commerce
1615 H Street NW
Washington, DC 20062
202-463-5580

U.S. Department of Commerce
14th Street and Constitution Avenue NW
Washington, DC 20230
202-482-2000
http://www.doc.gov

U.S. Consumer Information
U.S. Government Printing Office
Washington, DC 20402
202-512-2250

Library of Congress
101 Independence Avenue SE
Washington, DC 20540
http://www.oweb.loc.gov

Small Business Assistance Center
554 Main Street
P.O. Box 15014
Worcester, MA 01615-0014
508-756-3513

Internal Revenue Service
U.S. Department of Treasury
1111 Constitution Avenue, NW
Washington, DC 20224
202-622-5164
http://www.irs.ustreas.gov

Small Business Administration
409 Third Street SW
Washington, DC 20416
202-205-6600
http://www.sbaonline.sba.gov

U.S. Government Printing Office
Superintendent of Documents
U.S. Government Printing Office
Washington, DC 20402
202-783-3228
http://www.access.gpo.gov/

National Association of Woman Business Owners
1010 Wayne Avenue, Suite 830
Silver Springs, MD 20910
301-608-2590
http://www.nawbo2.org

National Business Owners Association
1033 N. Fairfax, Suite 402
Alexandria, VA 22314
202-737-6501

Additional Resources

Small Business Development Centers (SBDCs). Call your state university or the Small Business Administration (SBA) to find the SBDC nearest you. Far and away the best free management program available, SBDCs provide expert assistance and training in every aspect of business management. Don't ignore this resource.

Service Corps of Retired Executives (SCORE). Sponsored by the U.S. Small Business Administration, SCORE provides free counseling and also a series of workshops and seminars for small businesses. Of special interest, SCORE offers a Business Planning Workshop that includes a 30-minute video produced specifically for SCORE by Upstart Publishing and funded by Paychex, Inc. There are over 500 SCORE chapters nationwide. For more information, contact the SBA office nearest you and ask about SCORE.

Small Business Administration (SBA). The SBA offers a number of management assistance programs. If you are assigned a capable Management Assistance Officer, you have an excellent resource. The SBA is worth a visit, if only to leaf through their extensive literature.

Colleges and Universities. Most have business courses. Some have SBDCs, others have more specialized programs. Some have small-business expertise—the University of New Hampshire, for example, has two schools that provide direct small-business management assistance.

Libraries. Do not forget to take advantage of the information readily available at your local library.

Online Bookstores

Amazon
http://www.amazon.com/
Our favorite online bookstore. A vast selection of titles, author interviews, lists of books by
author, field, genre, and lots more. Worth visiting even if you don't buy books!

Powell's Bookstore—used, new, and out of print
http://www.powells.com
Another online bookstore, with many unusual titles that are hard to find elsewhere.

Small Business Oriented Web Sites

About Work: **Ask the Experts**
http://www.aboutwork.com/experts/
Staff experts from *About Work* cover topics ranging from "Work from Home" to "Career
Planning." You post your question; they post their replies. Bulletin boards, chats,
links, and resources.

ABN Entrepreneurs
http://www.all-biz.com/entrepr.html
Has excellent small business links.

Adam Home Page
http://www.uexpress.com/ups/comics/ad/
Some comic relief for us home workers.

American Home Business Association
http://www.homebusiness.com/
One of the better home business associations.

Nolo Press
http://www.nolo.com
Nolo specializes in legal do-it-yourself advice. They have an excellent product line, and
command our respect for their down-to-earth editorial policy.

America's Business Funding Directory
http://www.businessfinance.com/
Helpful information on where and how to find capital for your business.

American Demographics / **Marketing Tools**
http://www.marketingtools.com/
Books, publications, resources, research tools, links. This is *the* site for market research.

American Express
http://www.americanexpress.com/smallbusiness/
Lots of good small business how-to information, monthly articles on specialized topics,
and a long list of references to other sites of interest.

Apple Small Biz Site
http://smallbusiness.apple.com/
Some how-to information, especially helpful for us Mac aficionados. Expert advice, links,
success stories.

Better Business Bureau
http://www.bbb.org
The ethical watchdog. Does everything the old BBB did, but quicker.

BizInfoSearch: Business Information on the Web
http://www.bizinfosearch.com/
This is Prentice-Hall's Directory of Online Information. Good search function. The site is (apparently) always under construction.

CCH Business Owner's Toolkit
AOL only: keyword CCH
CCH (Commercial Clearing House) has a battery of superb small business articles and forms.

Claris Small Business
http://www.claris.com/smallbiz/
Generally a good site. Some how-to; some expert advice. Includes shareware templates for many business functions.

Committee on Small Business
http://www.senate.gov/~sbc/
This is one of the best entry points into the federal maze. Great links to government resources.

Community Center—Work and Family
http://www.smalloffice.com/cooler/keep.htm
Home Office Computing's family business area, devoted primarily to home-based businesses.

D&B Company Information
http://www.smalloffice.n2k.com/cgi-bin/canvas/co_info.htm
Worth a visit. You can get business credit info, but at a cost.

Dearborn Publishing Group, Inc.
http://www.dearborn.com/dearborn.htm
My publishers, bless their hearts!

Digital Daily Welcome—IRS
http://www.irs.ustreas.gov/prod/
Welcome to the IRS. They really are trying to be more user-friendly. Contains updated information and a strong section on taxes for small business.

Doing Business on the Internet
http://www.smartbiz.com/sbs/dobiz.htm
A fine site for those of us interested in doing business on the Internet (as the title says). Articles, links, tips, and useful information.

Home Based and Small Business Resource Center
http://members.tripod.com/~WorkinMoms/
Newsletter, kids, parents working at home site. Chatty and fun for the work-at-home mother.

Home Office Computing
http://www.smalloffice.com
Home Office Computing is far and away the best small business magazine going these days, bar none. While focused on businesses based on computer applications, they have a lot more to offer—how-tos, technical advice, interesting copy, even editorial differences of opinion. A must-visit site.

How to Start a Business
http://www.inreach.com/sbdc/book/
An SBDC-based compendium of odd bits. Could be helpful.

HR in a Box Home Page
http://www.ultranet.com/~windog/hr/index.html
Sylvia Ho is a human resources lawyer. She's an entrepreneur—and her site is superb. A must-visit for any personnel or human resources question.

IBM's Patent Server
http://patent.womplex.ibm.com/
A treasure for patent seekers! This is a real public service. Thanks, Big Blue! (From a Kasparov fan.)

Innovation Network / Corporate Innovation
http://www.thinksmart.com/index.html
Innovation is a buzzword these days, and with good reason: It's emerging as one of the most important duties of management. Contains stories, articles, links, and useful resources.

Internet Start
http://home.microsoft.com/
Another way into Microsoft's excellent Web presence. Well worth a site trip.

Khera Communications
http://www.kciLink.com/
Great free info on marketing, finance, and other matters. Locally focused (Washington, D.C. area) but with a much wider appeal.

Microsoft's Small Business Page
http://www.microsoft.com/smallbiz/
Similar to Apple and Claris: good how-tos and links to other sites. Frequently updated.

MIT Enterprise Forum
http://web.mit.edu/afs/athena.mit.edu/org/e/entforum/www/index.htm
The Enterprise Forums are a must for anyone seeking serious venture capital. This site has examples, names, dates of meetings, and more.

National Foundation for Women Business Owners
http://www.nfwbo.org/
A trade association for women business owners. Fascinating research articles about women and minority businesses. Good links.

National SBDC Research Network Home Page
http://www.smallbiz.suny.edu/
One of the best sites for small business on the Internet. Puts the capacities and capabilities of the SBDCs nationwide network to work for you. Don't miss this site.

Roger Parker's Home Page
http://www.rcparker.com
A brilliant example of a personal/business Web site. If you plan to have a Web presence, you have to visit with Roger. His new book on Web content and design is the standard for this burgeoning market. Plus, he's a friend of mine—and he's very entertaining.

SBDC Roster
http://WWW.SMALLBIZ.SUNY.EDU/roster.htm
The fastest way to find the nearest SBDC.

SCORE On Line
http://www.scn.org/civic/score-online/
Online, real-time assistance from retired executives. Somewhat hit or miss, but improving daily. Worth a visit.

Small and Home-Based Business Links

http://www.ro.com/small_business/homebased.html

Another of those must-visit sites. There is so much material on the Web that sites like this are great to stumble across!

Small Business Administration

http://www.sbaonline.sba.gov/

The Small Business Administration is the first place any small business owner should visit. Their range of services—from counseling to financial guarantees—is very impressive. With the advent of the Small Business Development Center program, their quality rocketed upwards. Any entrepreneur who ignores this resource is being willfully self-destructive.

Small Business Advancement Center (University of Arkansas)

http://www.sbaer.uca.edu/homepage.html

This site is a sleeper. It's full of gems: marketing tips, financing ideas, links, and more. A must-visit site. Even has a fine search engine built into it.

Small Business Home

http://smallbusiness.apple.com/

Apple's small business home page. See Microsoft's site, immediately below.

Small Business Resource

http://www.microsoft.com/smallbiz/

Microsoft's small business home page. See Apple's site, immediately above.

SoHo Central Home Office Resources

http://www.hoaa.com/index.html

The Home Office Association home page. Has very good links, ideas, tips, and resources.

Survey Research Center Home Page

http://www.princeton.edu/~abelson/index.html

If you are serious about market research, you have to use this site. A terrific help to anyone planning to survey a market. Plus a lot more.

The CNBC About Work Career Center

http://cnbc.aboutwork.com/

About Work's supersite for people interested in furthering their careers. If you are questioning your own path, this is a place to find solace as well as solid advice.

The Information House Free Information Area

http://www.informationhouse.com

A great Web site for people interested in doing business on the Web. Although they are looking for customers (and why not?), they exemplify one of the great things about this new medium: freely shared information.

The Occupational Safety and Health Administration

http://www.osha.gov/

OSHAs home page.

U.S. Business Advisor

http://www.business.gov/

Truthfully labeled "the one-stop electronic link to government."

U.S. Federal Trade Commission

http://www.ftc.gov

Major resource, especially if you plan to grow a consumer oriented business. Plenty of free information.

United Media
http://www.unitedmedia.com/
Snoopy, Dilbert, and many more entertaining things to view. Purely recreational.

Venture Capital Web Site Links
http://pacific.commerce.ubc.ca/evc/vc_title.html
The University of British Columbia's site for those seeking cash. Plenty of links and good tips on how to approach the venture capital community.

Welcome to Be the Boss
http://www.betheboss.com/
This site is for the franchise community.

Welcome to Hoover's Online!
http://www.hoovers.com/
Good for info on publicly traded companies, IPOs, and so forth. Some areas are by subscription only.

Welcome to Lycos
http://lycos.com/
Powerful search capabilities.

Welcome to the Angenehm Law Firm Home Page
http://www.Angenehm.com/
This site is devoted to intellectual property concerns. Worth a visit if you are involved in any way with patents, copyrights, and similar issues.

Welcome to the New Officeproducts.com Site
http://www.officeproducts.com/
"Office products, office tips, and office solutions." Some helpful material interspersed with ads.

Work at Home Moms
http://www.wahm.com/
The name says it best! Great place to visit, even for non-moms. It's local (Northwest) but has worldwide appeal.

Work @ Home
http://www.gohome.com
"Making a life while making a living" is their motto. I like it! How-tos, chats, links.

Working Today
http://www.workingtoday.org
Membership organization that has a sporadic newsletter and focuses on health and insurance issues.

Your Small Office (HOC)
http://www.smalloffice.com
Another way to get to *Home Office Computing*, our favorite paper and ink snail mail subscription.

G L O S S A R Y

"acid test" ratio   Cash, plus other assets that can be immediately converted to cash, should equal or exceed current liabilities. The formula used to determine the ratio is as follows:

$$\frac{\text{cash plus receivables (net)}}{\text{current liabilities}}$$

The "acid test" ratio is one of the most important credit barometers used by lending institutions, as it indicates the abilities of a business enterprise to meet its current obligations.

aging receivables   A scheduling of accounts receivable according to the length of time they have been outstanding. This shows which accounts are not being paid in a timely manner and may reveal any difficulty in collecting long overdue receivables. This may also be an important indicator of developing cash flow problems.

amortization   To liquidate on an installment basis; the process of gradually paying off a liability over a period of time, i.e., a mortgage is amortized by periodically paying off part of the face amount of the mortgage.

assets   The valuable resources, or properties and property rights owned by an individual or business enterprise.

balance sheet   An itemized statement that lists the total assets, liabilities, and net worth of a given business to reflect its financial condition at a given moment.

capital   Capital funds are those funds that are needed for the base of the business. Usually they are put into the business in a fairly permanent form such as in fixed assets, plant and equipment, or are used in other ways that are not recoverable in the short run unless the entire business is sold.

capital equipment   Equipment used to manufacture a product, provide a service, or to sell, store and deliver merchandise. Such equipment will not be sold in the normal course of business but will be used and worn out or be consumed over time as business is conducted.

cash flow   The actual movement of cash within a business — cash inflow minus cash outflow. A term used to designate the reported net income of a corporation plus amounts charged off for depreciation, depletion, amortization, and extraordinary charges to reserves, which are bookkeeping deductions and not actually paid out in cash. Used to offer a better indication of the ability of a firm to meet its own obligations and to pay dividends, rather than the conventional net income figure.

cash position   See **liquidity.**

collateral   An asset pledged to a lender in order to support the loan.

current assets   Cash or other items that will normally be turned into cash within one year, and assets that will be used up in the operations of a firm within one year.

current liabilities   Amounts owed that will ordinarily be paid by a firm within one year. Such items include accounts payable, wages payable, taxes payable, the current portion of a long-term debt, and interest and dividends payable.

current ratio   A ratio of a firm's current assets to its current liabilities. Because a current ratio includes the value of inventories that have not yet been sold, it does not offer the best evaluation of the firm's current status. The "acid test" ratio, covering the most liquid of current assets, produces a better evaluation.

debt   Debt refers to borrowed funds, whether from your own coffers or from other individuals, banks, or institutions. It is generally secured with a note, which in turn may be secured by a lien against property or other assets. Ordinarily, the note states repayment and interest provisions, which vary greatly in both amount and duration, depending upon the purpose, source, and terms of the loan. Some debt is convertible, that is, it may be changed into direct ownership of a portion of a business under certain stated conditions.

demographics   The statistical study of human populations, especially with reference to size and density, distribution, and vital statistics.

demographics   (2) Relating to the dynamic balance of a population, especially with regard to density and capacity for expansion or decline   .

demographic segmentation   A marketing analysis that targets groups of prospects by factors such as sex, age, marital status, income, occupation, family size, and education (from *Forecasting Sales and Planning Profits*, Kenneth E. Marino).

distribution   The delivery or conveyance of a good or service to a market.

distribution channel   The chain of intermediaries linking the producer of a good to the consumer.

equity   Equity is the owner's investment in the business. Unlike capital, equity is what remains after the liabilities of the company are subtracted from the assets—thus it may be greater than or less than the capital invested in the business. Equity investment carries with it a share of ownership and usually a share in profits, as well as some say in how the business is managed.

gross profit   Net sales (sales minus returned merchandise, discounts, or other allowances) minus the cost of goods sold.

guaranty   A pledge by a third party to repay a loan in the event that the borrower cannot.

income statement   A statement of income and expenses for a given period of time.

inventory   The materials owned and held by a business firm, including new materials, intermediate products and parts, work-in-process, and finished goods, intended either for internal consumption or for sale.

liquidity   A term used to describe the solvency of a business, and that has special reference to the degree of readiness in which assets can be converted into cash without a loss. Also called *cash position*. If a firm's current assets cannot be converted into cash to meet current liabilities, the firm is said to be *illiquid*.

loan agreement   A document that states what a business can or cannot do as long as it owes money to (usually) a bank. A loan agreement may place restrictions on the owner's salary, or dividends, on the amount of other debt, on working capital limits, on sales, or on the number of additional personnel.

loans   Debt money for private business is usually in the form of bank loans, which, in a sense, are personal because a private business can be harder to evaluate in terms of creditworthiness and degree of risk. A secured loan is a loan that is backed up by a claim against some asset or assets of a business. An unsecured loan is backed by the faith the bank has in the borrower's ability to pay back the money.

long-term liabilities   These are liabilities (expenses) that will not mature within the next year.

net worth   The owner's equity in a given business represented by the excess of the total assets over the total amounts owed to outside creditors (total liabilities) at a given moment in time. Also, the net worth of an individual as determined by deducting the amount of all personal liabilities from the total value of personal assets. Generally refers to tangible net worth, that is, does not include goodwill, and so forth.

note   The basic business loan, a note represents a loan that will be repaid, or substantially reduced 30, 60, or 90 days later at a stated interest rate. These are short term, and unless they are made under a line of credit, a separate loan application is needed for each loan and each renewal.

partnership   A legal relationship created by the voluntary association of two or more persons to carry on as co-owners of a business for profit; a type of business organization in which two or more persons agree on the amount of their contributions (capital and effort) and on the distribution of profits, if any.

positioning   A marketing method based on determining what market niche your business should fill and how it should promote its products or services in light of competitive and other forces.

pro forma   A projection or an estimate of what may result in the future from actions in the present. A pro forma financial statement is one that shows how the actual operations of a business will turn out if certain assumptions are realized.

profit   The excess of the selling price over all costs and expenses incurred in making a sale. Also, the reward to the entrepreneur for the risks assumed by him or her in the establishment, operations, and management of a given enterprise or undertaking.

sole proprietorship or **proprietorship**   A type of business organization in which one individual owns the business. Legally, the owner *is* the business and personal assets are typically exposed to liabilities of the business.

Subchapter S corporation or **tax option corporation**   A corporation that has elected under Subchapter S of the IRS Tax Code (by unanimous consent of its shareholders) not to pay any corporate tax on its income and, instead, to have the shareholders pay taxes on it, even though it is not distributed. Shareholders of a tax option corporation are also entitled to deduct, on the individual returns, their shares of any net operating loss sustained by the corporation, subject to limitations in the tax code. In many respects, Subchapter S permits a corporation to behave for tax purposes as a proprietorship or partnership.

takeover   The acquisition of one company by another company.

target market   The specific individuals, distinguished by socioeconomic, demographic and/or interest characteristics, who are the most likely potential customers for the goods and/or services of a business.

term loans   Loans that are either secured or unsecured, usually for periods of more than a year to as many as ten. Term loans are paid off like a mortgage: so many dollars per month for so many years. The most common uses of term loans are for equipment and other fixed asset purposes, for working capital, and for real estate.

working capital   The difference between current assets and current liabilities. Contrasted with capital, a permanent use of funds, working capital cycles through your business in a variety of forms: inventories, accounts and notes receivable, and cash and securities.

I N D E X